COASTS

COASTS

An Introduction to Coastal Geomorphology

Third Edition

Eric C. F. Bird

Basil Blackwell

© Geostudies 1984

This edition first published in the United Kingdom 1984
by Basil Blackwell Publisher Limited
108 Cowley Road, Oxford OX4 1JF, England

and in the United States 1984
by Basil Blackwell Inc.
432 Park Avenue South, Room 1505, New York NY 10016, USA

British Library Cataloguing-in-Publication Data

Bird, Eric C. F.
    Coasts.
    1. Coasts. 2. Geomorphology.
    I. Title.

    551.4'5   GB451.2

    ISBN 0 631 13567 7
    ISBN 0 631 13568 5 Pbk

Library of Congress No. 83-72678

PREFACE TO THE THIRD EDITION

This book is designed as an introduction to the subject of coastal geomorphology. It is based on courses given by the author in the Australian National University and the Universities of London, Sydney and Melbourne. The aim is to provide an introductory account of the data and problems of coastal evolution and coastline changes, with examples from various parts of the world. Inevitably there is some bias towards coasts that the author has examined in detail, notably in Europe, North America and Australasia, but an effort has been made to draw upon experience from other areas to balance this.

Definitions of terms, given when these are first encountered in the text, can be located by using the index. As a rule the terms and definitions used are those commonly accepted by coastal geomorphologists, but more advanced students interested in the origins and historical connotations of coastal terminology will need to consult the standard geological and geographical glossaries. The selected bibliography is intended to lead advanced students into the substantial research literature of the subject.

The metric system is used in preference to other units of measurement in order to bring the subject in line with customary scientific practice. In coastal work there is the complication that many marine charts still give soundings in fathoms, distances in nautical miles, and current velocities in knots. Conversion to metric units raised problems when the measurements quoted were approximations, and an effort has been made to render such measurements in metric units without implying different orders of accuracy from those originally intended. Where confusion is possible, non-metric alternatives have been included.

In preparing a third edition, further additions and amendments have been made, based on my experience during the past few years, and on suggestions made by teachers and students who used earlier editions. The intention is still to retain *Coasts* as an introductory textbook: it is required as preliminary reading for my courses in Melbourne. It is obvious that many of the general statements included could be expanded and qualified in terms of detailed work on particular coasts. Indeed, students are urged to examine their local coasts for examples of the features and relationships described in this book, and to attempt explanatory descriptions of the coastal landforms they encounter.

In addition to acknowledgments made in previous editions I would like to thank Rob Bartlett for his work on the figures, Wendy Godber for assistance with the plates, and Ruth Terrell-Phillips for help in revising the text. The various people and organisations who have contributed plates are acknowledged in the respective captions. I am grateful also to Catherine, Philippa, and Jennifer Bird for their help as I assembled this third edition, and particularly for revising the Index.

Eric Bird

CONTENTS

FIGURES

PLATES

I

INTRODUCTION

Coastal geomorphology is the study of coastal landforms, their evolution, the processes at work on them, and the changes now taking place.

It is convenient to begin by defining the terms used to describe coastal features. The *shore* (Fig. 1) is the zone between the water's edge at low tide and the landward limit of effective wave action; it comprises the foreshore, exposed at low tide and submerged at high tide, and the backshore, extending above normal high tide level, but inundated by exceptionally high tides or by large waves during storms. The *shoreline* is strictly the

1　*Coastal terminology*

water's edge, migrating to and fro with the tide (Fig. 2). The *nearshore zone*, between this and the line where waves begin to break, also migrates as the tides rise and fall: it includes the surf zone, with broken waves, and the swash zone, covered as each wave runs up on the foreshore. Outside the breaker line, extending to an arbitrary limit in deep water, is the offshore zone, but the term offshore is also used, together with onshore and long-shore, to describe directions of flow of wind, water, and sediment.

A *beach* is an accumulation of loose sediment, such as sand, gravel, or boulders, sometimes confined to the backshore but

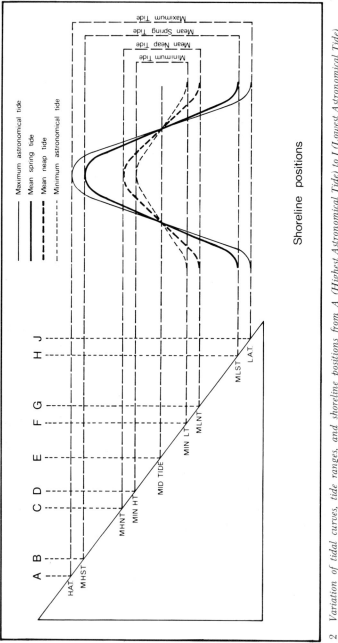

2 *Variation of tidal curves, tide ranges, and shoreline positions from A (Highest Astronomical Tide) to J (Lowest Astronomical Tide)*

often extending across the foreshore as well. The British term shingle has been widely used to describe beach gravels, especially where the stones are well-rounded. A bank of beach material which lies offshore and is exposed at high tide is called a *barrier*, but a similar feature submerged for at least part of the tidal cycle is called a *bar*. A *spit* is a beach that diverges from the coast, often terminating in one or more landward projections, known as recurves.

The *coast* is a zone of varying width, including the shore and extending to the landward limit of penetration of marine influences: the crest of a cliff, the head of a tidal estuary, or the solid ground that lies behind coastal dunes, lagoons, and swamps. The coastline is usually taken as the land margin in the backshore zone. It is useful to refer to the sea area adjoining the coast, comprising the nearshore and offshore zones, as coastal waters.

Some coastlines are straight or gently curved in outline (e.g. the Ninety Mile Beach in SE Australia); others have a more intricate configuration, with branching inlets and ramifying peninsulas (e.g. the Kimberley coast in NW Australia). The length of a coastline can be estimated by dividing it into a series of straight segments of equal length, and counting these. The result is an underestimate, because straight segments cut across bays and headlands; it becomes more accurate as the intercepts are shortened. Thus the Australian coastline is about 16,000 km long, measured in one hundred kilometre intercepts, increasing to almost 24,000 km when one-kilometre intercepts are used (Galloway and Bahr, 1979).* The total length of the world coastline is more than 500,000 km, and of this, only a small proportion has yet been studied in detail. For a sector-by-sector account of the world's coastline see Bird and Schwartz (1983).

Coastal evolution

The geomorphological processes at work on coastal landforms are influenced by a number of environmental factors, notably geological, climatic, biotic, and tidal and other oceanographic factors, including salinity. These vary from one sector of the coast to another, the variation being zonal in terms of climatic regions, and irregular in terms of geological outcrops.

---

* References are listed on pp. 297–306.

The geological factor is obvious in the evolution of cliffed coasts, which show features related to the structure and lithology of rock formations which make up the hinterland, the coast, and the nearshore zone. Depositional coasts are also influenced by the geological factor in terms of the sources of sediment derived from adjacent cliffed coasts, hinterland drainage basins, or the sea floor.

The climatic factor is important in terms of the weathering of coastal rock outcrops, which results from physical, chemical, and biological processes, related partly to subaerial climatic conditions and partly to the presence or proximity of the sea. Rocks are decomposed or disintegrated by such processes as repeated wetting and drying, solution by rain water, thermal expansion and contraction and freeze-thaw alternations, all related to temperature, precipitation, and evaporation regimes in the coastal environment. Climate also conditions modes of subaerial erosion, coastal slopes washed by runoff showing various kinds of wastage ranging from soil creep and solifluction to gulleying, landslides, and mudflows, but marine erosion plays an important part in undercutting coastal slopes, initiating instability, and removing superficial materials to expose fresh rock outcrops for further subaerial weathering.

Regional variations in climate (Bailey, 1958) may be marked by contrasted modes of geomorphological evolution. Thus in the humid tropics (Bird, 1981) rapid chemical weathering in progress at high temperatures results in deep decomposition of many of the rock formations which outcrop at the coast, and bold headlands are restricted to the formations which resist such weathering, notably quartzites. Hinterlands carry a dense tropical forest vegetation, and typically the rivers deliver an abundance of fine sediment (silt and clay) to the coast, rather than the sands and gravels which the same rock outcrops would yield under the weathering regimes of cooler or drier environments. In cold regions, by contrast, cliffed coasts are modified by rock shattering and solifluction resulting from repeated alternations of freezing and thawing, which yield an abundance of rock fragments for the building of beaches, spits, and barriers of gravel along the coast. Where glaciers reach the coast, glacifluvial and morainic material is delivered to the shore, while in high latitudes ice coasts form a distinct category. In arid regions the limited runoff from the land carries only small quantities of

terrigenous sediment to the coast, so that many of the beach
and barrier systems consist largely of biogenic sediments
derived from marine shells and coral debris, mainly calcium
carbonate. Sparseness of coastal vegetation results in rugged-
ness of cliff topography and the mobility of coastal dune systems. An elucidation of the climatic factor in coastal geomorphology requires comparative studies of coastal sectors that are
similar geologically, but differ in climatic regime. On the eastern
seaboard of Australia, for instance, the humid tropical sector in
North Queensland shows distinctive features related to its climatic environment that differ from those on other parts of the
Australian coast (Bird and Hopley, 1969).

The biotic factor is strongly influenced by climatic conditions
which limit the range of many significant organisms. Corals and
associated reef-building organisms are confined mainly to the
inter-tropical zone, and mangrove swamps are restricted to
estuaries and sheltered coastal environments in low latitudes
—environments which are occupied by salt marshes in the
temperate zone. The effects of organisms may be erosional,
protective, or constructional. The shore fauna and flora often
include species, the growth and metabolism of which lead to the
decomposition or dissolution of coastal rock outcrops, especially
limestone. There are also species which variously graze, excavate, or drill into the rock surfaces. On the other hand a dense
growth of kelp or a firm encrustation of algae may protect a
rocky shore from abrasion. Salt marsh, mangroves, or dune
vegetation may colonise and stabilise depositional landforms on
the coast, or promote accretion of sediment in such a way as to
build new landforms, and a variety of reef formations can be
built by coral, algae, oysters, and other organisms on the shore
and in coastal waters.

Wind is a climatic factor of particular importance in coastal
evolution, building coastal dunes and generating the waves and
currents that, together with tides, create the pattern of nearshore water circulation which influences the sculpturing of
cliffed coasts, shaping of sea-floor topography, movement of
coastal sediment, and patterns of marine deposition. Variations
in the strength and frequency of winds result in contrasts in
modes of coastal evolution. Some coasts border stormy seas;
others face comparatively calm waters. Some receive ocean
swell, generated by distant storms and transmitted across the

oceans; others are protected from prevailing ocean conditions by promontories and islands, depositional barriers, or offshore reefs and shoals, and receive only the waves generated locally by winds blowing over coastal waters. The geomorphological effects of plants and animals are suppressed on stormy coasts, especially where waves move sand and gravel to and fro, abrading the shore.

Tidal conditions also vary from coast to coast. On some coasts the tide range is negligible; on others it measures several metres and strong currents are generated as the tides ebb and flow.

The oceanographic factor derives from the nature of sea water, with variations in salinity from almost fresh, in parts of the Baltic Sea, to relatively strong salinity in the Red Sea and other ocean areas in the arid zone, where it is concentrated by high evaporation. The average salinity of the oceans is about 35 parts per thousand of dissolved solids (mainly chlorides). Salt water and sea spray have corrosive effects which influence the weathering of coastal rock outcrops; they also produce distinctive ecological conditions, the habitats of marine and estuarine flora and fauna, many of which influence weathering, erosion, transportation, and deposition of rock materials in the coastal environment.

Coastal evolution can be considered in terms of geomorphic systems, within which these various factors influence processes acting upon the coast. There is an input of energy (e.g. wind, tide, living organisms) and materials (e.g. water, rock, sediment) which interact to generate landforms, and there is 'feedback' in the sense that the developing morphology has influenced geomorphic processes, and has thus become a factor influencing subsequent coastal evolution. Variations in geomorphic systems on the world's coasts have been outlined by Davies (1972). It is also necessary to bear in mind the possible existence of relict features, inherited from contrasted geomorphic environments in the past, and modifications of coastal systems resulting from human activities during the past few centuries.

Landforms related to past conditions are found on many coasts. They include some which developed when the sea stood higher, relative to the land, and others related to submergence following relatively low sea level phases. There are coastal landforms inherited from earlier episodes when the climate was warmer or cooler, wetter or drier, than it is now. Existing geomorphological systems became established only within the past ten thousand years (geologically the Holocene epoch), and the landform legacy of the preceding Pleistocene period, when marked variations of climate and sea level accompanied the waxing and waning of ice sheets over a period of at least a million years, is still evident on many coasts. The Holocene is sometimes referred to as 'post-glacial', but this is unsatisfactory because such regions as Greenland and Antarctica are still in a 'glacial' phase despite the late Quaternary warming ('deglacial') of the world's climate.

Time scales in coastal geomorphology must be related to the relatively brief period (up to 6,000 years) over which the sea has stood at or near its present level relative to the land; long-term changes are those measured over periods exceeding the Holocene (i.e. 10^4 years), medium term over the range 10^2 to 10^4 years, and short term less than 10^2 years (i.e. the past few years, or recent decades).

Modification of coastal landforms by human activities may be either direct or indirect. The building of sea walls, groynes, and breakwaters, the dredging of harbour entrances, and the dumping of material on the coast and offshore, are all direct modifications of coastal topography. Major reclamation schemes in the Netherlands, and in densely populated areas in Tokyo Bay, Hong Kong, and Singapore have created new land behind artificial coastlines. Human interference often has indirect effects, accentuating erosion or deposition on adjacent sectors of the coast. Reduction of coastal vegetation by cutting, burning, grazing, or pollution has often led to changes in patterns of erosion and deposition on the coast, in estuaries and lagoons, or on the sea floor.

Attempts to modify coastal changes—to halt erosion or prevent deposition—require an understanding of the factors and processes at work in the coastal geomorphic system: the pattern of change, the sources of sediment, the paths of sediment flow, and the quantities involved over given periods of time. Such knowledge enables the effects of various kinds of human interference to be predicted and offset, or allowed for, in coastal engineering works. Studies of the effects of human activities on the coast are also important in planning the management and conservation of natural resources, including scenery and wildlife, in coastal areas.

The need for accurate data has introduced new techniques to coastal geomorphology, supplementing traditional methods of observation, mapping, and measurement of the landforms, processes, and changes on the coast. Aerial photography has been used for some time as an aid to mapping and measurement of coastal changes, but modern developments in colour photography from the air are extending these studies to the sea floor, and satellite photography holds possibilities for synoptic recording of ocean wave conditions. Aqualung diving has been used to supplement the older methods of sounding and sampling in the offshore zone, stimulated by the realisation that sea floor morphology and sediments greatly influence the evolution of coastal landforms. Depositional formations on the coast are subjected to modern stratigraphical and sedimentological analyses, using radiometric as well as palaeontological and archaeological methods of dating, and tracers are used to follow and measure currents and coastal sediment flow. Laboratory simulation of coastal processes requires the use of scale models such as water tanks in which waves, tides and currents can be generated. These models have limitations in practice because it is difficult to scale down materials and processes without modifying their physical properties (e.g. coherence, friability, expansion and contraction of sediments; viscosity and surface tension in water), but they can be useful in exploring potential responses to selected coastal processes. Monitoring of nearshore processes and changes is conducted from piers equipped for instrumental surveys and computerised recording, as at Duck (N Carolina) and Sochi (Soviet Black Sea coast).

Many problems in coastal geomorphology require long-term investigation, continued over several years, with repeated surveys of landforms to identify and measure changes, and relate these to correlative studies of processes (Wright and Thom, 1977). The ideal of a complete quantitative understanding of a coastal system is more easily advocated than achieved, but it is realistic to formulate and attempt to solve specific problems, and to establish empirical relationships between process and change that can be put to practical use in coastal management.

Each of these topics will be considered in more detail in subsequent chapters. Before proceeding to describe the various kinds of coastal landforms it is necessary to examine the processes at work in coastal waters (Chapter II) and the evidence of past changes of land and sea levels, which preceded the development of the environments in which we now find coastal landforms (Chapter III).

II

TIDES, WAVES, AND CURRENTS

The processes at work in coastal waters—tides, waves, and currents—interact to produce an energy input which shapes and modifies the shore. Under some conditions one process augments another; a rising tide, for example, generates shoreward movement of water, setting up current flow through narrow straits and inlets. As a rule the nearshore zone is concave-upward in profile and thus deepens as the tide rises, thereby increasing the height and effectiveness of waves that reach the shore. Under other conditions, one process may act against another: a tidal current flowing in one direction can reduce the velocity and dimensions of waves moving in a contrary direction. Nevertheless, it is convenient to separate the three components, astronomically-generated tidal movements, wind-generated wave action, and various forms of current flow, for the purposes of discussion.

Tides
Tides are movements of the oceans set up by the gravitational effects of the sun and the moon in relation to the earth. They are important in coastal geomorphology because they lead to regular changes in the level of the sea along the coast, and because currents are generated as the tide ebbs and flows. It is not necessary here to consider in detail the nature and origin of tides; they are essentially oscillations of water in ocean basins with characteristics determined partly by the size and shape of the basin. They move in harmony with the gravitational forces of the sun and the moon, with an additional gyratory motion imparted by the earth's rotation (Russell and MacMillan, 1954). They circulate around a number of nodal (amphidromic) points, and their effects are most strongly marked in shallow and relatively enclosed ocean areas such as the English Channel and the North Sea bordering the British Isles. In the open oceans, tides are essentially long waves that become modified as they move across continental shelves and approach the coastline. Fig. 3 shows the pattern of tidal movements around Australia by means of co-tidal lines that show the position of the tide wave

9

3   *The tidal regime around Australia, as indicated by the pattern of co-tidal lines. The tides take the form of long-period waves moving in from the Pacific and Indian Oceans. Note the convergence in Bass Strait north of Tasmania and the amphidromic circulation in the Gulf of Carpentaria. Variations in tide ranges are indicated by mean maximum tide range at selected stations*

crest (i.e. high tide) at successive hourly intervals. The convergence of tides in Bass Strait, north of Tasmania, and the amphidromic point in the Gulf of Carpentaria are noteworthy features.

The rise and fall of the tide on a coast is measured by tide gauges, located chiefly at ports. The tides recorded shortly after new moon and full moon, when earth, sun, and moon are in alignment, and have combined gravitational effects, are relatively large, and are known as spring tides. Maximum spring tide ranges occur about the equinoxes (late March and late September), when the sun is overhead at the equator. At half-moon (first and last quarter), when the sun and moon are at right angles in relation the earth, their gravitational effects are not combined; tide ranges recorded shortly after this are reduced, and are known as neap tides. There are also long-term variations in tide range in response to astronomical cycles of the relative positions of sun, moon, and earth; the moon, for example, returns to a similar position relative to the earth once every 27.5 days, but its orbit is such that it returns to exactly the same position only once in 18.6 years. Accurate determination of mean sea level from tide gauge records therefore requires tidal observations over a longer period than this, but a reasonable estimate can be made on the basis of one or two years' observations.

Further complications are introduced by meteorological effects. Onshore winds build up tide levels in coastal waters whereas offshore winds lower them. A fall in atmospheric pressure is accompanied by elevation, and a rise by depression, of the ocean surface: a fall of 1 millibar raises the ocean level about 1 cm. Storm surges are produced when strong onshore winds build up coastal water to an exceptionally high level, and are most serious when the onshore winds coincide with high spring tides. In 1953 a storm surge produced by a northerly gale in the North Sea raised the level of coastal water about 3 m, flooding extensive areas in E England and low-lying parts of the Dutch and German coasts. A similar surge accompanied the passage of a deep depression across the North Sea in January 1978 (Steers *et al.*, 1979), and there have been several such events in this region in recent centuries (Plate 1). High tides augmented by meteorological effects are known as king tides on the N coast of Australia, where heavy rains accompany onshore winds during the summer monsoon and cause widespread flooding in coastal districts. Hurricanes raise sea level as much as 6 m along the shores of the Gulf of Mexico, and disastrous storm surges are experienced from time to time at the head of the Bay of Bengal, when large areas of the Sundarbans are devastated by submergence. Short-term changes on these low-lying coastlines have proceeded on such a scale as to be obvious when comparisons are made of 1972 and 1979 satellite imagery (Landsat) covering the Bangladesh coast.

Observations of ocean levels during the International Geophysical Year (1957-8) showed fluctuations distinct from changes that could be explained by weather conditions, and these fluctuations are thought to be the result of seasonal variations in the

1   *Levels of storm surges recorded on a pole at Ribe, Denmark. From top to bottom the collars indicate levels attained in 1634 (+6.10 metres), 1825 (+5.33 metres), 1911 (+4.41 metres), 1909 (+4.11 metres), and 1904 (+3.98 metres). Since this photograph was taken there have been further storm surges, in 1976 (+3.44 metres) and 1981 (+5.02 metres). Information supplied by J. T. Møller.*

temperature and salinity of the oceans. The volume of a mass of sea water increases when rising temperature or diminishing salinity change its density, and this increase results in a slight rise in sea level. There are also local variations in tide range due to the configuration of the coast, the effects of outflow from rivers, and the modifications introduced where breakwaters and jetties have been built at harbour entrances. It is therefore necessary to consider the situation of a tide gauge when deciding the extent of coast to which a particular tide record is applicable.

Tide range in mid-ocean is small, of the order of 0.5 m, but it increases where the tide invades shallow coastal waters, particularly in gulfs and embayments. Where the spring tide range is less than 2 m, the environment is termed *microtidal*; between 2 m and 4 m *mesotidal*; and more than 4 m *macrotidal*. Microtidal ranges are typical of the coasts of the Atlantic, Pacific, Indian, and Southern Oceans and of certain landlocked seas (Baltic, Mediterranean, Black, Red, and Caribbean Seas). Around the

Pacific Basin mean spring tide range exceeds 2 m only in certain gulfs, notably the Gulf of Siam (Bangkok, 2.4 m) and the Gulf of California (9 m at the mouth of the Colorado River). On the Australian coast microtidal conditions prevail from Brisbane S to Cape Howe, thence along the whole of the S and W coasts, with the exception of certain embayments. Tide range increases into Spencer Gulf (Port Augusta, 2.0 m) and Gulf St Vincent (Port Wakefield, 2.1 m), but the narrow entrance to Port Phillip Bay (Fig. 8, p. 27) impedes tidal invasion, and tide ranges within the bay (0.85 m at Port Melbourne) are smaller than those outside (1.47 m at the entrance). Macrotidal ranges are characteristic of the N coast of Australia, especially between Port Hedland (up to 5.8 m) and Darwin (up to 5.5 m), with very large ranges recorded in the gulfs; Derby, on the shore of King Sound, has a spring tide range of 10 m. Macrotidal areas are also found in the Bay of St Michel in NW France, where maximum tides exceed 9 m, the Bristol Channel, where mean spring tide range increases eastwards to 12.3 m at Avonmouth, and the head of the Bay of Fundy, where more than 15.2 m is recorded. It is thought that the world's largest tide ranges, more than 20 m, occur within Leaf Bay, in N Canada.* Where large tides enter estuaries a visible wave, known as a tidal bore, may develop as the tidal front steepens (Tricker, 1964). In the Amazon River the tidal bore, migrating upstream, attains a height of about 9 m. Little is known of the dimensions of tidal bores developed in rivers draining to the marine gulfs of the N coast of Australia, but the bore that develops in the Victoria River runs at least fifty km upstream from Joseph Bonaparte Gulf.

Contrasts in tide range have important consequences in coastal geomorphology (Davies, 1972). A large tide range implies a broad inter-tidal zone, more than 20 km of sandflats and mudflats being exposed at low spring tides in the Bay of St Michel. Wave energy is expended in traversing such a broad shore zone and the waves which reach the backshore at high tide are much diminished by friction in their shallow water passage. Cliff erosion and beach building proceed only intermittently during the brief high tide, wave action being withdrawn from the backshore for most of the tidal cycle. On sheltered coasts with a

---

* Tidal information may be obtained from the three volumes of *Admiralty Tide Tables* (I. *European Waters and Mediterranean*, II. *Atlantic and Indian Oceans*, III. *Pacific Ocean and Adjacent Seas*) published annually in London by the Hydrographer of the Navy.

macrotidal range, as in Bridgwater Bay in the Bristol Channel, extensive salt marshes may develop. Where tide range is small, wave energy is concentrated at a more consistent level, facilitating cliff erosion and impeding the development of coastal marshlands. Larger tide ranges tend also to generate stronger tidal currents (see below, p. 26).

Waves

Waves are superficial undulations of the water surface produced by winds blowing over the sea (Bascom, 1959). The turbulent flow of wind energy over water sets up stress and pressure variations on the sea surface, initiating waves which grow as the result of a pressure contrast that develops between their windward and leeward slopes. Waves consist of orbital movements of water which diminish rapidly from the surface downwards, until motion is very small (0.04 × surface orbital diameter) where the water depth (d) equals half the wave length (L) (Fig. 4). In fact the orbital motion is not quite complete, so that water particles move forward slightly as each wave passes, producing a slight drift of water in the direction of wave advance. Waves are essentially a means of transmitting energy through water with relatively small displacement of water particles in the direction of energy flow.

4   *Wave terminology*

Wave height (H) is the vertical distance between adjacent crests and troughs, and wave steepness is conventionally the ratio between the height and the length: H_0/L_0.* The dimensions of waves are determined partly by wind velocity, partly by fetch (the extent of open water across which the wind is blowing), and partly by the duration of the wind. In coastal waters where fetch is limited the height of the waves is proportional to wind velocity and the wave period to the square root of wind velocity. Observations from ships in mid-ocean suggest that the largest waves, generated by prolonged strong winds over fetches of at least 500 km, may be more than 20 m high, and may travel at more than 80 km/hr.

In deep water, wave velocity (C_0), the rate of movement of a wave crest in metres per second, is the ratio of wave length $(L_0$, measured in metres) to wave period, the time interval between the passage of successive wave crests (T, measured in seconds). Wave velocity can be calculated from the following formula, in which g represents gravitational acceleration (approximately 980.62 cm/sec² at latitude 45°):

$$C_0^2 = \frac{gL_0}{2\pi}$$

Or, since $L_0 = C_0T$,

$$C_0 = \frac{gT}{2\pi} = 1.56T \text{ in metres per second.}$$

From this it is evident that

$$L_0 = 1.56T^2$$

and it is convenient to calculate wave length from measurement of wave period by using this formula.

As waves move into shallow coastal waters $(d < L/2)$ they are modified in several ways. Their velocity $(C_s$ in shallow water) is diminished according to the formula

$$C_s^2 = \frac{gL}{2\pi} \tanh \frac{2\pi d}{L}$$

As velocity diminishes, so do wave length (L_s) and period (T). Wave height first diminishes as the ratio of water depth to wave length (d/L) falls below 0.5, but when this ratio becomes less than 0.06 there is a revival of wave height, the crest rising immediately before breaking. Correspondingly, wave steepness

---

* The suffix '0' is used where still-water depth (d) is greater than half the wave length.

falls at first, then rises, the wave crest becoming narrower and sharper, the trough wider and flatter. Orbital movements within the wave become more and more elliptical, and shoreward velocity in the wave crest increases until it is greater than the wave velocity. The orbital motion can then no longer be completed, and the unsupported wave front collapses, sending forth a rush of water from the breaker line through the surf zone and thence, as swash, up across the foreshore.

These features can be demonstrated in a glass-sided water tank, using injected dyes to trace the wave motion, but under natural conditions the waves approaching a shore are far more varied and complex than this, and the relationships between wave parameters given above are of value as theoretical illustrations rather than practical guides. In practice the coastal geomorphologist is concerned primarily with the incidence and dimensions of waves that actually reach the shore, with the forms in which they break, and with the patterns of water flow that result. These features are complicated by the effects of local winds, by changes in nearshore water depth accompanying the rise and fall of tides, by currents other than those resulting from wave motion, and by the gradient and topography of the adjacent sea floor. There is usually considerable variation in the dimensions of waves reaching the shore, but the difficulty of estimating 'typical' wave lengths and wave heights can be overcome by using the concept of the significant wave. This is based on the calculation of the mean wave length ($L_{1/3}$) and the mean wave height ($H_{1/3}$) of the highest one-third of all waves observed over a period of 20 minutes. The dimensions thus obtained can be used in comparisons of conditions in coastal waters at different times, or on different coastal sectors.

Waves thus become breakers, which are said to plunge when the wave front curves over and collapses with a crash, or to spill when the crest breaks more gradually into a swash running forward on to the shore; the distinction is important in terms of the net movement of beach material on to or away from the shore (Chapter V). The swash is followed by a withdrawal (backwash), and the water that has been carried shoreward by wave action returns to the sea either as undertow (sheet flow near the sea bed) or in localised rip currents (Shepard *et al.*, 1941) with water flowing back through the breaker line in sectors up to 30 m wide, and attaining velocities of up to 8 km/hr before dispersing seaward. These various movements associated with wave action are known as the nearshore water circulation (Fig. 5).

Rip currents occur in definite patterns on many beaches. A light or moderate swell produces numerous rip current systems, and a heavy swell produces a few concentrated rips, fed by strong lateral currents in the surf zone; they become stronger and more widely spaced as incident wave energy increases, scouring hollows across the nearshore zone with fans of deposition at their seaward limits. When waves arrive at an angle to the shoreline they deflect the nearshore water circulation, so that resultant currents travel in one direction along the shore. The effects of these wave-induced longshore currents are not easily distinguished from the direct effects of waves arriving at an angle to the shore and breaking on the beach, for both processes move sediment along the shore, the action of oblique wave swash causing lateral *beach drifting*, while the wave-induced currents cause *longshore drifting* in the nearshore zone (see Chapter V). Rip currents that develop when waves approach obliquely head away diagonally through the surf instead of straight out to sea (Fig. 6).

A distinction is made between irregular patterns of waves generated directly by wind stress (a 'sea' in nautical terminology) and the more regular waves transmitted away from the generating area as *ocean swell*, which may eventually arrive on some distant coastline. Storms in mid-ocean produce a spectrum of waves of various lengths and heights, fanning out 30° to 40° on either side of the generating wind direction and travelling in a Great Circle course across the oceans (Davies, 1972). As long waves travel faster than short waves and low waves persist longer than high waves (which have to overcome greater internal friction), the long, low waves travel far beyond the storm region as a relatively regular ocean swell. This is the swell that arrives on the Pacific coast of New South Wales on a calm day with wave periods of 12–16 seconds; the wave crests gain in height and steepness as they enter shallow water, and break to produce the surf that is famous on the Sydney beaches.

Similar swells are observed on the shores of the Pacific, Atlantic, and Indian Oceans, and may have travelled vast distances. It has been shown that an ocean swell arriving on the shores of San Clemente Island on the Californian coast originated in

NEARSHORE WATER CIRCULATION

Beach

Rip — — — — Rip

Wave | approach

5 *Nearshore water circulation with waves approaching parallel to the shoreline*

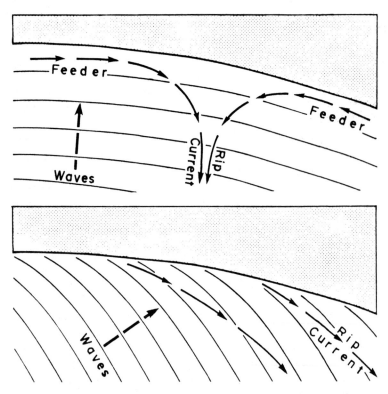

Feeder

Feeder

Waves

Rip Current

Waves

Rip Current

6 *Rip current patterns developed when waves arrive parallel to the shoreline (top) and at an angle to the shoreline (bottom)*

storm regions of the Southern Ocean, SW of Australia and New Zealand; it had travelled more than 16,000 km from the source region across the Pacific Ocean to the coast of California (Munk *et al.*, 1963). The swells that arrive on the S coast of Australia, passing into Bass Strait and reaching the W and S coasts of Tasmania, also originate in storms in the 'Roaring Forties', as do those reaching the W coasts of Africa and South America. Storms in the Atlantic Ocean produce waves typically of 6–8 seconds period which lengthen as they approach the coasts of W Europe, and occasionally the shores of SW England are washed by waves with periods of up to 20 seconds that have travelled more than 11,000 km from storm centres in the vicinity of the Falkland Islands.

Storms in northern latitudes generate similar ocean swell, especially in winter. North-westerly swell from the N Pacific then reaches the coasts of California, Central America and Ecuador, and in the Atlantic a similar swell extends to the coasts of Portugal and West Africa. Thus on the Californian coast a winter NW swell alternates with a summer SW swell, explaining the seasonal contrasts seen at Boomer Beach (p. 123).

Interactions of ocean swell arriving from different sources can produce variations in wave height as sequences of waves break on the shore. Sometimes there is a systematic increase in height of successive waves to a combined in-phase maximum, followed by a diminution as the waves move out of phase. Known as surf beat, this variation can produce maximum waves at intervals of 1 to 3 minutes. Consequent variations in breaker energy are accompanied by pulsations in longshore and onshore–offshore current flow in the nearshore zone (Komar, 1976).

Also associated with arriving swell are edge waves, standing oscillations at right angles to the coastline, the crests of which produce augmented waves as swash salients, with lateral flow into intervening troughs, where outflowing rip currents begin. As edge waves have the same periodicity as incident waves the two motions combine to produce a regularity in nearshore water circulation which leads to the formation of rhythmic morphological features such as beach cusps (p. 146).

Waves generated by wind action in coastal waters are typically shorter (wave period less than 6 seconds) and less regular than ocean swell; they may be superimposed on ocean swell in coastal waters, an onshore wind accentuating the swell and adding shorter waves to it and a cross wind producing shorter waves which move at an angle through the pattern of swell. Offshore winds tend to diminish ocean swell, producing rela- tively calm conditions in the nearshore zone. Sectors of ocean coast protected by promontories, reefs, or offshore islands receive swells in a much modified and weakened form, and may even be exempt from them. In these conditions, as in the land- locked seas of the Mediterranean and the Baltic, in the Arabian Gulf and the Gulf of California, and within embayments that have constricted entrances (e.g. Port Phillip Bay, Fig. 8), locally wind-generated waves predominate, influencing shore pro- cesses and coastal evolution. Around the British Isles, wave regimes are largely determined by wind conditions in coastal waters, ocean swell penetrating the English Channel, the Irish Sea, and the North Sea only on a very limited scale. On Van- couver Island, off W Canada, there are marked contrasts between the Pacific coast, which receives ocean swell as well as waves generated by local winds, and the shores of the Strait of Georgia, where wave action is related entirely to local wind conditions. The stormiest sectors of ocean coast are the west- facing coasts of Europe, Canada, and Patagonia within latitudes subject to frequent westerly gales. Tropical cyclones occur most frequently in the Caribbean, the north and west Indian Ocean, the China Sea, and northern Australia, the coastal waters of equatorial regions being relatively calm (e.g. NE Brazil and Indonesia), except where they receive ocean swell of distant derivation (e.g. Gulf of Guinea, SW Sumatra, and the Pacific coast of Central America). Much of the Australian coast is sub- ject to the effects of swell generated in the Southern Ocean, exceptions being the coast of Queensland where barrier reef structures lie offshore, and the coast of the Gulf of Carpentaria, partly sheltered from the ocean by Arnhem Land and the Cape York peninsula.

Ocean swell has parallel wave crests in deep water, but as the waves move into water shallower than the wave length they begin to 'feel bottom' and are modified in the manner pre- viously described. At first the pattern of wave crests is only slightly modified, but where the depth diminishes to less than half the wave length and the free orbital motion of water is impeded, the frictional effects of the sea floor retard the advancing waves. Sea floor topography thus influences the pattern of swell approaching the coast, bending the wave crests until they are parallel to the submarine contours. This is known as wave refraction. Where the angle between the swell and the submarine contours is initially large, this adjustment is often incomplete by the time the waves arrive at the shore, so that they break at

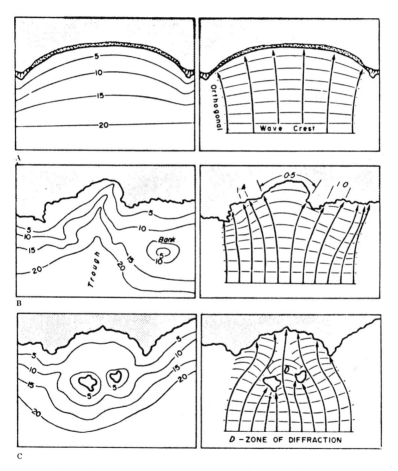

7 A *Wave refraction pattern in an embayment of simple configuration (depths in fathoms)*

B *Wave refraction pattern in an embayment with a trough offshore and a submerged bank (some refraction coefficients are indicated)*

C *Wave refraction and diffraction patterns formed where a coast is bordered by islands* an angle (usually less than 10°); where the angular difference is small, the waves are refracted in such a way that they anticipate and fit the outline of the shore, breaking simultaneously along its length. Waves entering a broad embayment become refracted into gently curved patterns, the wave in the middle of the bay moving on in deeper water while, towards the sides, in shallower water, it is held back (Fig. 7A). Sharp irregularities of the sea floor have stronger effects: a submerged bank holds back the advancing waves, but a submarine trough allows them to run on (Fig. 7B). Emerged features, such as islands, or reefs awash at low tide, produce complex patterns of wave refraction, and waves that have passed through narrow straits or entrances are modified by diffraction, spreading out in the water beyond (Fig. 7C).

Patterns of wave refraction in coastal waters can be traced from vertical air photographs, but methods have been devised for determining them graphically or by use of a computer program. Given basic knowledge of the direction of approach of waves in deep water, their length or period, and the detailed configuration of the sea floor, it is possible to construct diagrams predicting the patterns of refraction that will develop as they approach the coast. The modifications are best shown by orthogonal lines, drawn at equal intervals perpendicular to the alignment of waves in deep water, which converge where they pass over a submerged bank or reef, and diverge where deeper water is traversed; in general, they converge towards headlands and diverge in embayments. Orthogonals indicate how the wave energy is distributed, convergence towards a section of coast indicating a concentration of wave energy, whereas divergence of orthogonals indicates a weakening. The change in wave heights as waves are refracted is inversely proportional to the square root of the relative spacing of adjacent orthogonals. A refraction coefficient (R) can be derived as follows:

$$R = \sqrt{\frac{S_0}{S}}$$

where S_0 is the distance between a pair of orthogonals in deep water and S their spacing on arrival at the shoreline. Calculated from a wave refraction diagram, this coefficient is an approximate expression of the relative wave energy on sectors of the coastline.

Diagrams of this kind have been used to examine the effects of waves on the profile of sandy beaches, and it has been found that the positions of such features as stream outlets or lagoon entrances are related to wave energy distribution as indicated by the spacing of orthogonals. The outline in plan of many beaches (Plate 2) is related to patterns of approaching waves (Davies, 1959), and diagrams of wave refraction can also be used to predict the direction of longshore currents that develop where waves arrive at an angle to the shore. Longshore currents also disperse from sectors of coast where wave energy has been concentrated by refraction.

The direction, height, and frequency of waves approaching a shore are of great importance in coastal studies. These parameters are subject to much variation, and it is usually necessary to make a statistical analysis of several years' records to establish characteristic annual and seasonal patterns (Helle, 1958). Direct observations are made from lightships and from certain coastal stations, but it is generally necessary to supplement these by analyses of meteorological data. On some coasts a particular wave direction is clearly dominant. The S coast of England has

2 *Curved sandy coastline related to the arrival of refracted ocean swell (cf. Fig. 41) on Seven Mile Beach, Tasmania*

dominant waves from the direction of the prevailing SW winds, and the New South Wales coast receives a dominant SE swell. There is greater variation on coasts sheltered from regionally prevailing wind-wave and ocean swell patterns, such as the N Norfolk coast, where the prevailing SW winds blow offshore, and waves arrive from the NE, the N, or the NW according to local wind conditions. Records of onshore winds at Blakeney Point indicate that NE winds were dominant in 1958, and NW winds in 1960. Long-term records are necessary to determine dominant wave directions in these conditions.

Attempts have been made to correlate regional meteorological records with nearshore wave conditions. Silvester (1956) found that depression centres in one area off Western Australia produced waves approaching the coast from the NW, whereas depression centres in another area yielded southwesterly waves. Analysis of meteorological charts over a ten-year period gave the duration of depression centres in each area, and thus the relative incidence of northwesterly and southwesterly waves at the coast. Darbyshire (1961) outlined methods of predicting wave characteristics over the N Atlantic from synoptic records of wind velocity and direction applicable to 200 mile (320 km) grid squares in the ocean area. Characteristics of ocean swell spreading beyond a generating storm area were computed from diagrams of the angular distribution of wave energy, and added to the wind-wave pattern in each grid square. If wave refraction is taken into account, it is possible to predict wave conditions in coastal waters on sectors of the N Atlantic coast. Meteorological records can be analysed to indicate the relative duration of various kinds of wave regime over long periods, and to calculate resultants applicable to the study of process and change on coastal landforms. Few ocean areas are as well served by synoptic meteorological observations from ships, aircraft, and weather stations as the N Atlantic, but recent developments in satellite photography may produce useful data on wave patterns in less frequented ocean areas.

Coasts exposed to ocean swell and stormy seas are known as high wave energy coasts. Those that are sheltered from strong wave action are termed low wave energy coasts, and it is useful to recognise an intermediate category of moderate wave energy coasts. High wave energy coasts could be defined as those with mean annual significant wave height exceeding 1.0 m, moderate wave energy coasts 0.3 to 1.0 m, and low wave energy coasts less than 0.3 m. The stormy Atlantic coasts of Europe, and the ocean coasts of southernmost Africa and southern and western Australia are high wave energy coasts subject to frequent strong wave action, with rugged cliffs and bold sweeping beach outlines. At the other extreme are low wave energy coasts bordering narrow straits, land-locked embayments, and island or reef-fringed seas where limited fetch or intense refraction prevent the development of strong wave action. Examples are found in the Danish archipelago, in some of the embayments sheltered by the Great Barrier Reefs on the Queensland coast, and on the shores of many estuaries and lagoons. The Florida sector of the Gulf Coast of the United States has wave action reduced by a broad, gently-shelving offshore profile (Tanner *et al.*, 1963) and shows features typical of a low wave energy coast: limited beach development, lack of cliffing, an intricate shore configuration with minor spits, deltas, and coastal swamps, and persistence of offshore shoals. The distinction should be made in terms of normal prevailing wave regimes, for this kind of coast is occasionally subject to drastic modification by strong wave action during hurricanes. Variations in tide range introduce a complication, wave energy being more effective on microtidal than on macrotidal coasts, where it is dissipated over a broad shore zone; wave energy also shows marked variations with aspect on coasts of irregular outline. Many coasts fall into the intermediate category of moderate wave energy coasts, being partly cliffed, but having such features as spits, deltas, and swamps which diversify the outline of depositional sectors. Much of the E coast of England can be classified in this way and similar conditions obtain in gulfs and landlocked embayments around the Australian coast, for example in Port Phillip Bay, Gulf St Vincent and Hervey Bay.

Currents

Ocean currents are drifts of water in response to prevailing wind patterns, and are also due, in part, to density variations in the oceans resulting from differences in the salinity and temperature of water masses. There is an analogy here with air masses in the atmosphere, where density variations resulting from differences in humidity and temperature produce atmospheric currents (i.e. winds). These ocean currents should not be confused with currents associated with waves and tides, or currents that develop locally in coastal waters when strong winds are blowing. True ocean currents are slow movements of water, and are not important in coastal geomorphology, except where they bring in warmer or colder water, which affects ecological conditions near the coast and thereby influences the world distribution of such landforms as coral reefs and mangrove swamps.

Tidal currents, produced by the ebb and flow of tides, alternate in direction in coastal waters, reversing as the tide ebbs; their effects may thus be temporary or cyclic. In the open ocean tidal currents rarely exceed 3 km/hr, but where the flow is channelled through gulfs, straits between islands, or entrances to estuaries and lagoons, these currents are strengthened, and may locally and temporarily exceed 16 km/hr. The velocity of tidal currents constricted in this way is related to tide range, the strongest currents being generated in macrotidal areas at spring tides. In the Raz Blanchart, between Alderney and Cap de la Hague in NW France, the tidal current attains about 16 km/hr under these conditions. Off the N coast of Australia, another macrotidal area, powerful currents develop in the straits bordering Melville Island, particularly in Apsley Strait, between Melville and Bathurst Islands. Tidal oscillations impinging on a coastline may set up longshore currents, as on the N Norfolk coast, where the longshore flow is westward during the two to three hours preceding high tide, then eastward for another two to three hours as the ebb sets in. These currents are of limited importance in terms of erosion, deposition, or sediment flow on the open coast, their effects being subordinate to the effects of waves, and the associated currents developed by wave action in the nearshore zone.

Wave action is generally accompanied by wind-driven currents produced where winds cause mass movement of surface water, building up sea level to leeward and lowering it to windward. Hydraulic currents then disperse water from areas where it has been piled up, until normal levels are restored. Strong currents are produced when winds drive surface water into gulfs or straits, or into and out of estuary and lagoon entrances. These may strengthen the currents produced by tides in similar situations, and it is often difficult to separate the effects of the two. Wind-generated currents are not as regularly alternating as tidal currents, however, and their effects are likely to be cumulative in the direction of the prevailing wind. Winds blowing offshore can set up a shoreward bottom current in the nearshore zone.

Currents produced by fluvial discharge carry sediment into the sea, maintain or enlarge river outlets, and form a seaward 'jet' which refracts approaching waves and acts as a breakwater impeding or interrupting longshore current flow. Discharge currents are strongest off streams fed by melting ice and snow from coastal mountains, as in Norway and Alaska during the summer months. In tidal estuaries, fluvial discharge is reduced, and possibly halted by the rising tide, but augmented by the ebb. Currents generated by wind and tide can be strong enough to move superficial sediment on the sea floor to prevent deposition and even to erode channels or colks (scour-holes) where water is driven through narrow straits such as the entrance to Port

8   *Tidal colk at the entrance to Port Phillip Bay (soundings in fathoms)*

Phillip Bay (Fig. 8) (Benson and Raeside, 1963). The sea floor between islands in Bass Strait shows deep, elongated channels, evidently formed by current scour (Jennings, 1959), and narrow entrances to lagoons and estuaries have often been deepened by the action of tidal currents (Fig. 75). Closed basins have been scoured in soft outcrops on the sea floor off the Dorset coast and in the Bristol Channel by tidal currents (Donovan and Stride, 1961), and off the Brittany coast paths of current flow are marked out by rocky or gravelly sectors on a sea floor that is generally sandy or muddy. Shoals of gravel sometimes develop adjacent to rocky headlands in sectors of current flow, examples being the Skerries, E of Start Point, and the Shambles, E of Portland Bill, on England's S coast (Fig. 45).

The effects of currents in transporting sediment were measured by the Swedish scientist, Hjulström, who showed that the most readily eroded particles were fine to medium sands, with grain diameters between 0.1 and 0.5 mm, which could be mobilised by currents of velocity greater than 15 cm/sec, but higher velocities are required to move larger and heavier particles, and also smaller particles, such as silt and clay, which are less easily moved because they are cohesive. On the other hand once in suspension, silt and clay can be kept moving by current velocities much lower than those required to maintain the flow of coarser material. In the nearshore zone, sediment is more readily transported by relatively weak currents, because particles are thrown into suspension by the water turbulence associated with breaking waves.

Currents are generally more effective in shaping sea floor topography than in developing coastal configuration, and the early view that long, gently-curving beaches on oceanic coasts were produced by currents sweeping along the shore has given place to the modern view that these outlines are determined by refracted wave patterns (see Chapter V). Nevertheless, changes in the topography of the sea floor, due to erosion by current scour or deposition from slackening currents, modify patterns of wave refraction and may thus indirectly affect coastal outlines. Currents often play a part in removing material eroded by waves from the coast, or in supplying the sediment that is built into depositional forms by wave action. In addition, currents are responsible for the development of inter-tidal spits and bars, as well as various kinds of ripple patterns on foreshores and tidal flats, on the floors of estuaries and lagoons, and on the sea bed. These points will be considered further in later chapters.

It is difficult to trace and measure currents accurately. Superficial movements of coastal water can be traced by introducing fluorescein, a coloured dye which indicates where the water is moving. Another technique is to use floats, submerged as far as possible to reduce wind resistance and carrying distinctive markers that can be observed, enabling their speed to be measured as they move with the current. Attempts have been made to trace sea floor sediment movement by bottom currents with the aid of sea bed drifters, plastic devices with slight negative buoyancy that sink to the bottom and then drift with the water flow (Phillips, 1970). The location of floats and drifters subsequently found indicates the resultant of current flow (and thus of sediment movement) over the intervening period, but not the routes that were taken. It can be of more value to measure the effects of nearshore processes (volumes of sediment eroded, in transit, and deposited) than the processes themselves—a theme that will be taken up again in Chapter V.

Catastrophic processes
Exceptional disturbances of ocean water occur during and after earthquakes, landslides or volcanic eruptions in and around the ocean basins. These produce waves several hundred kilometres long, with periods of up to half an hour, proceeding at velocities of up to 800 km/hr across the deep oceans. They are barely perceptible in mid-ocean, but on entering shallow coastal waters they build up into giant 'tidal waves' which may attain heights of more than 30 m by the time they reach the coast. The term 'tidal waves' is misleading, for they are not tidal in origin, and the scientific term for them is the Japanese word 'tsunami'. They are most common in the Pacific Ocean, which is bordered by zones of crustal instability, and they are responsible for occasional catastrophic flooding and erosion of Pacific coasts, often with much devastation and loss of life far from the originating disturbance. In April 1946 a tsunami was initiated by an earthquake off the Aleutian Islands, and waves travelling southwards arrived in the Hawaiian Islands, 3700 km away, in less than five 'hours, having moved at an average speed of 750 km/hr. Shepard, who happened to be in Oahu at the time, has described how, after a preliminary withdrawal of water, a succession of

giant waves broke at intervals of 12 minutes, each higher than
the last, sweeping across the coral reefs and rising up to 10 m
above normal sea level. The town of Hilo in Hawaii was hit by
waves rising 9 m, and at one point a wave reached 16.8 m.
Beaches were swept away, and the waves carried reef debris,
including large blocks of coral, on to the coast, and eroded
hollows on hillsides far above normal high tide level. Giant
waves were recorded at many other places around the Pacific
Ocean, and at Scotch Cap, Alaska, they destroyed a lighthouse
and a radio mast 30 m above sea level (Shepard, 1963).

After these events, a network of seismographic and tidal
observatories was set up by the U.S. Coast and Geodetic Survey
in the Pacific region to record the initiation and give warning of
the spread of tsunamis. The next major disturbance was an
earthquake of exceptional intensity off the coast of S Chile on
22 May 1960, when huge waves broke on the adjacent coast, and
very long waves spread radially across the Pacific Ocean. Soon
afterwards, abnormally high waves were recorded on tide
gauges on the Pacific coast of North America, and it was forecast
that giant waves would reach Honolulu. The waves arrived at
the predicted time, but they were only 1.2 m above normal; Hilo
was again devastated, this time by waves reaching 11 m, and a
few hours later waves up to 40 m high hit the coasts of Hokkaido
and Honshu in Japan, causing extensive damage and drowning
many people. Waves 3.3 m above normal were recorded at Port
Lyttelton, on the E coast of South Island, New Zealand, and the
tide gauge at Cronulla, on the coast of New South Wales,
recorded series of exceptional oscillations of water level up to
0.75 m above and below the predicted tidal curve. The Alaskan
earthquake of March 1964 initiated a tsunami in the Pacific, and
exceptionally high waves were recorded on the W coast of
North America. The effects were moderate, however, in
Hawaii, on the Japanese coast, and in the S Pacific; Sydney
recorded tides about a foot higher than usual.

It is now realised that tsunamis are not necessarily 'damped
down' by distance; the magnitude of waves received depends
partly on offshore topography, the waves being higher where
the offshore zone is gently shelving, and partly on the orientation of a coast in relation to the source of the disturbance. An
earthquake along a fault line is likely to produce higher waves
on coasts facing and parallel to the fault than on coasts which
run obliquely to it; the greatest effects of the 1960 tsunami were

on parts of the Japanese coast parallel to the line of disturbance of the Chilean earthquake. Wave heights are much reduced where coral reefs border the coast, where there is deep water close inshore, or where the waves have been refracted round reefs, shoals, or islands of intricate configuration.

The explosive eruption of Krakatau, a volcanic island in Sunda Strait, in 1883 generated a tsunami up to 30 m high on the nearby coasts of Java and Sumatra, hurling coral boulders and blocks up on to fringing reefs and triggering landslides in deeply-weathered rock outcrops on steep coastal slopes (Bird and Ongkosongo, 1980).

Huge waves can be generated in restricted areas by landslides and rockfalls. Miller (1960) gave details of the effects of a massive rockfall into Lituya Bay, an Alaskan fiord, in July 1960. Water swept 520 m up an adjacent mountainside, and a wave 15 m high raced down the fiord at 160 km/hr, sweeping across a spit at the entrance and dispersing in the sea area offshore. Disturbances of a similar kind develop in the vicinity of ice coasts as the result of iceberg calving.

Tropical cyclones can raise sea level and generate waves that reach several metres beyond high tide level on the coast. When the island of Mauritius received its first tropical cyclones for fifteen years in 1960, coastal rocks were dislodged, slumping occurred on cliffs, beaches were lowered, and sand and coral debris deposited at the storm swash limit (McIntire and Walker, 1964), but the changes on these steep coasts were minor compared with those observed on the low-lying Gulf Coast of the United States during hurricanes, some of which produced major changes in coastal forms and nearshore geometry (Warnke *et al.*, 1966). Cyclone Audrey in 1957 submerged parts of the Mississippi delta to depths of 3.6 m, and Hurricane Eloise in 1975 raised sea level at Panama City by up to 6 m. In Australia, Cyclone Althea in 1971 generated a storm surge that attained a maximum of 3.66 m on the Queensland coast north of Townsville. Sandy shorelines were cut back up to 14 m, but mangrove-fringed coasts proved resilient, even though waves washing into the mangroves moved sand and shell debris (Hopley, 1974). Features produced by cyclones include blocks of dune calcarenite up to 2 m in diameter thrown up on to a platform above high tide level at Quobba in Western Australia (Plate 3). Pacific tsunamis have piled up broken beach rock on the coast of Ecuador (Plate 4).

3 *Coastal terraces at Quobba, Western Australia showing large blocks thrown on to upper terrace by storm waves*

4 *Broken beach rock piled up by a tsunami on the coast of Ecuador*

These are unusual episodes. On most coasts the tides, waves, and currents operate, and influence the development of coastal landforms, within a zone above and below present mean sea level, the extent of the zone depending largely on tide range. Storm waves achieve erosion and deposition well above high spring tide mark, and the sea floor is subject to the effects of wave action, increasing in intensity shorewards from the line where water depth equals half the wave length. It is clear that, in the past, the zone of operation of marine processes has been at times higher than it is now, and also, at times, lower; there have been *stillstands* when the relative levels of land and sea remained constant at particular altitudes, and episodes when the levels of land and sea have changed. The evolution of coastal landforms has been much influenced by the sequence of still-stands and changing levels of land and sea, and it is necessary now to examine the evidence for these, to show how the history of such changes is being established, and to consider for how long marine processes have been operative with land and sea at their present relative level.

III

CHANGING LEVELS OF
LAND AND SEA

At various places on the coast there are stranded beach deposits, marine shell beds, and platforms backed by steep cliff-like slopes, all marking former coastlines that now stand above high tide level and beyond the reach of the sea. These are *emerged* coastlines, and they owe their present position either to uplift of the land, or a fall in sea level, or some combination of movements of land and sea that has left the coast higher, relative to sea level, than it was before. In addition, there are *submerged* coastal features, such as the drowned mouths of river valleys, submerged dune topography, and the former coastlines marked by breaks of slope that have been detected by soundings on the sea floor. Evidence of submergence has also been obtained from borings in coastal plains and deltas where freshwater peat and relics of land vegetation have been encountered well below present sea level, together with coastal deposits formed when the sea stood at a lower level relative to the land. Submerged coastlines may have been caused by subsidence of the land, sea level rise, or a combination of these movements. Where evidence of a change in the relative levels of land and sea is found, it is difficult to decide whether it is a result of an uplift or depression of the land (*tectonic movement*), a raising or lowering of sea level (*eustatic movement*), or a combination of the two (Fig. 9). Until this is known, it is best to use the neutral terms *emergence* and *submergence*.

Some parts of the coast show evidence of both emergence and submergence, the sea having been higher relative to the land at one stage, lower at another, and now in an intermediate position. A close investigation is necessary to determine the sequence and dimensions of successive changes in the levels of land and sea, and whether any changes are still in progress. Some coasts are now being submerged, others are emerging. If no changes of land or sea level are taking place, a condition of 'stillstand' has been attained. The various kinds of tectonic and eustatic movement will be considered first, before dealing with the evidence of such changes on coasts in more detail.

Movements of the land

Upward or downward movements of the land, termed *tectonic* movements, may be *epeirogenic, orogenic,* or *isostatic.* Epeirogenic movements are broad-scale elevations or depressions of continents and ocean basins, with warping restricted to a marginal hinge-line, whereas orogenic movements involve more complicated deformation, with folding, faulting, warping, and tilting of the land. Broad-scale epeirogenic movements took place in Aus-

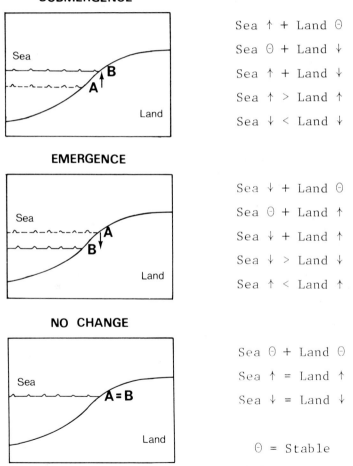

SUBMERGENCE

Sea ↑ + Land ⊖
Sea ⊖ + Land ↓
Sea ↑ + Land ↓
Sea ↑ > Land ↑
Sea ↓ < Land ↓

EMERGENCE

Sea ↓ + Land ⊖
Sea ⊖ + Land ↑
Sea ↓ + Land ↑
Sea ↓ > Land ↓
Sea ↑ < Land ↑

NO CHANGE

Sea ⊖ + Land ⊖
Sea ↑ = Land ↑
Sea ↓ = Land ↓

⊖ = Stable

9   *Submergence can result from five combinations of land and sea movements or stability; emergence also from five; no change from three*

tralia late in Tertiary times, when the Eastern Highlands and the large Precambrian shield region of Western Australia were elevated, while the intervening tract from the Gulf of Carpentaria southwards to the mouth of the Murray remained at a comparatively low level. Episodes of epeirogenic uplift have marked the evolution of the African continent, where broad planation surfaces initiated during intervening phases of tectonic stability are separated by bold scarps initiated during each uplift episode (King, 1962). Tectonic deformation at the margin of an epeirogenically-uplifted continent would be likely to run parallel to the general trend of the coastline, with elevation on the landward side and subsidence on the seaward side of a 'hinge-line'. Bourcart (1952) considered this 'continental flexure' responsible for the stairways of terraces in which the oldest is the highest and farthest inland, reported from many coasts, but other possible explanations of these terrace sequences must be considered (see below, p. 46).

Orogenesis is the process by which mountains are built; it begins with the formation of vast crustal depressions, known as geosynclines, which subside as sediment is deposited in them, and are subsequently upheaved as chains of mountains. Orogenic movements are in progress N of Australia, in New Guinea and Indonesia, where active deformation is accompanying the formation of the geosyncline that lies between the more stable crustal regions of the Sahul Shelf, bordering N Australia, and the Sunda Shelf beneath the China Sea. In Victoria, Port Phillip Bay (Fig. 8) occupies a tectonic depression, or *sunkland*, bordered on the eastern side by Selwyn Fault, an active fault along which earthquakes still occur from time to time: the Mornington earthquake of 1932 was traced to a displacement along this fault. Earth movements continuing into Recent times have also influenced the levels of coastal features around the margins of the Pacific Basin, notably in New Zealand, Japan, Alaska and California, and on the shores of the Mediterranean Sea. Coasts subject to active movements are termed *neotectonic* coasts, and rates of change may be determined by the dating of tectonically-displaced features. Near Aitape, New Guinea, Hossfeld (1965) obtained radiocarbon dates indicating that an emerged mangrove swamp had been uplifted about 50 m during the past five thousand years. Where warping has been transverse to the coastline, as in the Wellington district, New Zealand, there is a juxtaposition of uplifted and emerged coasts with downwarped and submerged coasts, and parts of the coastline have been determined by Recent faulting.

Isostatic movements are adjustments in the earth's crust where it is heavily loaded by ice, lava, or accumulating sedimentary deposits. Crustal subsidence is taking place in the vicinity of large deltas, where the load consists of sedimentary deposits accumulating at the mouth of a river, and borings have shown that the Mississippi delta is underlain by a great thickness of Quaternary sediment, occupying a crustal depression, the subsidence of which is partly due to isostatic adjustments of the earth's crust beneath the accumulating sedimentary load. A long history of subsidence can be deduced from this stratigraphic evidence, for the deposits on river terraces bordering the Mississippi valley can be traced down into the wedge of sediment beneath the delta (Fig. 118) (Russell, 1967). Other large deltas show similar evidence of subsidence as sediment accumulated.

Complicated isostatic movements have taken place in regions that were glaciated during Pleistocene times. As ice accumulated the earth's crust was depressed; when it melted, the crust was gradually elevated. In Scandinavia and N Canada the land is still rising because of the melting of glaciers and ice sheets. Isostatic recovery of depressed crustal areas continues for some time after the ice has gone, until the physical equilibrium of the earth's crust is restored, so that coasts bordering recently deglaciated areas have been subject to continuing uplift of the land; they show sequences of differentially elevated coastlines, as on the southern shores of Hudson Bay in N Canada and on the coasts of highland Britain. In northern Sweden coastlines only 10,000 years old have been raised by up to 286 m above the present level of the Gulf of Bothnia by the postglacial isostatic recovery, and the Danish island of Laesø in the Kattegat is an example of an island enlarged by such emergence.

Each of these kinds of land movement may have affected, or may be affecting, the evolution of coastal landforms. Coasts bordering a land area that had remained tectonically stable through Quaternary times would show evidence of successive episodes of submergence and emergence due entirely to upward or downward movements of the sea. It is only on such coasts that the record of Quaternary oscillations of sea level can

be established, but it is difficult to prove that a sector of coast
has been stable through Quaternary times. If such stable sectors
do occur, they will be found in regions without evidence of
earthquakes or volcanic action, where the coastal rocks are
relatively old, and where emerged and submerged shoreline
features, traced along the coast, are found to be horizontal,
above and below present sea level.

Movements of the sea

Upward and downward movements of sea level, termed *eustatic*
movements, are world-wide because the oceans are interconnected. Major changes of sea level are caused by the addition or
subtraction of water from the oceans, changes in the configuration and capacity of the ocean basins, or a combination of these
two factors (Fairbridge, 1961).

It is believed that the total quantity of water on and around
the earth has been more or less uniform through Quaternary
times, apart from relatively small accessions of 'juvenile' water
being supplied from the interior by volcanic processes. This
means that water lost from the oceans must be gained either by
the atmosphere or by the land. If the volume of water in the
oceans remains constant, sea level changes may result from
variations in the density of ocean water accompanying changes
in temperature: it has been calculated that a fall of 1°C in the
mean temperature of the oceans would contract their volume
so that sea level would fall about 2 m. Estimates of Pleistocene
variations of mean ocean temperature based on palaeotempera-
ture measurements on fossils from ocean floor deposits (see
below, p. 40) are within 5°C of the present temperature, so that
this process could only account for sea level oscillations of about
10 m. Geomorphological evidence indicates that Pleistocene sea
level oscillations amounted to more than 100 m, and so other
mechanisms must be involved.

Sea level would rise if water were added to the oceans, and
fall if it were removed. This is evidently what happened during
Pleistocene times, when world-wide climatic changes produced
a series of at least four main cold (glacial) phases separated by
warmer (interglacial) phases, and followed by a warmer (postglacial) phase in Holocene times; subsidiary mild (interstadial)
phases occurred during each glacial phase. As the climate
became cooler, with the onset of each glacial phase, the growing

glaciers and ice sheets were nourished by precipitation from the atmosphere, derived largely from evaporation over the oceans, but deposited and retained as snow and ice on the land. As a result, water was removed from the oceans, their volume diminished, and a world-wide lowering of sea level took place. When the glaciers and ice sheets melted, water was returned to the oceans, and world-wide marine transgressions carried the sea to relatively high levels. It has been calculated that, if all the ice remaining on the earth melted, sea level would rise about 60 m, submerging coastal plains and most of the world's major cities, but at the maximum of the Pleistocene glaciation sea level was more than 100 m lower than it is now. These large, world-wide movements of sea level during Quaternary times are termed *glacio-eustatic* oscillations, and various attempts have been made to establish their sequence and provide a time-table for the climatic changes which led to them.

Such changes are believed to be due to variations in solar radiation, and attempts have been made to project estimates of variations in solar radiation, based on astronomical theory, backwards through time. Graphs of hypothetical variations, compiled mathematically, show a sequence of warmer and colder periods during Quaternary times, and these have been correlated with interglacial and glacial phases.

An alternative approach uses oxygen isotope ratios measured in analyses of fossil foraminifera taken from sedimentary cores obtained from the floors of the oceans, where sedimentation has been very slow, and deposits marking the whole of the Quaternary era are only a few feet thick. The ratio of the oxygen isotopes O^{16} and O^{18} in fossil foraminifera is an indication of the temperature of the environment at the time they formed, and thus, compared with present ocean temperatures, an indication of warmer or colder climates in the past. Foraminifera obtained at successive levels from the stratified sequence of ocean floor sediments yield evidence of past changes of climate, with warmer and colder phases that are correlated with interglacial and glacial phases in the Pleistocene period (Emiliani, 1966). It is supposed that each climatic oscillation was matched by a glacio-eustatic oscillation of sea level, a warmer ocean indicating a higher sea level, and a cooler ocean a lower sea level. In other words, the temperature graph will do for a graph of changing sea levels if it can be calibrated with vertical dimensions. On this basis Fairbridge (1961) devised a curve of Quaternary sea level changes (Fig. 10) which is conceptually valid, but requires much refinement. Shackleton and Opdyke (1973) analysed oxygen isotopes and palaeo-magnetism in ocean-floor cores from the Equatorial Pacific, representing a sedimentation sequence over the past 870,000 years. Isotopic palaeotemperatures within the upper 2.2 m (deposited in the past 128,000 years) were used to deduce a glacio-eustatic world sea level curve which showed maxima correlative with those derived from work in Barbados (peaks at 120 and 80 to 100 thousand years ago) and New Guinea (peak 30 to 50 thousand years ago), with a Last Glacial minimum about 20 to 25 thousand years ago and the ensuing transgression (Fig. 11). The problems of relating this graph to the geomorphological evidence of higher and lower sea levels in Quaternary times will be discussed later.

Sea level changes may also result from variations in the capacity of the ocean basins, the volume of ocean water remaining constant. If the capacity of an ocean basin (measured below

10   *Eustatic oscillations of sea level during Quaternary times (after Fairbridge, 1961). The peaks in the graph mark interglacial phase high sea levels, the troughs glacial phase low sea levels (G = Gunz, M = Mindel, R = Riss, W = Würm, the four European glacial phases); the lower graph shows Quaternary temperature variations in tropical seas (after Emiliani, 1966)*

11 *A deduced sequence of sea level changes on tectonically stable coasts during the past 125,000 years, compiled from various sources. For Holocene variations see Fig. 17*

present sea level) were increased, sea level would fall; if it were reduced, sea level would rise. It should be noted that we are now no longer dealing purely with movements of sea level, for changes in the configuration and capacity of the ocean basins involve tectonic movements in the earth's crust beneath the oceans or on bordering coasts. Epeirogenic sinking of an ocean basin would increase its capacity, and cause a world-wide lowering of sea level, while orogenic or isostatic movements in and around the ocean basins would lead to a world-wide lowering or raising of sea level, according to whether they increase or diminish the capacity of the ocean basin. As tectonic movements anywhere within the ocean basins will influence sea levels all over the world, it is best to distinguish sea level changes of this kind as *tectono-eustatic.*

Deposition of land-derived sediment in the sea and outpouring of volcanic lava on the sea floor also reduce the capacity of the ocean basins and therefore raise sea level, but these modifications would not lead to sea level changes as large or as rapid as those due to glacio-eustatic or tectono-eustatic variations.

According to King (1959), transference of all the land above present sea level into the ocean basins would raise the level of the oceans by more than 250 m, but present estimates of denudation rates would only account for a secular rise of sea level of about 3 mm per century.

Bloom (1967) has indicated the possibility of an isostatic readjustment of the coastal fringe and continental shelf to loading and unloading as sea levels rose and fell during Quaternary times. The extent of such *hydro-isostatic* readjustment would vary in relation to the width and slope of the continental shelf in each sector (which determines the volume and weight of water gained or lost during a sea level change) as well as to the structure and strength of geological formations in the area affected. It is possible that sectors of steep coast were thus submerged more deeply than sectors of gently-shelving coast during the last major marine transgression, which may account for some of the discrepancies between 'eustatic' sea level curves derived from studies in various parts of the world (see below, page 59).

Further variations in ocean level may result from changes in transverse gradients that develop where ocean currents are strong. Off the east coast of the United States and in the China Sea the ocean is up to 2 m above its general level in areas adjacent to the poleward currents of the Gulf Stream and Kuroshio, and any variation in the velocity or extent of these currents could have led to anomalous changes of sea level on the nearby coasts. Moreover, the ocean envelope is related to the axis and velocity of the earth's rotation, and any variation in these will have caused differential changes of sea level around the world's coasts. Moreover, evidence from satellite sensing has shown that the oceans have a complex surface configuration, with bulges and troughs rising and falling several metres above and below a smooth geoid because of gravitational, hydrological and meteorological forces: although they are interconnected, the oceans have probably not responded equi-altitudinally to the various changes of water volume that have been deduced (Mörner, 1976), so that there may well be considerable variation in the elevations of changing 'eustatic' sea levels around the world's coasts. At best, it may prove possible to delineate oceanic regions, around the margins of which eustatic fluctuations have been similar.

The task of distinguishing between local land movement changes and world-wide sea movement changes is therefore a difficult one, and will remain so even if a record of world-wide eustatic movements can be firmly established on coasts where stability through Quaternary times is proved. Meanwhile it will be useful to collect evidence of the sequence of *relative* changes of land and sea level on particular coasts during Quaternary times, in the hope that it will eventually be possible to separate the effects of oscillations of sea level from those of upward and downward movements of the land.

Measuring changes of level
Where emerged or submerged coastlines are discovered, it is necessary to determine their levels above or below present sea level. Confusion has been caused by the use of different datum levels in surveys of this kind. Some workers have measured from mean sea level, the datum used on topographic maps in many countries; others from low water spring tide level, the datum used on nautical charts of coastal regions; and others from high water spring tide level, which is more easily determined and more readily accessible for surveying work on the coast.* Each of these has advantages for particular purposes, the first fitting in with surveyed contours and bench marks on topographic maps, the second enabling chart soundings and submarine contours to be used without modification, and the third being the most practical in field work, but the discrepancies between them increase with tide range, and it is necessary to adjust levels determined by different workers to the same datum before comparisons are made. Perhaps the best method would be to adjust all measurements of emerged and submerged shoreline features to mean sea level datum, stating the local spring tide range above and below this level.

Emerged shore features usually consist of benches or terraces, backed by abandoned cliffs, and sometimes bearing beach deposits or marine shell beds. Where possible, the level is measured at the back of the terrace, towards the base of the abandoned cliff, but this point is frequently obscured by beach deposits, dunes, or sediment washed down from adjacent slopes, and

---

* High tide levels are indicated by strandline drift material, or the vertical extent of rock-dwelling marine organisms such as the rock oyster, which is generally found to an upper limit close to high water neap tide.

it is rarely possible to determine it within ± 1.5 m. For this reason, the altitudes of emerged coastlines are usually given in approximate figures: e.g. '5 to 8 m above mean sea level'.

Sequences of terraces measured on one sector of coast may not be recognisable on adjacent sectors, for terrace preservation requires a particular relationship between rock resistance, the intensity and duration of marine denudation at the higher coastline phase, and the degree of subsequent degradation and dissection. As a rule, permeable sandstones, limestones (including coral), and gravel-strewn formations retain terraced forms better than impermeable rocks that are more resistant (restricted terrace development at the higher shoreline phase) or less resistant (greater destruction of terrace by subsequent denudation). Coastal terraces are rarely well preserved on rapidly-weathering rock formations.

Emerged coastlines have often been dissected by valleys incised by rivers as they extended their courses across the emerged sea floor, whereas submerged coastlines are more often preserved intact, and may be traced across the sea floor by sounding, providing they have not been obscured by later sedimentary deposition. Where fragments of emerged marine terraces occur at intervals along a coast, the problem of correlation arises. There are dangers in correlating terraces simply in terms of their altitude above present sea level, for where the land has been tilted laterally along the coast, fragments of the same terrace will be found at different levels, and fragments of different terraces may be found at similar levels. If there are sequences of terraces spaced at equivalent intervals above present sea level, correlation is less hazardous, and where this is possible the terraces indicate either a series of episodes of uniform uplift of the land without tilting or warping, or a succession of eustatic changes of sea level on the margins of a land area that has been stable.

Where marine deposits are associated with coastal terraces, correlation may be possible in terms of distinctive groups of fossils. Distinctive assemblages of minerals may occur in old beach sands, but the lateral variations in mineral composition of present-day beaches are such that correlation in terms of this evidence can only be tentative. A more promising means of correlation, developed in recent years, is based on radiocarbon measurements on samples of wood, peat, shells, or coral, obtained from deposits associated with former shorelines. The proportion of the carbon isotope C^{14} to stable C^{12} diminishes with the age of organic materials, and is thus a measure of the time that has elapsed since they were alive. Radiocarbon analysis permits estimates of the age of samples less than 35,000 years old, and is therefore a means of distinguishing Holocene deposits (less than 10,000 years old) from those formed during Pleistocene times. Dates obtained from radiocarbon analysis are stated in years B.P. (Before the Present), and there is an international agreement that the present should be defined as the year A.D. 1950. The margin of error is usually indicated as ± the standard deviation of the measurements made (e.g. 5,580 ± 200 years B.P.).

Certain difficulties in the application of radiocarbon dating have become evident in recent years. Radioactive contamination of the atmosphere by nuclear explosions has led to a sharp increase in the proportion of C^{14}, more than offsetting the dilution due to the combustion of fossil fuels, releasing 'ancient' carbon (i.e. with little or no C^{14}) into the atmosphere since the beginning of the industrial era. The C^{14} concentration in the atmosphere may also have varied in the past in relation to changes in the intensity of cosmic radiation, and to climatic variations. Dates obtained from shells or coral are less reliable than those from wood or peat because of the possibility that during their lifetime the calcareous organisms ingested an unknown proportion of ancient carbon derived from fossil organisms or dissolved carbonates, giving a deceptively high radiocarbon age. Alternatively, younger carbon from percolating groundwater may have replaced some of the fossil carbon, giving a deceptively low radiocarbon age. Carelessly collected or inadequately cleaned samples may also be contaminated by 'modern' carbon (e.g. if the roots of living plants have penetrated fossil wood or subsoil peat), traces of which can reduce the radiocarbon age to a fraction of the true age.

Other dating techniques recently developed permit correlation of pre-Holocene coastal deposits. Refinements of the potassium-argon method have been applied to the dating of volcanic rocks interbedded in the Pleistocene stratigraphy of the New Zealand coast (Stipp *et al.*, 1967). Another technique is based on the fact that uranium isotopes present in small quantities in living corals and other marine organisms yield daughterisotopes of thorium with the passage of time: fossil corals from progressively greater depths in a boring on Eniwetok Atoll had increasing proportions of Th^{230}. The U^{234}/Th^{230} ratio has been used to date marine carbonate rocks up to 300,000 years B.P. (Chappell, 1974, 1983).

Evidence of emerged coastlines
Emerged marine terraces have been found on many coasts at various levels, and submerged terraces indicative of former coastlines at lower levels have been discovered during surveys of sea floor morphology. Correlation of these former coastlines in terms of a sequence of Quaternary eustatic movements of sea level, allowing for the extent of tectonic movements in coastal regions during Quaternary times, has proved extremely diffi-cult, and there is little prospect of an early solution to these problems. At one time it appeared that the sequence of terraces reported half a century ago by De Lamothe in Algeria and Depéret on the French Riviera, sectors of the Mediterranean coast thought to have been stable during Quaternary times, was being confirmed by studies of 'coastal stairways' elsewhere (Zeuner, 1959). The Mediterranean sequence consisted of four main high sea level stages (named Sicilian, Milazzian, Tyrrhen-ian, and Monastirian), taken as equivalent to successive high stillstands of sea level during interglacial phases of the Pleisto-cene period. The Sicilian was equivalent to a sea level at 90–100 m, the Milazzian 55–60 m, the Tyrrhenian 28–32 m, and the Monastirian was subdivided into Main Monastirian, 18–20 m and Late Monastirian, 7–8 m. There was a tendency to correlate terraces discovered at these levels on other coasts with the Mediterranean sequence, and accept the correlation as evi-dence of the Quaternary stability of the coast concerned. In Britain, high-level marine deposits in SE England at about 200 m were assigned an early Pleistocene (Calabrian) age on palaeonto-logical grounds, their contained fossil assemblage matching marine deposits of this age elsewhere. Terraces at lower levels (especially 130 m and 50 m) were correlated with the Mediterra-nean sequence by Zeuner (1959), who postulated a high late Tertiary sea level followed by the glacio-eustatic oscillations with successive interglacial maxima of diminishing altitude, culmin-ating in the final low sea level of the Last Glaciation, and the succeeding Holocene marine transgression to present sea level.

The term Holocene marine transgression is not strictly accurate, because the sea level rise began about 18,000 years ago in late Pleistocene times, and had attained approximately − 30 m at the start of the Holocene (10,000 years B.P.) but as it is a convenient and widely used term it will be retained here. It should be noted that the contact between basal marine sediments deposited as this transgression proceeded and the underlying previously subaerial surface is diachronous when traced across the sea floor to the modern coast (cf. Fig. 15).

If all the ice that remains on the earth's surface were now to melt, the sea level would rise about 60 m, so that if the sea stood about 200 m higher at the beginning of Pleistocene times something more is required than straightforward glacio-eustatic oscillations. One suggestion has been that the ocean basins, notably the Pacific Ocean basin, have been subsiding epeirogenically during Quaternary times, resulting in successively lower interglacial sea levels, so that the sea level fluctuations are partly tectono-eustatic changes. Another is that the Antarctic ice sheet became progressively larger, taking up an increasing volume of ocean water, during Pleistocene times.

In the last few years, doubts have arisen concerning the validity of the Quaternary sea level sequence outlined by Zeuner. On the one hand, it is possible that some of the classic sites around the Mediterranean, on which the original levels and chronology were based, were not tectonically stable during Quaternary times; although some high level coastlines are horizontal for several kilometres, Hey (1978) found that they could not be correlated altitudinally around the Mediterranean, and concluded that vertical displacements had occurred. Elsewhere, altitudinal correlations of coastal terraces are not as good as was formerly thought. It has been all too easy to give emphasis to those terraces which appeared to lie within the range of levels quoted for the classic Mediterranean sequence or, admitting the possibilities of error in determining coastal levels, to agree that some of them were approximately equivalent to the Mediterranean sequence. When the results of detailed studies of coastal terraces are examined, they show considerable departures from the classic Mediterranean sequence of four or five main terraces up to and including the Sicilian (90−100 m): some workers have found many more terraces within this height range, others have found fewer, and former sea levels supposedly of Pleistocene

age have been reported at almost every altitude below 200 m
on various coasts.

Varying viewpoints have been expressed in the numerous
symposia that have considered these problems. At one extreme
are workers who accept most coasts as having been stable during Quaternary times, and envisage a sequence of eustatic
movements of sea level with terraces marking former higher
stillstands up to 200 m or more (Stearns, 1961) above present
sea level. At the other extreme are those who are doubtful if
Pleistocene sea levels ever stood more than 10 m above present
sea level (Russell, 1964), and who would presumably argue that
Quaternary coastal terraces and shorelines above this level owe
their present elevation, at least in part, to tectonic uplift. The
situation is analogous to solving a single equation with two
unknowns. The contradictory views may eventually be resolved
by carrying out world-wide studies of the sequences of coastal
terraces and associated stratigraphic features, with former
coastlines measured and dated as accurately as possible. If coastal terraces of Quaternary age up to 200 m above sea level are
as widespread as has been claimed, the former view requires
large-scale movements of the ocean surface during Quaternary
times, and the latter view requires large-scale tectonic uplift
over extensive areas during the same period. The discovery of
similar marine Pleistocene stratigraphic sequences at different
coastal altitudes indicates unequal vertical displacement of
former coastlines (Flint, 1966). At this stage it will be useful to
summarise briefly the record of coastal terraces, on which an
enormous literature now exists.

In the British Isles research on coastal terraces has been
dominated by the tracing of early Pleistocene coastline deposits
210 m above sea level in SE England, and 'erosion surfaces' at a
similar sea level in Wales. Beneath this level, fluvial terraces in
the river valleys descend towards former base levels estimated
at about 400, 200, 100, 50, 25, and 10 feet above present sea
level.* A correlative 'stairway' of coastal terraces has been
recorded by various workers along the S coast of England, and
assigned a Pleistocene age on the grounds that even the lower
terrace features and associated deposits are overlain by perigla-

---

* These estimates can be rendered, without much loss of real accuracy, as 120, 60, 30,
15, 7.5 and 3 m respectively.

cial drift. In E England coastal terrace levels have been modified by subsidence in the North Sea basin, and in N and W Britain the levels have been complicated by isostatic recovery following deglaciation. The assumption that southernmost England has been tectonically stable throughout Quaternary times, so that river and coastal terraces match former eustatic sea level still-stands, remains to be checked against world-wide evidence. Terrace sequences on the coasts of W Europe raise similar problems to those in S England.

In North America, the Atlantic coastal plain bears depositional terraces which have been correlated with successive alternations of sea level since Miocene times, the sea attaining levels of 13.5, 6, 7.5, 4.5, and 0 m respectively, with intervening low sea level phases (Oaks and Coch, 1963). On the Pacific coast, terraces have been dislocated by the San Andreas fault near San Francisco, and warped and uplifted terraces are found near Los Angeles and on Santa Catalina Island (Emery, 1960). In Chile, coastal terraces have been displaced tectonically in a region subject to earthquakes, and as the Chilean coast runs parallel to the main axes of Andean uplift there is a possibility that terraces found at the same height above sea level have been epeirogenically uplifted (Fuenzalida *et al.*, 1965).

Stairways of coastal terraces have been reported on the margins of continents assumed to have been relatively stable in Quaternary times, as on the coast of India, S Africa, and Australia, and equivalence with former eustatic sea levels has been considered probable. The dangers and difficulties of terrace correlation are more obvious in regions of Quaternary tectonic activity, such as Indonesia, New Guinea, Japan, and New Zealand.

The evidence so far obtained from the world's coasts thus supports the idea of a sequence of successively lower interglacial sea levels, but much work remains to be done. There are certainly marine terraces at various levels, and related series of river terraces bordering valleys that descend towards the coast, but few detailed surveys have been made, and terrace levels have often been stated within wide limits, based on reconnaissance surveys, or merely on inspection of contoured maps of uncertain accuracy. Facile correlations of terraces in terms of approximate heights may well have concealed evidence of tectonic deformation in coastal regions, and favoured too strongly

12   *Stranded beach ridges (calcarenite) marking emerged coastlines in the south-eastern region of South Australia*

the view that these terraces correspond to former eustatic sea levels on coasts assumed to have been stable.

Marine terraces have been reported on various parts of the Australian coast at about 130 m, 40 m, 12–15 m, and 6–9 m above present mean sea level. The last three could correspond with interglacial or interstadial eustatic stillstands of high sea level. Associated beach deposits have been found to contain marine shells of types that now occur in the warmer parts of the ocean, and oxygen isotope measurements have generally confirmed a warmer environment of origin. A Pleistocene age is suggested by the fact that associated deposits are beyond the range of radiocarbon dating (i.e. older than 35,000 years), and it is therefore likely that the beaches formed on the shores of warmer high-level interglacial seas, but there is as yet no means of deciding which interglacial they represent.

In the SE of South Australia (Fig. 12) a series of stranded beach ridges runs roughly parallel to the coast at successive levels up to more than 60 m above present sea level. It was once thought that these corresponded with the Mediterranean sequence of interglacial high sea levels, but it is now realised that they were tilted transversely when the Mount Gambier region rose and the Murray-mouth area subsided during Quaternary times. The levels of the successive beach ridges do not, therefore, correspond with Quaternary eustatic high sea levels, for their emergence results from land movements as well as sea level oscillations. The same is true of the NE coast of New Guinea where a remarkable series of emerged Quaternary coralline terraces gains elevation and multiplies across an axis of uplift in the vicinity of the Tewai gorge, where the highest attains more than 600 m above sea level. Radiocarbon dating of the younger terraces has been supplemented by U^{234}/Th^{230} dating of the earlier and higher terraces to indicate peaks in the Quaternary sea level curve at 6, 30, 40–50, 60, 80, 105, 120, 140, 185, and 220 thousand years B.P., supporting and extending results obtained from previous studies of emerged coralline terraces in Barbados (Chappell, 1974). As the terraces are warped it is difficult to separate the effects of eustatic oscillations of sea level from those of long-term uplift. The terrace 120,000 years old varies in elevation from 90 m to 360 m above present sea level within this 80 km sector of coastline, indicating a differential tectonic elevation of up to 22.5 cm per century along the former coastline. If, as some evidence suggests, the world ocean level 120,000 years ago was close to its present stand, this terrace represents actual uplift of between 90 and 360 m (i.e. between 7.5 and 30 cm per century) during the past 120,000 years. In further work on uplifted coral terraces on the north coast of Timor, Chappell and Veeh (1978) confirmed the sequence deduced in Barbados and New Guinea, and correlated stratigraphic evidence of seven successive marine transgressions between 700,000 and 120,000 years B.P. with phases of sharp O^{18} diminution recorded in a sedimentary core from the Pacific by Shackleton and Opdyke (1973).

Coastal terraces in the vicinity of Wellington, New Zealand, include shorelines uplifted as the result of earthquakes during recent centuries (Plate 5). The 1855 earthquake raised the coastline near Wellington (Fig. 13) by up to a metre, and in the vicinity of the airport there are emerged shore platforms, lifted above high tide level by this movement. Successive earthquakes have raised coastlines around Tokyo Bay, producing a sequence of emerged Holocene terraces, with shore platforms raised out of the sea by the 1703 and 1923 movements. An earthquake at

5   *Cape Turakirae, near Wellington, New Zealand, showing four emerged coastlines resulting from uplift of the land during successive earthquakes (D. L. Homer, New Zealand Geological Survey)*

Hawke Bay, New Zealand, in 1931 resulted in an uplift of up to 2 m, tidal mudflats near Napier emerging to form a coastal plain. The 1964 Alaskan earthquake raised intertidal shore platforms out of the sea, for example on Montague Island.

13   *The 1855 earthquake at Wellington, New Zealand, resulted in coastal progradation as shore areas were uplifted above high tide level. Earlier in Holocene times a similar emergence led to the formation of the isthmus at Miramar*

Submerged coastlines

The development of accurate sounding devices has led to a
more precise knowledge of the submerged topography of the
sea floor bordering coasts, and the search for oil, natural gas,
and mineral deposits is rapidly increasing our awareness of the
structure, morphology and sediment mantles of continental
shelves. Stairways of submerged terraces have been mapped off
various coasts, one of the clearest being the paired sequence of
seven terraces at successive levels down to 110 m bordering
Tsugaru Strait, between Hokkaido and Honshu, in Japan
(Emery, 1961). A submerged shoreline at a depth of about 18 m
has been reported off the coasts of the United States (Shepard,
1963) and detailed studies have been made of beach deposits
indicative of lower sea level stands on the floor of the Gulf of
Mexico (Curray, 1960). Off S California the sea floor has been
tectonically deformed (Emery, 1960), but around the Hawaiian
Islands Stearns (1974) has described a sequence of submerged
shorelines down to a depth of 1,100 m, regarding those above
− 140 m as glacio-eustatic and those at greater depths as the
outcome of earlier tectonic subsidence. In some areas it is possible that smoothing of sea floor contours by wave action during
episodes of marine transgression has obliterated or concealed
evidence of submerged shorelines, and many sea floor beaches
may now be hidden beneath a veneer of finer deep-water sediments.

In Australian waters the classic evidence of a low sea level
stage is the sediment with nearshore fossils dredged from a
depth of 130 m off the New South Wales coast (Smith and
Iredale, 1924). Jennings' investigation of the submarine topography of Bass Strait revealed a well-marked break of slope,
indicative of a submerged coastline at a depth of 60 m (Jennings, 1959). These features probably date from episodes of low
sea level corresponding with glacial phases in Pleistocene times.

Lowering of sea level during the Last Glacial phase has been
estimated from the volume of water taken up to form the
calculated extent of glaciers and ice sheets during this phase.
According to Donn *et al.* (1962) the sea stood between 110 and
130 m below its present level before the start of the succeeding
marine transgression. Another estimate, based on extrapolation
of the pre-Recent floor of the Mississippi valley out to the edge
of the continental shelf, indicates a lowering of 140 m (Fisk and

McFarlan, 1955). It is clear that a broad tract of the continental shelf was laid bare at this stage, and that the coastlines of Pleistocene interglacial phases were left high and dry, some distance inland. Britain was a peninsula of W Europe, and Australia, linked to Tasmania and New Guinea, had the outline shown in Fig. 14. Rivers then extended their courses seaward across the continental shelf, incising valleys that were submerged during the ensuing marine transgression and have been largely filled with sediment in Holocene times. It is often difficult to trace their offshore alignments in existing sea floor morphology, but they can be readily located by seismic surveys, from which the form of the incised channel can be deciphered and the nature of the infilling sediment (which may include mineral deposits) deduced.

It is probable that mild interstadial episodes during glacial phases were accompanied by sea level rises, and it has been

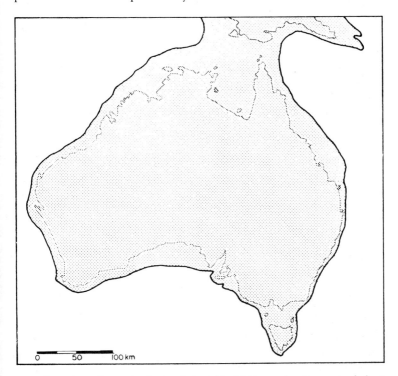

14 *The outline of Australia during the Last Glacial phase, when the sea stood about 140 m below its present level*

suggested that one or more interstadial sea level rises during the
Last Glacial phase attained or exceeded present sea level. This
suggestion, based on anomalous dates from emerged shore
features, has been discussed by Thom (1973) who, after a comprehensive review of the literature, concluded that there was no
convincing evidence of a warm interval during the Last Glacial
comparable in intensity or duration with that now existing or
those that occurred during the Last Interglacial.

Holocene marine submergence

The subsequent transgression which carried the sea to its present general level and established the broad outlines of the
world's existing coasts took place within the range of radiocarbon dating, and has been investigated from samples obtained
from the sea floor, and from borings in deltas and coastal plains
in various parts of the world. Valley mouths drowned by Holocene submergence contain the marine, estuarine, and deltaic
deposits that accumulated during and since the phase of submergence. Carbonaceous materials found in these sediments
can be dated by radiocarbon analysis and correlated with
former sea levels. Dates have been obtained from samples of
beach shells or shallow-water organisms, such as oysters, refer-
able within narrow limits to sea level at the time of their formation, but more reliable ages are given by peat deposits and tree
stumps found in borings and occupying levels slightly above the
sea level at the time of their formation. In some cases these may
now be below the level at which they formed, because of subsequent compaction of underlying peat or clay, or because of the
isostatic subsidence that has taken place beneath many deltas. If
attention is confined to coastal regions thought to have been
stable since the late Pleistocene (and evidence from tide gauge
records or repeated geodetic surveys is preferable to local affir-
mation) radiocarbon dates plotted against sea level at the time
of formation of these organic materials give a picture of an
oscillating rise of sea level beginning about 18,000 years ago; in
Europe this is known as the Flandrian transgression.

The question of Recent emergence

It is widely agreed that a rapid transgression of the sea took
place between 18,000 and 6,000 years ago, but there is less
agreement concerning changes during the past 6,000 years.

Shepard (1963) took the view that sea level stood 6 to 9 m lower 6,000 years ago than at present, and that during this period it rose gradually to its present level: it may still be rising (see below, p. 60). Coleman and Smith (1964) considered that the sea attained its present level between 3,000 and 5,000 years ago, since when there has been a stillstand. Fairbridge (1961) believed that the sea rose to higher levels during the past 6,000 years, and that there have been three brief stillstands 3, 1.5 and 0.5 m above the present level within this period (Fig. 15). Shepard and Coleman and Smith based their views on the chronology of levels established on the Gulf Coast of North America, and supported by measurements from many other parts of the world. Fairbridge based his view on the radiocarbon dates

15   *The Holocene marine transgression. Alternative interpretations of sea level changes during the past 6,000 years are indicated in Fig. 17. Fairbridge considered that the sea rose to higher levels (O.P. = Older Peron, Y.P. = Younger Peron, A = Abrolhos, R = Rottnest stages, named from W Australia); Shepard thought that it attained present level without exceeding it during Holocene times*

16   *Coastal platforms near Fremantle, Western Australia. Fairbridge (1961) correlated the three platforms with higher Holocene sea level stillstands shown in Fig. 15*

obtained from deposits associated with coastal terraces of Western Australia (Fig. 16), and similar dates for low terraces have been reported elsewhere around the Indian, Pacific and South Atlantic Oceans, on a scale suggestive of world-wide eustatic oscillations rather than tectonic uplift. The differences focus on the interpretation of coastal terraces and associated features suggestive of emergence found below the 6 to 9 m coastline of late Pleistocene interglacial times and generally within 3 m of present sea level. Many reefs and atolls in the Pacific Ocean have been uplifted tectonically, and even tilted (see p. 271); and these cannot be accepted as evidence of a higher Holocene sea level and subsequent eustatic lowering.

Much more detailed work is needed to resolve this problem. It is necessary to confine attention to features definitely indicative of emergence, ruling out those that could have been formed by weathering processes, storm wave activity or depositional processes with the sea at its present relative level. It is then necessary to find materials suitable for dating in a context that will give the age of the emerged feature, indicating whether it is Pleistocene or Holocene. Emerged shore forms of Pleistocene age must have persisted through at least one phase of glacially-lowered sea level, when stream incision and dissection will have occurred. Emerged shore forms of Holocene age could be indicative of a phase of higher stillstand of sea level if such features are indeed ubiquitous on coasts that can be shown to have been tectonically stable since Pleistocene times. Tectonic uplift is likely to have been localised to particular sectors of coast, and variable in extent of vertical displacement, but the possibility of broad-scale, possibly continent-wide, epeirogenic uplift giving equivalent emergence over large areas cannot be ruled out.

17 *Holocene variations in world sea level: A—according to Fairbridge (1961);*
    B—according to Shepard (1963); C—New Zealand; D—Southern England;
    E—New England; F—Arctic Canada (based on Pirazzoli, 1977)

During the past decade an international project on 'sea level movements during the past 15,000 years', set up to collate information from around the world and establish definitive graphs of the trend of mean sea level over this period has led to the compilation of an Atlas of Sea Level Curves (Bloom, 1979). Some regional patterns of eustatic correlation have been suggested, but there has been much variation in the sequence and dimension of vertical changes on the world's coastlines in the Holocene (Fig. 17). The sequence around the Mediterranean Sea, for example, is complex, for some of the coastal settlement sites of ancient civilisations are now on the sea floor while others are stranded well inland (Kraft *et al.*, 1977; Pirazzoli, 1977).

t the present time

ords over the past few decades show evidence
n the relative levels of land and sea are still in
n sea level, determined by averaging high and low
er a period of several years, is often found to have
n when compared with levels determined fifty or a
hundr ars ago (Gutenberg, 1941; Valentin, 1952). The
changes thus recorded are again caused by movements of the
land, movements of the sea, or combinations of both. The
majority of tide gauges, including all those on coasts believed to
be tectonically stable, show evidence of submergence during the
past few decades, and as this evidence is widespread it is probable that a world-wide eustatic rise of sea level has been taking
place, accompanying the melting of the margins of glaciers and
ice sheets during this period. Ice recession is widely in evidence
in the northern hemisphere, and the release of water of the
oceans has evidently exceeded the loss incurred in the increase
of Antarctic ice volumes over this period (Wexler, 1961). There
appears to have been a slight warming of atmospheric temperatures, accentuated by the increasing proportion of carbon dioxide resulting from combustion of fossil fuels, particularly during
the industrial era. In 1981 the U.S. Council on Environmental
Quality estimated that global carbon dioxide is now 15 to 25 per
cent higher than before the Industrial Revolution. Within the
next century, if this trend continues, warming could accelerate
ice melting and produce a sea level rise of several metres, with
drastic implications for coastal geography.

It has been calculated that the sea has risen at the rate of
1 mm per year, or about 4 inches during the past century. Tide
gauges that show a more rapid rate of submergence than this
indicate that the local coast has been sinking tectonically; those
that show a smaller submergence, or an emergence, indicate
that the land has been rising. Donn and Shaw (1963) have summarised the variations in tidal levels on the United States coast
during the past century. In Britain, tide gauge records suggest
uplift in the N and continuing subsidence of the E and S coasts.
The floor levels of Roman London are now about 4 m below
high-tide level in the Thames estuary, indicating an average rate
of submergence of about 2 mm per year in this area, twice the
world rate. At Newlyn in Cornwall, mean tide level in the 1960s
was 12 cm above that recorded for 1915–21, when the mean sea

level at this site was calculated to establish a datum for British
topographical surveys: a rise of 2.4 mm per year. By contrast,
mean tide level at Dundee in Scotland fell just over 2 mm per
year in this period. Figure 18 shows typical trends of mean sea
level change from tide gauge records on emerging, submerging,
and apparently stable coastal stations. Repetition of precise
geodetic levelling from time to time can provide an independent check on the results obtained from tide gauge records, and
a means of determining areal patterns of crustal deformation
more accurately than from measurements of tide levels at scattered coastal stations. In Finland, for example, the uplift and
tilting that had been detected from tide gauge records and from

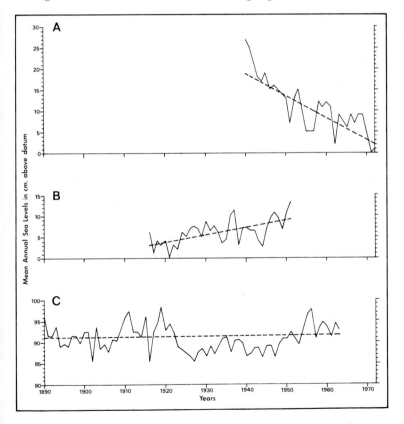

18   *Mean annual sea levels and regression lines (pecked) determined from tide gauge*
     records: A—an emerging coast (Yakutat, Alaska), B—a submerging coast (New-
     lyn, SW England), C—a 'stable' coast (Sydney, Australia) (from Bloom, 1979)

the evidence of secular emergence and extension of the land from shallow bordering seas has been confirmed by geodetic surveys in 1935 and 1959 (Fig. 19). Over the next century it should be possible to decide which indeed are the stable areas of the earth's crust, and to isolate more accurately the extent of contemporary eustatic sea level changes.

A number of geomorphological effects have been attributed to the rise in sea level over the past century. They include the renewal of coral growth on planed-off reef surfaces off the coast of Western Australia, the onset of erosion on most of the world's sandy shores (Chapter VI), and the prevalence of erosion on the seaward margins of many marshlands (Chapter VII). In each

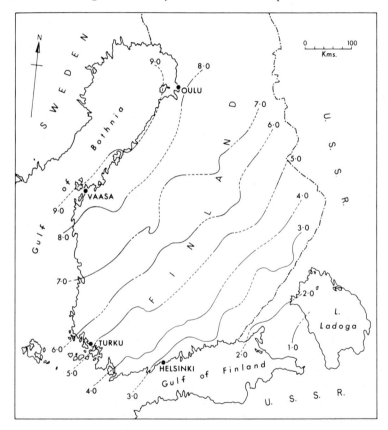

19   *The pattern of mean annual uplift of the land (in mm per year) in Finland, determined from comparison of precise geodetic levellings in 1935 and 1959. Based on a map in the Atlas of Finland 1960 by permission of the Geographical Society of Finland*

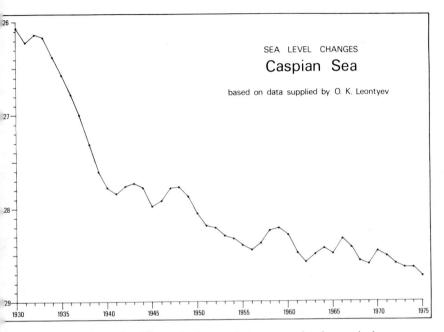

SEA LEVEL CHANGES
Caspian Sea
based on data supplied by O. K. Leontyev

20   *The Caspian Sea has fallen in level since 1930 as a sequel to large-scale dam construction and reservoir impoundment in tributary rivers. It is possible that increasing aridity in SW Asia has contributed to this change. The outcome has been extensive coastal emergence around the Caspian Sea*

case it is possible to indicate other relevant factors and processes, but the continuance of a slow marine transgression should be borne in mind in considering the dynamics of existing coastal features.

Features of emerging coasts can be seen around the Caspian Sea, the level of which fell by 2.67 m between 1930 and 1975, partly because of dam construction in tributary rivers and partly because of drier climatic conditions (Fig. 20). Sea floor shoals have become islands, beaches have prograded, and deltas, especially the Volga, have enlarged rapidly. A similar fall of about 1.5 m has occurred in the Aral Sea as a sequel to damming of inflowing rivers. Soviet proposals to divert water from north-flowing Siberian rivers (Pechora, Ob, Yenisei) into these southern regions could restore the levels of the Caspian and Aral Sea, but could also modify the existing regime of sea freezing in the Arctic, thereby changing climatic conditions in the Northern Hemisphere and possibly leading to world-wide changes of sea level.

IV

CLIFFED COASTS

The retreat of cliffed coasts takes place mainly during storms, and is achieved largely by wave action: the hydraulic pressure of impact and withdrawal, and the abrasive action of water laden with rock fragments (sand and gravel) hurled repeatedly at the cliff base. After a storm the backshore is littered with debris eroded from the cliff. Agitated by wave action, this becomes broken and worn down (a process known as attrition), and is either retained as a beach, or carried away along the shore or out to sea by the action of waves and currents. The simplest type of cliffed coast is found where marine erosion has attacked the margins of a stable land mass of homogeneous and relatively resistant rocks, removing a wedge of material to leave a steep cliff at the back of a gently-sloping platform, which extends from high tide level to beneath low tide level (Fig. 21A). There are, however, many variants of this simple form, for complications are introduced by the lithology and structure of coastal rock formations, the degree of exposure to wave attack,

21   *A   Cliffed coast with an inter-tidal shore platform*
         B   Cliffed coast with shore platform at about high tide level
         C   Cliffed coast with shore platform at about low tide level
         D   Plunging cliff, with no shore platform

the effects of subaerial processes of denudation on the coast, and the history of changing land and sea levels. The platform is often termed a wave-cut, or abrasion platform, but these genetic terms can be misleading and the purely descriptive term, shore platform, is preferred here.* A misconception repeated in many textbooks is that the platform extending beneath low tide level is continued by a wave-built terrace constructed by deposition at its outer margin. There is little evidence that such a terrace actually exists off sea coasts (Dietz, 1963).

The morphology of cliffs

Examination of almost any section of cliffed coast soon reveals features that are related to variations in lithology and structure, picked out by marine erosion. It is obvious that the more resistant parts of coastal rock formations protrude as headlands, or persist as rocky stacks and islands offshore, whereas the weaker elements are cut back as coves and embayments. Resistance in this context means the hardness of rocks attacked by the physical forces of marine erosion, or their durability in face of other processes at work on the coast, including the physical and chemical effects of repeated wetting and drying or freezing and thawing of rock surfaces, and the purely chemical effects of solution by sea water, notably on limestone coasts. Solid and massive formations are generally eroded more slowly than formations that disintegrate readily, such as friable sandstones, or rocks with closely-spaced joints and bedding-planes, or rock formations shattered by faulting. Weathering and marine erosion penetrate these lines of weakness, excavating caves and coves, so that patterns of jointing and faulting influence the outline in plan of a cliffed coast. This is exemplified on the north coast of Cornwall, where coves and headlands are closely related to the intricacies of local geology (Wilson, 1952). Natural arches, formed where less resistant rock has been excavated from a promontory or islet, are illustrated by the Green Bridge of Wales, an arch that consists of massive Carboniferous Limestone beneath which thinly-bedded strata have been cut out along joint planes, and various 'London Bridges', notably at Torquay in Devon and Portsea on the Victorian coast in Australia. Where the forces produced by the hydraulic action of waves

---

* The term 'solution platform' is similarly misleading, for it is doubtful if any shore platform can be ascribed solely to solution processes, and the term 'beach platform' should be avoided, for it could indicate a depositional rather than an erosional feature.

6   Some of the stacks known as the Twelve Apostles, bordering the cliffed coast near Port Campbell, Victoria

7   The Needles, stacks in hard Upper Chalk at the W end of the Isle of Wight, England. The promontory is a ridge of steeply-dipping Chalk, with fresh cliffs on the side exposed to predominant SW waves (Scratchells Bay, right) and partly degraded cliffs on the more sheltered side, bordering Alum Bay (left) (Aerofilms Ltd)

and the compression of trapped air puncture the roof of a cave, water and spray are driven up through blowholes, as on Porth Island, near Newquay in Cornwall and on the Old Red Sandstone coast near Arbroath in eastern Scotland. An Australian example occurs at Kiama, N.S.W. Spectacular steep-sided clefts are produced where the roofs of caves collapse or where rock is excavated along lines of weakness at an angle to the shore. Examples can be found on many cliffed coasts: they are known as geos or yawns on the coast of Scotland, and zawns in Cornwall. Deep gorges of this kind are incised into the bold sandstone cliffs of the Jervis Bay district in New South Wales, and near Port Campbell in Victoria, where powerful wave action has penetrated joints and bedding-planes to sculpture a variety of forms, including stacks and natural arches (Plate 6). Similar coastal topography is found on the red sandstones of the Devon coast, notably at Ladram Bay, and in northernmost Scotland, where huge cliffs of Old Red Sandstone face powerful wave action from the north Atlantic. The Old Man of Hoy is a spectacular stack in front of towering cliffs of Old Red Sandstone on the west coast of the Orkneys, but probably the best known stacks are the Needles, residual ridges of hard chalk at the W end of the Isle of Wight (Plate 7).

Certain kinds of lithology yield characteristic cliff forms. The castellated granite cliffs of the Lands End peninsula in Britain are related to cuboid jointing (Plate 8). Distinctive profiles develop on columnar basalts (Plate 9), as in the Giant's Causeway, N Ireland, and there are similar features on columnar dolerites in SE Tasmania. In limestone areas the sea may penetrate and widen fissures that originated as subterranean solution passages: the caves of Bonifacio in S Corsica, are believed to have formed in this way. On soft clay formations, as in Bournemouth Bay and parts of the Norfolk and Yorkshire coast in England, and at Palos Verdes in California, cliffs are subject to recurrent slumping, particularly after wet weather. Subsequent removal of slumped material by waves from the base of the cliff then rejuvenates the profile, preparing the way for further slope failure, so that the cliffs recede as the result of alternating marine and subaerial effects (Plate 12). Figure 22 shows such a sequence on the Norfolk coast, and Figure 23 is a model of coastal evolution in Lyme Bay. It can be argued that such retreating coasts are in dynamic equilibrium when considered over time scales of about a century (Cambers, 1976; Brunsden and Jones, 1980), these sequences being fluctuations about that equilibrium as retreat proceeds. Recession of vertical cliffs by intermittent rock falls and basal rejuvenation provides a similar sequence (Fig. 24).

22   *Changes in the transverse profile of the coast near Cromer, E England, as the result of a landslide in glacial drift deposits. The cliff crest receded from A to D, but the undercliff (BC) advanced as a lobe (to EF), which was subsequently cut back (to GH) by marine erosion. After Hutchinson, 1976*

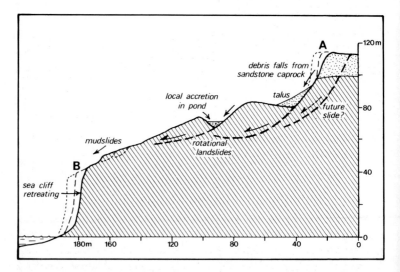

23   *A cliff subject to recurrent landslides and basal undercutting near Lyme Regis, S England. During the past century recession of the cliff crest (A) has been about the same as undercliff recession (B), but there have been complex variations in the intervening landslide topography. After Brunsden and Jones, 1980*

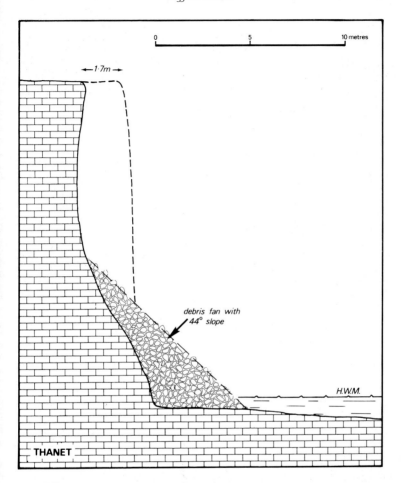

0   5   10 metres

← 1·7m →

debris fan with
44° slope

H.W.M.

THANET

24   *Cliff recession on a Chalk coast in Thanet, SE England, has produced a basal debris
fan which is gradually reduced by solution and attrition and removed by wave
action, until the cliff base is again exposed to wave attack. Undermining then
produces further rock falls so that the cliff crest recedes intermittently*

Where the dip of coastal rock formations is seaward, undercutting by marine erosion often leads to landslips and rock falls,
the undercut rock sliding down bedding-planes into the sea,
leaving the exhumed bedding-planes as a coastal slope. On the S
coast of England, coastal landslips are common where the permeable Chalk and Upper Greensand formations dip seaward,
resting on impermeable Gault Clay. Water seeping through the

8　*Castellated cliffs in granite at Lands End, England (Aerofilms Ltd)*

9　*Columnar basalts on the coast at Fingal Point, New South Wales*

permeable rocks moves down the clay plane, and if marine erosion has exposed the junction at or above sea level, lubrication of the interface leads to slipping of the overlying rocks. A spectacular landslip occurred in this situation on the E Devon coast near Axmouth in 1839 (Arber, 1940), and similar slides have occurred on the S side of the Isle of Wight, and between Folkestone and Dover, where a railway built along the undercliff is damaged from time to time by falling rock (Plate 10). The physical effects of wetting and lubrication of the Gault Clay surface are probably accompanied by chemical processes, involving base exchange. The seeping water is rich in dissolved calcium carbonate, and when it reaches the glauconitic Gault Clay, calcium ions displace potassium ions from the clay, alkalinity increases, and the clay is deflocculated. Conversion of the upper layers of Gault Clay into a soft wet slurry which flows out at the base of the cliff hastens the undermining of the Chalk and Upper Greensand beds. Similar features are seen west of Moonlight Head, Victoria, where a series of amphitheatres backed by cliffs in Tertiary sandstone are fronted by tumbled rocks where landslips have occurred on the underlying Palaeocene clay. On the Oregon coast there have been major slides at Humbug Mountain forming lobate slump promontories that have temporarily prograded the shoreline. Similar such lobes at Fairlight in Sussex have formed natural breakwaters, intercepting the eastward drift of shingle, while on the shores of Lyme Bay festoons of boulders commemorate former lobes from which finer sediment has been dispersed by wave action.

Where relatively resistant coastal rock formations are backed by weak outcrops, penetration of the outer wall by marine erosion is followed by the excavation of coves and embayments. The classic example of this is on the Dorset coast E of Weymouth, where several stages can be seen. Stair Hole, near Lulworth, is an early stage, a narrow breach in the outer wall of steeply-dipping Jurassic limestone. Close by, Lulworth Cove has a wider entrance through the limestone wall, and an almost circular bay carved out of Cretaceous sands and clays, backed by a high ridge of Chalk (Plate 11). Farther E a much broader embayment has developed, opening up the clay lowland corridor in front of the Chalk ridge at Worbarrow Bay (Fig. 25), while to the W the Jurassic and Wealden rocks have been removed almost completely, leaving only the small peninsula at Durdle

10 *Coastal landslip near Folkestone, England*

11 *Lulworth Cove (cf. Fig. 25), on the Dorset coast, S England, a cove excavated in Wealden sands and clays behind a breached wall of strongly-folded Jurassic limestone and backed by a high ridge of Chalk (Aerofilms Ltd)*

25   *Configuration of the Dorset coastline in S England shows embayments cut in soft sands and clays (Wealden Beds) where the coastal rampart of Jurassic limestone has been breached, especially at valley mouths, where gaps have been widened by marine erosion*

Door and some outlying reefs. Penetration by marine erosion has been facilitated here by subaerial denudation, especially the Late Quaternary incision of valleys in the softer outcrops.

Where the recession of cliffs cut in a relatively weak formation such as glacial drift or dune calcarenite uncovers outcrops of harder basement rock at or near sea level, the latter become persistent headlands as the weaker formation is cut back in embayments. There are good examples of such 'contraposed shores' on the west coast of Eyre Peninsula, in South Australia, where cliffs of dune calcarenite extend behind and between exhumed promontories of harder Pre-Cambrian rock, and in NW Brittany where granite surfaces have been exposed as overlying periglacial deposits are removed by the sea.

Cliffs exposed to powerful wave action are often shaped entirely by marine erosion. This is true of the high wave energy coast near Port Campbell, in W Victoria, where steep cliffs have been cut by marine erosion in horizontal stratified Miocene sedimentary rocks, and the huge waves that break against these during storms have cut out ledges along the bedding-planes at various levels up to 60 m above high tide mark (Baker, 1958). The ledges are rarely more than 3–6 m wide, and it is important to note that they are the product of present-day storm wave erosion; they should not be confused with coastal terraces that bear 'raised beach' deposits indicative of emerged coastlines (Plate 13). In North America there has been rapid recession of cliffs cut in Miocene sandstones and shales and exposed to a storm wave environment on the Washington coast south from Cape Flattery, but on the equivalent sector of the European coast, from the Bay of Biscay to Norway, the coastal rocks are generally older and harder, and recession rates have been slow.

Cliffs on more sheltered sections of the coast, where strong wave action is intercepted by headlands, islands, or reefs off-shore, or attenuated by a gentle offshore slope, may show features that have been formed by subaerial denudation as well as those shaped by marine attack. Cliffs in these situations often consist of a coastal slope shaped by rainwash and soil creep, the lower part of which is kept steep and fresh by wave attack. At Black Rock Point, Port Phillip Bay, a cliff in soft sandstone has been cut back by alternations of rilling produced by runoff during occasional downpours and dispersal of basal fans by wave action when storms accompany high tides.

The profiles of steep coasts on similar rock formations show intricate variations related to exposure to wave attack. It is instructive to compare the bold profiles of cliffs of massive sandstone facing the ocean in the Sydney district with the gentler, often vegetated, slopes on the same geological formation on the sheltered shores of Sydney Harbour and Broken Bay. The

12 *Slumping coast in Tertiary clays, Barton, England*

degree of cliffing developed in these situations is closely related to the local fetch, which limits the strength of attack by local wind-generated waves.

When marine erosion of a cliffed coast is halted (by accumulation of protective beaches or barriers, by coastal emergence, or by the construction of sea walls to prevent wave attack), subaerial processes become dominant and the sea cliff is 'degraded' to a coastal bluff of gentler inclination, comparable with escarpment and valley-side slopes inland, and determined by the geotechnical properties of the rock outcrop: usually between 8° and 10° on soft clays (Hutchinson, 1976) and steeper on more resistant formations. On the N Norfolk coast a line of bluffs, formerly cliffs, were cut off in a similar way by the development of spits, barrier islands, and marshlands (Fig. 48). In this case the sea reached the cliffs in late Pleistocene times, the raised beach at Stiffkey dating from a late interglacial or interstadial phase, and deposition in front of them took place during and since the Holocene marine transgression, which reworked glacial drift deposits left behind on what is now the floor of the North Sea. In Australia, enclosure of former embayments by the growth of coastal barriers has been followed by the degradation of the former sea cliffs on the enclosed coast, as in the Gippsland Lakes region in Victoria (Bird, 1978a).

The active cliffs that we now see on the coast have assumed their present form only since the Holocene marine transgression brought the sea to its present general level within the last 6,000 years (Fig. 26). Cliffed coasts undoubtedly existed before

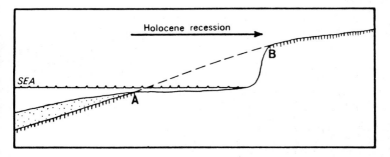

26   *Where it is possible to find on the sea floor, or at the outer edge of a shore platform, the weathered horizon (A) equivalent to the cliff-top weathering mantle (B) an estimate may be made of the extent of cliff recession since the Holocene sea attained its present level relative to the land*

13 *Cliff profile formed by differential erosion of horizontally-bedded limestone strata near Port Campbell, Victoria*

the Last Glacial phase of low sea level, but during that phase, in the absence of marine attack, they were degraded by subaerial denudation. As a rule, the bluffs thus formed were undercut as the Holocene sea attained its present level and rejuvenated as receding cliffs, but it is possible to find sectors where the Pleistocene bluffs have been preserved, usually behind areas of Holocene deposition. The Port Campbell coast in Victoria consists of vertical cliffs, except at Two Mile Bay, where these pass into Pleistocene bluffs to the rear of a raised beach area that has not yet been eroded away by the Holocene sea.

In high latitudes this degradation took place partly under periglacial conditions, when the cliff became a slope mantled by frost-shattered debris. Since the Holocene transgression, periglaciated slopes of this kind have been undercut by marine erosion, but some coasts retain part of the periglaciated slope, the lower part having been cut back by wave attack to produce a 'slope-over-wall' profile (Plate 14). The slope, mantled by frost-shattered debris, is clearly a legacy of past periglacial conditions; it cannot be explained in terms of processes now at work. Residual outcrops of more resistant rock, such as massive quartzite, which survived this frost-shattering, protrude from the debris-mantled coastal slopes as tors or buttresses. Coastal landforms of this type are found in SW England, where the proportion of relict periglaciated slope to actively-receding wall depends on the degree of exposure of a coastal sector to storm wave attack. On sheltered sectors of the S coast of Cornwall, the relict slope is well preserved, extending down almost to high tide level, but on the more exposed north coast of Cornwall, open to Atlantic storm waves, the relict slope has been largely, and on some sectors (e.g. Watergate Bay, N of Newquay) completely destroyed by Holocene marine erosion. The inferred

27   *Evolution of 'slope-over-wall' cliffs on coasts subjected to Pleistocene periglaciation. A, pre-periglacial sea cliff; B, cliff degraded under periglacial conditions and mantled by rubble drift (shaded) during Pleistocene glacial phases of low sea level; C, 'slope-over-wall' form produced by marine erosion of the base of the cliff after the sea rose to its present level in Recent times*

sequence of cliff forms is shown in Fig. 27. Similar features are
found in Brittany and S Ireland, on parts of the coast of Washington and Oregon, in Korea, and on the shores of islands in the
Southern Ocean, notably on Auckland I. (Fleming, 1965). On
rocky sectors of the Antarctic coast, and on parts of the Canadian and Siberian arctic coast, formation of degraded slopes by
periglacial activity still continues.

On the shores of the St Lawrence estuary sectors of rocky cliff
and shore platform developed alongside narrow straits where
the fetch is limited are the outcome of frost shattering and shore
ice plucking, the waves merely washing away the products of
cold-climate rock disintegration.

The influence of subaerial denudation on the form of cliffed
coasts is also important in humid tropical regions, where many
coastal rock formations, weakened as the result of decomposition by chemical weathering, do not form steep cliffs. Bluffs with
a soil and vegetation mantle occur on steep coast sectors in NE
Queensland, where the Great Barrier Reefs prevent strong
wave action, and within the Indonesian archipelago, where
weak waves across limited fetches achieve little more than the
removal of material that moves downslope and would other-
wise accumulate on the shore (Bird and Ongkosongo, 1980).
Yampi Sound in N Australia is bordered by low crumbling cliffs
of deeply-weathered metamorphic rocks, from which protrude
bolder promontories of quartzite, a type of resistant rock less
readily modified by chemical weathering. Marine erosion therefore works upon coastal rock formations, the resistance of which
is more a function of their response to weathering under humid
tropical conditions than of their original lithology. Tricart (1962)
has described the persistence of a dolerite headland at Mamba
Point in Liberia, where adjacent outcrops of thoroughly weathered granite and gneiss do not form bold cliffs, and the rarity of
cliffed coasts in the humid tropics is also apparent in Brazil
(Tricart, 1959).

Cliff forms are also influenced by the geomorphology of the
immediate hinterland, in particular the topography which is
intersected as the cliff recedes. Other things being equal, cliffs
that intersect high ground recede more slowly than cliffs cut
into low-lying topography, so that interfluves tend to become
promontories between valley-mouth embayments. This has

happened on the coast near San Remo, Victoria, where a crenu-
late coastal outline has developed on the margins of hilly dissected country on Jurassic formations, and rather similar terrain
has been sculptured in the same way on the Yorkshire coast N
of Flamborough Head. Where the hinterland slopes away from
the coast, there are receding cliffs of diminishing altitude, as in
the vicinity of Childers Cove near Warrnambool in Victoria.
Streams which drain valleys truncated by cliff recession pour out
as waterfalls cascading on to the shore, as at Ecclesbourne Glen,
on the Sussex coast near Hastings, and deep coastal ravines
known as chines in the Isle of Wight and Bournemouth Bay
have been cut by runoff from land adjacent to rapidly-receding
cliffs. Accordant valley mouths, with unaggraded stream channels opening to the shore, are rare features that occur where
cliff recession has matched the rate of stream incision, or where
coastal uplift has prevented valley-mouth submergence during
the Holocene transgression: they are found on the steep coast
of the Otway Ranges in Victoria. Dry valleys truncated by recession of chalk cliffs on the Sussex coast produce the undulating

14   *Slope-over-wall cliff topography on the W side of Dodman Point, Cornwall, England. The promontory consists of intensely folded slates and phyllites, exposed in
the lower part of the cliff, but mantled by periglacial rubble in the upper slope
(C. T. Bird)*

15 Chalk cliffs at Seven Sisters on the Sussex coast. The cliffs truncate ridges and valleys on the coastal margin of the South Downs, and there is an inter-tidal shore platform at their base, with a sanded sector (A—see Fig. 30) at Birling Gap (C. T. Bird)

16 Erosion on the South Devon coast at Hallsands

crest line of the Seven Sisters (Plate 15); locally, valleys that ran parallel to the coast have been dismembered by cliff recession, as in the vicinity of Beachy Head.

Measurements of cliff recession may be linear (Fig. 28), areal, or volumetric, and are usually expressed as annual averages. Cliff-crest recession in glacial drift on sectors of the Polish coast has averaged a metre a year, with up to 5 m in a stormy year (Zenkovich, 1967). May (1977) measured an areal loss of 3,264 m^2 over 12 years on chalk cliffs in Sussex, 97 per cent of which was removed in winter periods, and 42 per cent in two particularly cold, wet and stormy winters. It is useful to take account of variations in cliff height and calculate the volume of rock removed as the cliff was cut back. Williams (1956) recorded 12 m of recession on cliffs 12 m high and 27 m of recession on cliffs 3 m high on a mile-long sector of the Suffolk coast at Covehithe during the 1953 storm surge, when the loss of material over a 24-hour period amounted to about 300,000 metric tonnes. Because of the intermittency of such events, and lateral variations in their effects, measurements of average annual rates of cliff retreat can be misleading. Along the Port Campbell cliffs in W Victoria the mean rate of cliff recession is only a few centimetres per year, achieved by a series of localised and occasional rock falls, when segments up to 200 m long and 20 m wide suddenly collapse into the sea. One such collapse in 1939 near Sentinel Rock left a freshly exposed scar that was still discernible as a less weathered cliff sector forty years later, its base aproned by fallen debris being slowly consumed by marine erosion.

Accumulation of large quantities of fallen rock or deposited beach material on the backshore serves to protect the base of a cliff from wave attack, storm wave energy being expended upon the beach. Smaller quantities of beach material that can be mobilised and hurled on the cliff base during storms accentuate abrasion by waves. Herein lies the risk of removing beach material from the shore. Removal of shingle from the foreshore at Hallsands, in S Devon, for construction work at Plymouth during the 1890's, has led to accentuated cliff erosion and the destruction of the fishing village of Hallsands, which used to stand on a coastal terrace near the base of the cliffs (Robinson, 1961) (Plate 16). On the Holderness coast, Pringle (1981) correlated phases of accelerated cliff erosion with the passage of low

28 *Recession (in metres) of the cliff crest at selected points along the Holderness coast, E England, between 1852 and 1952 (after Valentin, 1954). The + symbols indicate two sectors that prograded during this period*

sectors of beach (ords) in the southward-drifting beach system. Complete absence of rock material in front of cliffs would leave waves unarmed with abrasive material and capable only of hydraulic action at the cliff base, but as a rule some beach sediment is present, and one way of halting recession of cliffs on weak outcrops is to build and maintain a broad beach by constructing groynes to intercept longshore drifting, augmented if necessary by the dumping of supplementary beach material on the foreshore or updrift. Groynes which intercept longshore drifting may starve the coast downdrift of sediment, accentuating erosion there. This has happened on the Sussex coast since the building of Newhaven breakwater intercepted eastward shingle drift, leading to depletion of beaches at Seaford, where the seafront is repeatedly damaged in storms, and under Seaford Head where the chalk cliffs are now receding rapidly (Fig. 29). Sea walls may stabilise a shore, but unless a protective beach is maintained in front of them they will need frequent repair (Plate 17). Where sea walls have been built to halt coastline recession, beaches that front them are usually soon depleted by scour due to the reflection of storm waves from the wall (Bird, 1979).

29   At Newhaven, on the S coast of England, the construction of a breakwater W of the harbour interrupted the eastward shingle drift, so that only a narrow fringe of shingle persists from Seaford Esplanade eastwards (cf. Plate 17)

17 *Sea walls and groynes at Seaford, England*

The outline in plan of a cliffed coast often becomes simplified and smoothed with the passage of time, except where there are marked contrasts in the structure and lithology of coastal rock formations, which may perpetuate irregular outlines as the cliff recedes. Where the coastal outcrops are comparatively uniform, a receding cliffed coast tends to develop an outline in plan related to the prevailing wave patterns, although it is possible for crenulations to develop and persist even on receding cliffs of generally homogeneous material, as on sectors of the Nullarbor coast in S Australia (Plate 18). Where the predominant wave patterns are refracted by offshore topography or adjacent headlands, the cliffed coasts develop gently-curved outlines in plan, much like those on depositional coasts (Chapter V); indeed a curved cliffed sector may pass smoothly into a curved depositional sector, as in some of the asymmetrical embayments on the Victorian coast, notably Waratah Bay W of Wilsons Promontory. Similar curved outlines have developed on the Tertiary cliffs of Bournemouth Bay, in S England, in relation to refracted waves approaching from the SW.

Shore platforms
On the simplest form of cliffed coast, the cliffs are bordered by platforms extending across the shore zone and sloping gently, but not always uniformly, to pass beneath the sea. These platforms are evidently developed and widened as the cliffs recede, and shaped by the action of waves and other marine processes. They extend from high tide mark, at the base of the receding cliff, to a level below and beyond low tide mark, in the nearshore zone, and it is convenient, though not strictly accurate, to describe them as inter-tidal shore platforms (Fig. 21A).

Such platforms are best developed where the coastal rock formations are homogeneous, without structural or lithological variations, but it is difficult to find ideal examples. Vertical cliffs and sloping inter-tidal platforms are found on the Chalk coasts of S England and N France (Prêcheur, 1960), but these are not simply the product of wave abrasion (see below, p. 87). The ideal form is sometimes found where structureless sandstone or shale formations have been eroded by wave action, but its development requires a delicate balance between rock resistance and the intensity of wave attack. If the rocks are too resistant, the cliff and the intertidal shore platform will not have developed

18   *Cliffs near the Head of the Bight, in South Australia. The coast consists of almost horizontal Eocene and Miocene limestones (Australian Tourist Commission).*

19   *Serrated foreshore topography on Palaeozoic rocks at Barraga Point, New South Wales, showing shore platform development along corridors of less resistant rock (O. F. Dent)*

in the time available since the sea reached its present level; if they are too weak they will be unable to sustain a steep cliff profile, and will either show recurrent landslides or will recede until they are reached by the sea only briefly at the highest tides and develop subaerially degraded profiles. Relatively resistant formations may be eroded into steep cliffs and inter-tidal shore platforms on a high wave energy coast, and relatively weak formations may develop these features on a low wave energy coast; under such a balance of conditions, a dynamic equilibrium may be attained, the coastal morphology persisting with parallel recession of cliffs and inter-tidal platforms. In practice there are usually several complicating factors, but the balance of these may sometimes yield a deceptively simple cliff-and-platform profile, as on certain Chalk coasts. More often, variations in structure and lithology in the shore zone persist in irregularities of profile with tracts of platform locally developed between ridges of harder rock, and channels where less resistant outcrops have been excavated (Plates 19, 20 and 21).

Waves armed with rock fragments (sand, shingle, cobbles) are undoubtedly powerful agents of abrasion. Without such fragments, waves are capable of only limited abrasion, mainly on soft clay and shale formations. Rock fragments may be of local derivation, eroded from the cliff or the shore platform, or they may have been brought in by longshore drifting from adjacent sectors of the coast, or shoreward drifting from the sea floor. Evidence of wave abrasion can be seen on shore platforms where the more resistant elements of rock persist as reefs and stacks and intervening areas have been scoured out as pools and clefts. Debris used by the waves as an abrasive tool is found littered on the shore platform, particularly after stormy periods; the rock fragments are generally smooth and round as the result of abrasion. Smoothed and scoured abrasion ramps slope gently upward to the base of the receding cliff, which has sometimes been undercut to form a definite abrasion notch. Rock fragments that become trapped in a crevice on a shore platform may be repeatedly moved by wave action in such a way as to excavate circular potholes, smoothly-worn basins containing smoothed and rounded pebbles—clear evidence of the potency of waves armed with abrasive debris (Plate 22).

The depth to which abrasion is active is an important factor in the evolution of shore topography. Sand grains in sea floor

20 *Cliff and shore platform in dipping Silurian sandstone and mudstone, Cape Liptrap, Victoria (N. Rosengren)*

21 *Structural shore platform developed on a horizontal limestone layer in the Jurassic rocks of the Dorset coast near Kimmeridge, England*

sediments off the Californian coast have been shown to become well worn and rounded in depths of less than 10 m below low tide level; in deeper water they show less evidence of wear, and often remain angular. As the wearing of these particles implies the abrasion of the rock surface upon which they rest, this evidence suggests that on coasts exposed to ocean swell, abrasion of the platforms is effective only to a depth of 10 m. On a tideless coast, such abrasion platforms could develop shoreward from a depth of 10 m to the cliff base, and with an average inclination of 1° such a platform would be about 0.5 km wide. The possible width increases with tide range, and would be about 0.8 km with an average slope of 1° where the tide range is 5 m. Where much broader shore platforms are found, they can only be explained as abrasion platforms if they developed during a phase of slow marine transgression, the land margin being planed off by waves as the sea rose.

The Chalk cliffs and inter-tidal shore platforms on the English and French coasts bordering the English Channel are to some extent the product of wave abrasion, the waves being armed with flint nodules eroded out of the Chalk (Prêcheur, 1960). Chalk is a relatively homogeneous limestone formation, apart from the flint nodules, which are usually in layers along the bedding-planes. The best development of vertical cliffs and sloping inter-tidal shore platforms is on the Kent coast near Dover and the Sussex coast E of Brighton, where stratified chalk dips gently seaward. Fresh white chalk exposed on the shore platform and at the base of the cliff after stormy periods is evidence of the wearing and scouring of chalk by waves armed with flints, but other processes are also at work. Cliff recession is marked by recurrent rock falls, particularly after wet weather, or when a spring thaw releases rock masses that had been loosened by frost action along vertical joints and horizontal bedding-planes during the preceding winter. Fans of chalk and flint talus thus produced are subsequently dispersed or consumed by the sea (Fig. 24). Examination of boulders that have fallen in this way shows that the chalk surface is pitted by solution, and that the rock has been modified by the physical and biochemical effects of shore flora (chiefly marine algae) and fauna (limpets, mussels, and winkles). These processes play an important part in the reduction and eventual disappearance of the chalk, releasing further flint nodules which can then be used in abrasion. Wave

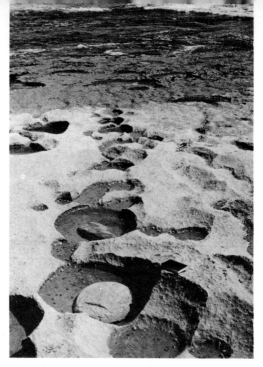

22   *Potholes scoured on foreshore of aeolian calcarenite near Rye, Victoria*

23   *Base of Chalk cliff near Birling Gap, Sussex, England, showing flint shingle and rounded boulders of chalk on the beach and layers of flint in the face of the cliff (C. T. Bird)*

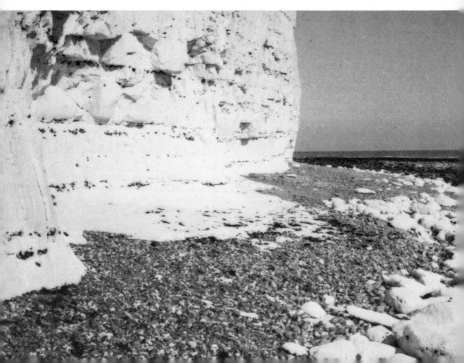

action contributes to the wearing and reduction of rock debris and also clears away material that has fallen from the cliffs, thereby ensuring continued recession at the cliff base (Plate 23).

Shore platforms in front of such receding cliffs are interrupted at the mouths of valleys where rivers incised deeper channels at low sea level stages. On the Sussex coast the chalk platform is interrupted by sanded sectors off the mouths of dry valleys that were excavated during a low sea level stage, then partly infilled with periglacial drift deposits. Their evolution is explained in Fig. 30.

30 *Evolution of a sanded sector interrupting the rocky shore platform opposite the mouth of a valley incised into a Chalk coast during a Pleistocene low sea level phase (AC) and subsequently aggraded by accumulation of periglacial drift deposits (Combe Rock) to form a dry valley (AD) truncated by cliff recession. Based on Birling Gap, Sussex (A in Plate 15)*

Structural and lithological variations in coastal rock formations can strongly influence the development of cliff and shore platform profiles. In the Sydney district, on the coast of New South Wales, stepped profiles have developed on the outcrops of Triassic sandstones, the steps being 'structural' in the sense that they coincide with the upper surfaces of resistant strata:

24   *Structural benches on bedded sandstone in the cliffs at Cape Solander, New South Wales (O. F. Dent)*

25   *High tide shore platforms on the New South Wales coast near Scarborough*

they are horizontal where the bedding is flat, and inclined where the rocks are dipping (Plate 24). It is possible to follow a particular bench along the shore, down the dip of a resistant sandstone layer, until it passes below sea level, when the bench on the next higher resistant rock outcrop begins to dominate the shore profile as it declines into the sea. This kind of coastal topography results from storm wave activity, with erosion along bedding-planes and joints and the removal of dislocated rock masses to lay bare a structural bench. Where the rock formations dip gently seaward the profile may resemble an inter-tidal shore platform, passing below low water mark. Where benches or platforms have developed on flat or gently dipping formations above high tide level, it may be tempting to regard them as emerged features, developed during an earlier phase of higher relative sea level, but on high wave energy coasts storm waves may develop 'structural' benches as much as 60 m above present sea level on horizontal or gently-dipping stratified formations (p. 73). A platform above high tide level is more likely to indicate an earlier phase of higher relative sea level if it is cut *across* the local structures of coastal rock formations, and, even then, confirmatory evidence of associated 'raised beach' materials is desirable.

Structural benches of the kind found on the Sydney coast are developed elsewhere on horizontal or gently-dipping sandstones, and occasionally on stratified limestone formations. In Britain, the Old Red Sandstone of northernmost Scotland has benches of this kind, and they are also found locally on the Triassic sandstones of the S Devon coast between Torquay and Sidmouth and on limestone ledges in Dorset (Plate 21).

Much attention has been given in coastal geomorphological literature to horizontal, or nearly horizontal, shore platforms found on many coasts, which truncate local geological structures and cannot be explained in terms of lithological control. Originally observed and studied in New Zealand, Hawaii, and Australia, these are in fact of widespread occurrence on the islands and shores of the Pacific and Indian Oceans, and have also been noted locally on the Atlantic coast. They fall into two main categories: those developed at, or slightly above, mean high tide level ('high tide shore platforms') (Fig. 21B), and those developed slightly above mean low tide level ('low tide shore platforms') (Fig. 21C).

Shore platforms at relatively high levels have been interpreted in various ways (Cotton, 1963). In SE Australia they are
typically submerged at high spring tide, and when storms drive
waves across them, but on calm days they remain dry at high
neap tide (Plate 25). It has been suggested that they are essentially 'storm wave platforms' produced by waves driven across
them during storms when the cliff at the rear is cut back; in
calmer weather, wave action is limited to the outer edge, which
gradually recedes, the width of the platform being a function of
the relative rates of front and rear recession. It is difficult to
accept this as an explanation for horizontal shore platforms,
except in the special case where the platform coincides with the
upper surface of a horizontal rock stratum. Attempts to argue
that storm waves achieve planation because they concentrate
their energy at a particular level have not proved convincing,
since storm waves come in a variety of dimensions, and operate
over a height range related to the rise and fall of tides. High tide
shore platforms are often as well, or better, developed on sectors of the coast that are sheltered from strong storm wave
activity as on the New South Wales coast, where the strongest
storm waves arrive from the SE, but the high tide shore platforms are at least as broad and often better developed on the
northern sides of headlands and offshore islands. On the more
exposed southern sides the platforms show evidence of dissection and destruction at their outer margin and along joints and
bedding-planes, and there is evidence that this recession accom-
panies the development of an inclined platform at a lower level
(Bird and Dent, 1966). It appears that wave abrasion, operating
alone, tends to develop the simple profile of steep cliff, bordered
by 'inter-tidal' shore platform, within restraints imposed by the
structure and lithology of coastal outcrops. Horizontal platforms
truncating local geological structures cannot be explained in
terms of storm wave attack, which appears to have a secondary
and modifying influence on these features.

It has been suggested that shore platforms at or slightly above
mean high tide level are the product of wave abrasion at an
earlier phase when sea level was higher (Fairbridge, 1961), the
platforms merely being kept fresh by the surf that washes over
them at high spring tides and during storms. The hypothesis
accords with the idea that the Holocene marine transgression
attained a maximum slightly above present sea level before

dropping back during a phase of 'Recent emergence', and where high tide shore platforms are backed by degraded cliffs which have not been kept fresh by marine attack the evidence for this view appears strong (Plate 26); dissection of the outer edge of the platforms can then be interpreted as the result of the cutting of a new platform by wave abrasion at a lower level following emergence. However, it is difficult to explain why high tide shore platforms are horizontal, or nearly so, whereas the platform being cut by wave abrasion at a lower level has a seaward inclination. Moreover, the cliffs behind high tide platforms are not always degraded. Some are clearly active and receding, but the degradation of others could be simply a function of intermittency of storm wave attack, and a relatively long phase of quiescence since they were last trimmed back by the sea. It is necessary to consider what other processes are at work on these cliffs and platforms before deciding if it is necessary to invoke an episode of higher sea level in Holocene times to account for their development.

Examination of shore features in the vicinity of high tide shore platforms yields evidence that weathering processes are at work on coastal rock outcrops unprotected by a soil or vegetation cover in the zone at and above mean high tide level. Superficial decomposition of exposed rock surfaces results from repeated wetting and drying, accompanied by salt crystallisation, in the zone subject to the action of spray. Tricart (1959) claimed that salt spray weathering is a dominant process in shore platform development on the tropical coast of Brazil, where absence of coarse detritus impedes abrasion by waves and high insolation rapidly dries off rock surfaces wetted by saline spray. It is, however, difficult to dissociate the physical effects of wetting and drying from the physico-chemical effects of crystallisation from drying spray. Salt crystallisation probably has specific corrosive effects, and may accelerate weathering compared with wetting and drying in freshwater environments: laboratory tests suggest that this is so, but the problem requires further investigation in the field.

Sandstone outcrops subject to wetting by seaspray and rainfall, and subsequent drying, become pitted and honeycombed as sand grains are loosened by the decomposition of the cementing material that formerly bound them. Other fine-grained rock formations, such as siltstones, mudstones, shales,

26 *Inner margin of high tide shore platform cut in basalt on Broulee Island, New South Wales, showing the degraded cliff*

27 *Plunging cliffs of granite at the southern end of Wilsons Promontory, Victoria (Australian News and Information Bureau)*

schists, phyllites, and basalts, are subject to similar superficial decomposition and weathering effects. This kind of weathering is not effective at lower levels, where rock formations are permanently saturated by sea water, and so wave action washes away the disintegrating material above a certain level, gradually laying bare a platform which coincides with the upper level of permanent saturation. On the coast of SE Australia it is the fine-grained rock outcrops, which show evidence of pitting and cavity formation indicating that the exposed rock is gradually being disintegrated by weathering processes, that have shore platforms developed at or slightly above mean high tide level. Pools and channels on the platform surface become enlarged and integrated as their overhanging rims recede, and gradually the rock surface is 'peeled off' down to a level which remains intact because it is permanently saturated (Plate 26). The process has been described as 'water-layer weathering', and as the level of saturation need not coincide with bedding-planes it offers a mechanism by which coastal planation may operate, forming platforms which may transgress local geological structures (Hills, 1949). It also accounts for the fact that high tide shore platforms are almost horizontal, often with a raised rim at the outer edge which is permanently saturated by breaking waves. Finally, this type of weathering is less effective on massive coastal outcrops of granite and quartzite on the SE coast of Australia, which explains why some headlands, such as the granite mass of Wilsons Promontory in Victoria, are not bordered by high tide shore platforms (Plate 27).

Water-layer weathering explains many features of high tide shore platforms, but it cannot explain them entirely. Occasional storm wave activity is necessary to sweep away the disintegrated rock material, and to attack and rejuvenate the base of the cliff at the rear of these platforms. On extremely sheltered sectors of the coast it is possible that the weathered material would not be carried away sufficiently for the high tide shore platform to develop, and on sectors exposed to very frequent storms it is possible that abrasion would be sufficiently rapid to destroy the high tide platform as quickly as the removal of weathered debris laid it bare. The width of such a platform is determined by the relative rates of recession of the cliff at the rear (by removal of weathered material and occasional storm wave abrasion) and the frontal margin (by more continuous wave action on permanently saturated and unweathered rock). Where nearshore rock debris is available, accelerated dissection of the frontal margin may lead to the development of an inter-tidal shore platform. On the New South Wales coast high tide shore platforms give place to inter-tidal platforms on exposed sectors where wave abrasion is facilitated by the presence of locally-derived shingle (Bird and Dent, 1966). The nature and extent of shore platforms on such a coast vary in relation to a number of factors: lithology, structure, weathering processes, nearshore topography, wave regime, tidal range, and the availability of abrasive debris—factors that vary intricately on a coast of irregular configuration, with local variations in aspect. As the sea stood at higher levels relative to the land at certain phases during Quaternary times, existing shore platforms have often developed as the result of down-wasting and planation of presumably similar features that developed earlier at higher levels. Locally, fragments of older and higher platforms may persist as emerged terraces. High tide shore platforms on the SE coast of Australia are related to present sea level and wave conditions and it is not necessary to invoke an episode of higher sea level to account for them; on the other hand they cannot be taken as evidence that a higher stillstand has *not* occurred in Holocene times.

The development of shore platforms by the washing away of disintegrated material where rock formations have been weathered down to a certain level was described by Bartrum who termed these platforms of 'Old Hat' type, with reference to islands with residual central hills encircled by flat rock ledges formed in this way, within the low wave energy environment of the landlocked Bay of Islands, NE New Zealand (Cotton, 1974). In N Australia, Edwards (1958) similarly explained broad platforms on the shores of Yampi Sound in terms of removal by wave action of rock that had been deeply weathered, under tropical humid conditions, to expose a shore platform of unweathered rock. Climatic factors may also have influenced the development of strandflats, the extensive shallow-water and partly emerged platforms of problematical origin found on the fiord coasts of Norway, Spitzbergen, Iceland, and Greenland. They are up to 50 km wide locally, and numerous rocky islands rise above them. It is possible that they developed as the result of plucking and disintegration of coastal rock outcrops by shelf ice, followed by the sweeping away of debris by wave action when the ice melted. Alternatively, they may be the outcome of prolonged coastal periglaciation. The Norwegian strandflat appears to be a relict feature formed by repeated freeze-and-thaw action beneath Pleistocene shelf ice that rose and fell with the tide (Tietze, 1962), but the processes that produced it have not yet been identified on actively glaciated or periglaciated Arctic or Antarctic rocky coasts.

Low tide shore platforms may be defined as horizontal, or almost horizontal platforms exposed only for a relatively brief period when the sea falls below mean mid-tide level. They are best developed on certain limestone coasts, where they are broad and almost flat, except for an inclined ramp towards the rear, leading up to the cliff base, which frequently has a notch overhung by a visor (Plate 28). There is sometimes a slightly higher rim at the outer edge formed by an encrustation of algae (chiefly *Lithothamnion* species) in a zone that is kept wet by wave splashing even at low tide (Fig. 31).

31   *Low tide shore platform, as developed on Pleistocene dune limestone (aeolian calcarenite) on the S and W coasts of Australia*

As low tide shore platforms of this kind are typically developed on limestone formations, it is evident that solution of limestone (chiefly calcium carbonate) by water, in the presence of carbon dioxide, is an important factor in their formation (Wentworth, 1939). The dissolving of limestone is represented by the equation:

$$CaCO_3 + H_2O + CO_2 \rightarrow Ca(HCO_3)_2$$

the rock passing into solution as calcium bicarbonate, $Ca(HCO_3)_2$. Solution of limestone can also be accomplished by rainwater and by ground-water seepage provided that the water contains dissolved carbon dioxide and is not already saturated with calcium bicarbonate in solution. In fact, sea water off lime-stone coasts and ground water emerging from limestone cliffs is normally saturated with dissolved calcium bicarbonate, and thus incapable of dissolving more limestone on the shore. Rain water, on the other hand, is rich in dissolved atmospheric car-bon dioxide, and is capable of dissolving away a limestone surface. This is a contributory factory in the development of limestone shores exposed to rainfall at low tide, but the fact that low tide platforms are at least as well developed on the coasts of arid regions indicates that some other factor must be dominant.

The problem of how sea water, already saturated with cal-cium bicarbonate, can achieve further solution of limestone in the shore zone was analysed by Revelle and Emery (1957) on Bikini Atoll. They found that there were marked diurnal varia-tions in the dissolving capacity of sea water, related in part to variations in the temperature and carbon dioxide content of water in the shore zone. Nocturnal cooling of sea water increases its capacity to take up carbon dioxide (which is more

28   *Part of the low tide shore platform cut in Pleistocene calcarenite on the Victorian coast near Portsea, showing the notch and overhanging visor at the base of a stack*

soluble in water at lower temperatures), permitting it to dissolve more limestone, and the biochemical activities of marine organisms lead to the production of carbon dioxide (from plant and animal respiration) which is used by the plants (chiefly algae) in photosynthesis by day but which accumulates at night when the absence of sunlight halts photosynthesis. The nocturnal increase in the acidity of coastal water permits limestone to be taken into solution, and calcium carbonate dissolved during the night will be precipitated by day, when temperature rises and photosynthesis revives. The capacity of sea water to retain dissolved bicarbonate therefore diminishes. Much of the precipitated carbonate is quickly carried away from the limestone shore by waves and currents. As the nocturnal solution processes operate mainly within the tidal zone, they will remove calcium carbonate in solution down to a level at which permanently saturated and submerged limestone is evidently dissolved more slowly, if at all, by sea water, so that a low tide platform tends to develop. According to Hills (1949), shore platforms developed on calcarenites coincide with a horizon of secondary induration, where cementing calcite has been precipitated from percolating ground water encountering carbonate-saturated sea water: the calcarenite is less resistant both above and below this horizon, which thus becomes a secondary structural factor in shore platform evolution.

As with the water-layer weathering process effective on the coastal rock formations where high tide shore platforms have developed, solution processes are accompanied by occasional storm wave activity, which sweeps away precipitated calcium carbonate, and, if armed with suitable rock fragments, achieves abrasion of the outer margin of the platform and of the ramp and cliff at the rear. Chalk coasts, discussed previously, would evidently have developed similar low tide shore platforms, were it not for the availability of associated flints, which have been used in wave abrasion, leading to the development of a broad inter-tidal platform. The notch and visor feature typical of many limestone coasts (Plate 29) is not simply an abrasion notch; it is often as well developed on sheltered sectors of the coast as on sectors exposed to strong wave action, and extends uniformly around the stacks in the foreground of Plate 30. Exposure to strong storm wave activity is evidently inimical to the development of this feature, for storm waves have been observed to

29　*Notch and visor developed mainly by solution processes on emerged coral limestone on the Kenya coast near Mombasa*

30　*Coastal lapies on a limestone shore near Sorrento, Victoria*

snap off visors that had developed under quieter conditions. In Malaysia, Hodgkin (1964) found that the maximum solution of coastal calcarenites (about 1 mm/year) took place just above mean sea level, where the notch develops, indicating that it is essentially the outcome of solution processes. Marine organisms also contribute to the etching away of limestone in the shore zone, and Emery (1960) has indicated that in favourable conditions biochemical processes can consume rock at least as quickly as physical and purely chemical erosion. Some would go as far as to suggest that the notch has been almost literally eaten out by the shore fauna that occupy this horizon (e.g. Healy, 1968).

Shore morphology on limestone coasts shows variations related to zonal climatic factors. Guilcher (1953) outlined the characteristic features of limestone (excluding Chalk) coasts in the cool temperate, warm temperate, and tropical zones. In cool temperate regions (S Ireland, S Wales) limestones show pitting and honeycombing in the upper (spray) zone, shallow flat-floored pools with overhanging rims, tending to widen and coalesce as a platform, in the shore zone, and a more irregular network of ridges and pinnacles (coastal lapies) in the lower part of the shore zone (Fig. 32A). These predominantly solution forms are obliterated where waves armed with rock debris abrade the shore zone, and lithological variations introduce further complications, as on the stratified Jurassic limestones of the Dorset coast. In warm temperate regions Guilcher recognised two kinds of zonation, both with coastal lapies in the upper (spray) zone (Plate 28). On mesotidal coasts (Morocco, Portugal) the shore zone consists of flat-floored pools becoming larger and deeper towards low tide mark; on microtidal coasts (Mediterranean) there is a notch, with an overhanging visor, and a narrow shore ledge exposed at low tide (Fig. 32B and C). The warm temperate zonation gives place to the cold temperate zonation from S to N around the coastline of the Bay of Biscay (Guilcher, 1958). On coasts of tropical regions, especially on emerged coral, the pinnacles are developed on top of an overhanging visor, and the flat-bottomed pools occupy a ledge exposed at low tide (Fig. 32D).

On the calcarenite coasts of southern Australia the zonation is similar to that described from warm temperate environments, except that the shore platform is somewhat broader. In the spray zone the rock surfaces are intricately pitted as the

32 *Typical zonation of corrosion forms on coastal limestone (after Guilcher, 1958). A, cool temperate regions (British Isles); B, warm temperate regions, mesotidal (Morocco); C, warm temperate regions, microtidal (Mediterranean); D, tropical regions (Pacific atolls)*

result of muricate weathering, due to solution of carbonates by rain water, sea spray and surf, aided by corrosive exudations from marine organisms, notably algae. Monitoring of changes on a freshly-exposed surface of dune calcarenite on the shore at Portsea, Victoria showed only the earliest stages in development of intricate pitting after ten years. At higher levels in the cliff face the calcarenite is marked by honeycombs and cavities pro-duced by alveolar weathering, due to recurrent wetting-and-drying and associated internal solution and near-surface precipi-tation of case-hardening carbonates.

There are similar variations in the characteristic forms of cliffed coast on granites and basalts, related to the weathering regime under different climatic conditions, but the details of these have not yet been worked out. Recent work suggests that shore platforms on various kinds of rock have become indur-ated by weathering processes at work in the shore zone, the outcrops being significantly harder than those seen in quarries or encountered in boreholes in the same geological formation a short distance inland. Induration may result from superficial enrichment of shore outcrops by the precipitation of carbon-ates, or of ferruginous or siliceous cementing compounds; it contributes significantly to the persistence of shore platforms shaped by weathering rather than by abrasion processes.

Plunging cliffs

Plunging cliffs (Fig. 21D) are cliffs that pass steeply beneath low tide level without any development of shore platforms. These have several possible explanations. Plunging cliffs can be pro-duced by Holocene faulting, the cliff face being the exposed plane of the fault on the up-throw side, the down-thrown block having subsided beneath the sea. The cliffs along the line of the Wellington fault, on the W shore of Port Nicholson in New Zealand, have been explained in this way (Cotton, 1952); they slope at about 55°, show little evidence of marine modification at the shore level, and descend to the 12 fathom (about 22 m) submarine contour, close inshore and parallel to the coastline. Tectonic subsidence of coasts may lead to the development of plunging cliffs, possibly with former shore platforms submerged beneath low tide level; the plunging cliffs of Lyttelton Harbour and Banks Peninsula (Fig. 67) originated as the result of continu-ing subsidence of this area during and since the Holocene mar-ine transgression. The explosive eruption of Krakatau, a volcano in Sunda Strait, Indonesia, in 1883 left residual islands with steep plunging cliffs on the caldera rim, and similar features are seen on Santorini, north of Crete, which exploded about 3,500 years ago. Coasts built up recently by volcanic activity, as on the island of Hawaii, show plunging cliffs on sectors where there has not yet been time for shore platforms to develop. Absence of shore platforms on very sheltered sectors of coast bordering rias and fiords, and on sectors where the coastal rock outcrops are extremely resistant, may simply be due to the fact that the period of up to 6,000 years since the sea attained its present level has been too brief for marine processes to develop platforms. In Australia the plunging granite cliffs of Wilsons Promontory (Plate 27) are evidently too resistant for shore platforms to be developed within this relatively short period; the cliffs are the partly-submerged slopes of granite hills and mountains. On the Nullarbor coast, there are sectors where the vertical cliffs of homogeneous Eocene and Miocene limestones pass beneath low tide level without shore platforms, possibly because the great vigour of storm wave activity on this coast is achieving abrasion down to a level below low tide level as these cliffs recede (Plate 18).

It is useful to recognise a category of steep coasts which are not actively-receding cliffs, but rather coastal slopes that descend steeply to the shoreline. Some of these are plunging, in that the coastal slope continues below sea level, while others border shallow seas, the floors of which have been built up by deposition. Examples of steep coasts include the North Devon coast bordering Exmoor, and the coast of the French and Italian Riviera. In Australia the Otways coast and parts of the North Queensland coast (Plate 31) are in this category (Bird, 1970), and much of the New Zealand coast is similarly bold.

The morphogenic system leading to the evolution of cliffed coasts can be analysed in terms of the effects of geological structure and lithology, the action of marine and subaerial processes, tidal conditions, and the inheritance of changing levels of land and sea and changing climatic conditions. The tempo of change on a cliffed coast shows marked variations from place to place, even on adjacent flanks of an embayment or headland, according to rock resistance and degree of exposure to marine attack. At one extreme there are sections of coast, like Wilsons Promontory, which have changed very little in the period since

31 *Steep coast of Macalister Range, near Cairns, Queenland*

the Holocene marine transgression brought the sea to its present general level. At the other extreme there are sections of rapid cliff recession, as on the coast of W Victoria, near Port Campbell, and sectors of the E and S coasts of England, where relatively weak Tertiary formations confront stormy seas, and changes can be measured by referring to old maps and photographs (Fig. 33). Between these extremes there are many sections of cliffed coast that are developing slowly and showing variations which can be analysed to show the respective roles of rock resistance, wave attack, and coastal weathering processes in their developing morphology. Examples of such analysis, based on synoptic reviews of particular coasts, are given by Bird and Dent (1966) and Hills (1971).

33   *The betrunking of Elephant Rock, near Port Campbell, Victoria*

Studies of the evolution of cliffed coasts have generally been largely qualitative, concerned with identifying and attempting to evaluate the various factors and processes that have been at work. In quantitative terms it would be possible, given adequate data on wave direction and height in relation to tidal levels, to derive a time-integrated expression of the wave energy profile on a cliffed coast (Sunamura, 1977). Profiles of this kind have been used in engineering studies, notably in the design of sea walls, but there are difficulties in attempting to use such data to explain the configuration of a cliffed coast. Existing configuration is one of the important factors determining the wave energy profile so that there is a danger of circular argument. Moreover, as has been indicated, erosion of cliffed coasts is the outcome of a variety of processes, including weathering, solution, and biochemical activity, which are largely independent of wave energy profiles. It is perhaps because of these difficulties that satisfactory quantitative appraisals of the evolution of cliffed coasts have yet to be made.

V

BEACHES, SPITS, AND BARRIERS

Beaches are accumulations of sediment deposited by waves and currents in the shore zone. In terms of the Wentworth scale of particle diameters (Table 1) they are typically composed of sand or pebbles: granular beaches are uncommon, but silt beaches may occur on very sheltered coastlines. The proportions of each grain size can be determined by mechanical analysis, when a known weight of dried beach sediment is passed through a succession of sieves of diminishing mesh diameter, and divided into size grades which are weighed separately. As a rule, samples of beach sediment are well sorted, in the sense that the bulk of a sample falls within a particular size grade, as indicated by the graph in Fig. 34. Statistical parameters based on mechanical analysis indicate that the grain size distribution of beach sediment is commonly asymmetrical, and negatively-skewed, the mean grain size being coarser than the median; evidently the winnowing effect of wave action reduces the relative proportion of fine particles (Mason and Folk, 1958). Such parameters may

TABLE 1

Wentworth size class	Particle diameter		ø scale	
Boulders	>	256 mm	below	$-8ø$
Cobbles	64 mm −	256 mm	$-6ø$ to	$-8ø$
Pebbles	4 mm −	64 mm	$-2ø$ to	$-6ø$
Granules	2 mm −	4 mm	$-1ø$ to	$-2ø$
Very coarse sand	1 mm −	2 mm	$0ø$ to	$-1ø$
Coarse sand	$\frac{1}{2}$ mm −	1 mm	$1ø$ to	$0ø$
Medium sand	$\frac{1}{4}$ mm −	$\frac{1}{2}$ mm	$2ø$ to	$1ø$
Fine sand	$\frac{1}{8}$ mm −	$\frac{1}{4}$ mm	$3ø$ to	$2ø$
Very fine sand	$\frac{1}{16}$ mm −	$\frac{1}{8}$ mm	$4ø$ to	$3ø$
Silt	$\frac{1}{256}$ mm −	$\frac{1}{16}$ mm	$8ø$ to	$4ø$
Clay	<	$\frac{1}{256}$ mm	above	$8ø$

Note: The ø (phi) scale is a logarithmic scale of particle diameters defined by Krumbein as the negative logarithm to base 2 of the particle diameter in millimetres: ø = $-\log_2 d$

assist in the identification of former beach deposits, permitting a distinction from positively-skewed grain size distributions typical of fluvial, aeolian, and lagoonal deposits (Friedman, 1961). Chappell (1967) used this method to identify shoreline sediments in the Quaternary deposits of the W coasts of the North Island, New Zealand. Granulometric studies can also be used to describe and elucidate the origin and dynamics of present-day beach systems (Folk and Ward, 1957; Bird, 1971).

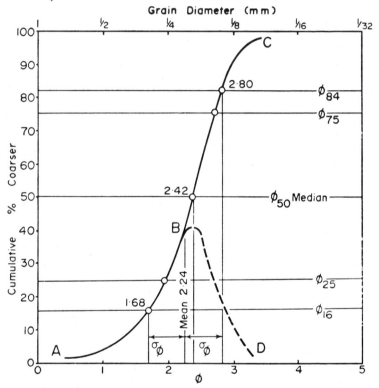

34 *Graphic representation of a grain-size analysis of a beach sand. Measured in ø units, the median diameter, $Md_ø$ (50th percentile) is 2.42, the 16th percentile ($ø_{16}$) 1.68, and the 84th percentile ($ø_{84}$) 2.80. Values for the mean ($M_ø$), sorting ($σ_ø$) and skewness ($α_ø$) are calculated as follows:*

$$Mean = M_ø = \tfrac{1}{2}(ø_{16} + ø_{84}) = \tfrac{1}{2}(1.68 + 2.80) = 2.24$$

$$Sorting = σ_ø = \tfrac{1}{2}(ø_{84} - ø_{16}) = \tfrac{1}{2}(2.80 - 1.68) = 0.56$$

$$Skewness = α_ø = \frac{M_ø - Md_ø}{σ_ø} = \frac{(2.24 - 2.42)}{0.56} = -0.32$$

(i.e. the mean (2.24) is coarser than median (2.42), the sample is moderately well sorted and the grain-size distribution is strongly negatively skewed – see Table 2).

Beach sediments composed of larger particles tend to develop steeper gradients (Table 3), chiefly because of their greater permeability. Wave swash sweeps sediment forward on to a beach, and backwash tends to carry it back, but the greater

TABLE 2

Descriptive categories for sorting and skewness

Sorting (σ_ϕ)	Category
Less than 0.35	Very well sorted
0.35 to 0.50	Well sorted
0.50 to 1.00	Moderately well sorted
1.00 to 2.00	Poorly sorted
2.00 to 4.00	Very poorly sorted
More than 4.00	Extremely poorly sorted

Skewness (α_ϕ)	Category
-1.00 to -0.30	Strongly negatively skewed
-0.30 to -0.10	Negatively skewed
-0.10 to $\;\;\;0.10$	Nearly symmetrical
-0.10 to $\;\;\;0.30$	Positively skewed
$\;\;\;0.30$ to $\;\;\;1.00$	Strongly postively skewed

Source: Folk and Ward (1957)

TABLE 3

Wentworth size class	Mean slope of beach face
Cobbles	24°
Pebbles	17°
Granules	11°
Very coarse sand	9°
Coarse sand	7°
Medium sand	5°
Fine sand	3°
Very fine sand	1°

Source: Shepard (1963)

permeability of gravel and coarse sand beaches diminishes the effects of backwash, leaving swash-piled sediment at relatively steep gradients. Fine sand beaches are more affected by back-wash, and have gentler slopes, often of firmly-packed sand across which it may be possible to drive a car. Where the sands are well-sorted, and composed of well-rounded and highly-polished sand grains, the beach may emit a squeaking noise when walked upon (Lindsay, 1976).

The origin of beach sediments

The nature of beach sediment is clearly related to the nature of material supplied by rivers from the adjacent cliffs and fore-shore, or brought in from offshore or alongshore sources. Gra-vel or shingle beaches are found where coastal rock formations yield debris of suitable size, such as fragments broken from thin resistant layers in stratified sedimentary rocks, or eroded out of conglomerates or gravel deposits, or derived from intricately-fissured igneous outcrops. Much of the shingle on the beaches of SE England has been derived, directly or indirectly, from flint nodules eroded out of the Chalk; some of it has had a long and complex Tertiary and Quaternary history. On the world scale, coasts bordering regions which are, or have been, subject to glaciation and periglaciation have relatively abundant supplies of rock fragments derived from the erosion of rubble drift, gravelly moraines, or drumlins, for the formation of shingle beaches; elsewhere sandy beaches are predominant unless a shingle source exists locally. Shingle is rare on tropical coasts, except where it is derived from coral (Chapter IX), or from lateritic crusts outcropping in coastal cliffs, as in the ironstone gravels of the Darwin district, or where torrential rivers have delivered gravels to the shore, as at Lae, in New Guinea, which has a cobble beach supplied with gravels from the Markham River.

Sandy beaches may be supplied with sand eroded from coas-tal arenaceous outcrops, as in Bournemouth Bay on the S coast of England, and on the eastern shores of Port Phillip Bay, Austra-lia, both of which have beaches derived mainly from receding cliffs of Tertiary sandstone. At Bournemouth the progressive extension since 1900 of a promenade on the seafront has halted cliff recession and cut off the sand supply; the beach is gradually diminishing on a wasting foreshore, with little if any replenishment of sand carried away by longshore drifting. It has since been restored artificially (p. 174).

Sand may also be delivered to the shore by rivers, as on the coast of S California, where the beaches consist of sand of fluvial origin that drifts southwards from river mouths, accumulating against the northern flanks of promontories (such as Point Dume), or lost into the heads of the submarine canyons that run out from the southern ends of several embayments. There are thus distinct compartments of beach material on this coast (Emery, 1960). In NE Queensland, rivers deliver sandy sediment to the coast during floods, to be subsequently distributed along-shore by wave action as beaches and spits (Plate 32). Sediment delivered to the coast by rivers in flood is usually deposited on the sea floor off the river mouth, then sorted and distributed by wave and current action, the coarser fractions (sand, gravel) often moving shoreward to nourish beaches around the river mouth or down-drift.

In 1967, torrential rainfall in the Serra do Mar, SW of Rio de Janeiro, led to extensive erosion, catastrophic river flooding, and the delivery of vast quantities of sand, silt and clay to the sea, notably in Caraguatatuba Bay, where wave action has subse-quently sorted this material and washed the sandy fraction onshore, to be added to the beaches (Cruz, 1982). When the fluvial sand supply is intercepted, following construction of reservoirs in the river valleys, beaches are reduced and shore-line erosion accelerated. Fluvial catchment yields, augmented as the result of man-induced erosion (following deforestation, over-grazing, or unwise cultivation), can add to the supply of sand delivered to beaches such as these, as can the addition of mining waste to river loads, as in New Caledonia and Bougainville. Hinterland earthquakes and volcanic eruptions can also increase sediment yield, for example in Java where successive eruptions of such volcanoes as Merapi increase the fluvial sedi-ment supply to the nearby coast south of Yogyakarta, where beaches and dunes of grey volcanic sand are extensive.

The large-scale sandy beaches on the SE coast of Australia cannot be explained in these ways. The Ninety Mile Beach in Victoria, for example, is not adjacent to eroding sandstone cliffs; it forms part of a barrier system that seals off river mouths as coastal lagoons in which the fluvial sand supply is intercepted. It appears that the beach sand here has been swept shoreward

32 *Sandy sediment in the channel of the River Don, North Queensland, is washed down to the coast during floods and added to beaches and spits that drift northwards from the river mouth*

from the sea floor, during and possibly since the Holocene marine transgression. The possibility that sand is still being delivered from the sea floor receives support from experimental work in wave tanks, which show that waves moving towards a coast generate a shoreward current at depth, close to the sea floor. In addition, winds blowing offshore may set up a shore ward movement of water close to the sea floor. Both processes are capable of delivering sediment to a beach, but the depth from which material can be carried shoreward varies in relation to sea floor topography, wave conditions, and the size, shape and specific gravity of the available sediment. Submarine vegetation is also a factor, sediment flow being inhibited where such plants as *Zostera*, *Posidonia*, and *Cymodocea* form luxuriant growths, as in parts of the Mediterranean and off the South Australian coast. In favourable conditions it appears that sea floor sediment can be drifted shoreward from depths of up to 18 m. In the Mediterranean, Van Straaten (1959) found that waves are moving sand on to beaches on the French coast from a depth of 9 m, and on coasts receiving long ocean swell the process may be effective from greater depths than this. Off S California there is only limited and occasional movement of sea-floor sand by ocean swell in depths exceeding 18 m, indicating the probable maximum limit. Sand dumped in water 12 m deep off the New Jersey coast failed to move shorewards to replenish an eroding beach (Harris, 1955), and was therefore beyond the limit for shoreward drifting in that environment. In view of these limitations, it seems probable that the bulk of shoreward sand drifting on the SE Australian coast took place during the Holocene marine transgression, when the near shore zone migrated shoreward over unconsolidated deposits stranded during the previous sea regression, and that beach progradation took place in the ensuing stillstand as ocean waves swept sand in from nearshore shoals (Bird, 1978b). Relics of such shoals persist in sheltered areas, e.g. to the east of Wilsons Promontory and in the shallows between Robbins I. and Hunter I. off NW Tasmania.

In general, sandy beaches are supplied partly by material eroded from adjacent parts of the coast, partly by fluvial sediment, and partly by sand carried shoreward from the sea floor, the relative proportions being determined by local conditions. In addition, quantities of sand may be blown from the land into the sea, particularly on desert coasts, and thence delivered to the beach (Plate 33). The dynamics of a beach sediment system are thus determined by the balance of nourishment from these various sources against alongshore and offshore losses, the removal of sand by wind to build landward dunes, and the washing of sand into estuaries and tidal inlets. Davies (1974) has discussed beach systems in terms of *coastal sediment compartments* delimited laterally by protruding headlands, rocky shores, river mouths, or the heads of submarine canyons close inshore (Fig. 35).

On steep and rocky coasts, beaches of sand or gravel develop and persist in suitable niches, such as relatively shallow bay-heads, coves and inlets; many such beaches are locally derived, but some are interceptions of sediment carried alongshore, or washed in from the sea floor. Just as there are catchments on land from which sediment is derived and delivered to the coast at river mouths, so are there 'sea floor catchments', areas of tributary shelf from which material has been, and may still be, carried shorewards.

Beach systems

Measurement of wave processes and their effects close to the shore has been developed by Kirk (1973), who devised a dyna-

33   *Sand supplied to beach by dune spilling on to the shores of Corner Inlet, Victoria*

35   *On the Caucasian Black Sea coast rivers supply sand and gravel to the beaches,
which drift south-eastwards until they are lost into the heads of submarine
canyons. After Zenkovich, 1973*

mometer to register swash and backwash velocities in association with a depth gauge and with mounted nozzles as sediment
samplers. Another approach to the study of beach dynamics is
by setting up scale model tanks with simulated waves and currents (Saville, 1950), although there are difficulties over the
scaling down of natural sediment calibre to fit model conditions.
Sand grains can be used in a model to represent a shingle beach,
but the representation of a sandy beach to scale may involve the
use of silts, which have different physical properties, and may
not reproduce the correct response of sand to wave and current
action.

   More recently there have been theoretical studies of the dynamics of natural beach systems. Miller and Zeigler (1958) pre-
sented a theoretical model relating nearshore processes to sediment characteristics on shores where an equilibrium has been
attained between process and form. They considered the dynamics of shoaling waves entering shallow water, of turbulence in
the breaker zone, and of sheet flow in the zone of swash and
backwash, and postulated trend maps of sediment size (maximum in the breaker zone) and sorting (best on the shoreward
side of the breaker zone) related to these dynamics. The theoretical model was tested against maps of median grain size and the

sorting of nearshore and foreshore sectors of four American beach systems, with generally good results. Krumbein (1963) proposed a process-response model for the analysis of beach phenomena in which the process side is influenced by the energy factor (waves, tides, currents), the geological material factor, and the overall geometry of a coastal sector, and the response side is the form of the beach and the nature of its component sediments. In quantifying this model, 'feedback' is recognised: the beach morphology and sediments influence the processes at work on them. Numerous variables can be defined and measured, and their relationships investigated with the aid of a computer.

Application of this kind of analysis soon reveals the complexity and variability of natural beach systems. An example is given by Harrison (1970), who collected data on fifteen process and response parameters on a beach over a 26-day period, and subjected these to correlation-analysis in the hope of finding empirical equations that would permit prediction of changes in selected beach features, notably changes in the quantity of sand on the foreshore, the advance or retreat of mean high tide line during a tidal cycle, and the slope of the foreshore at the end of the cycle. The analysis showed that ground water flow, determined by the beach water table, was a major factor influencing the response of the beach to wave processes: a wet sandy beach is more easily eroded by wave scour than a dry one. Prediction of changes was hampered by rapid variation in processes (often before the beach response to a particular process had been completed), by the interdependence of process variables, and by the fluctuating range of frequency, magnitude and duration of component variables, with some combinations yielding a unique beach response.

Composition of beach sediments

Beach sands of terrigenous origin generally have quartz as the most abundant mineral, accompanied by felspars, mica, and varying proportions of heavy minerals. Sand supplied from erosion of adjacent cliffed coasts or brought down from river catchments reflects the mineral composition of the source areas. The concentration of rutile, ilmenite, and other heavy minerals in beach sands on the N New South Wales and S Queensland coast has been related to fluvial supply from the Mesozoic sandstones of the Ipswich-Clarence basin, sandstones derived earlier from denudation of Permian granites on the New England plateau, within which these heavy minerals originally formed.

Sand supplied from the sea floor may earlier have been of terrigenous origin, laid down during phases of low sea level and subsequently reworked by wave action during marine transgressions. On the New South Wales coast, sand delivered from the sea floor has smaller proportions of the less resistant felspar and mica grains than freshly supplied fluvial sand, the beaches being predominantly quartzose away from river mouths. Calcareous sands derived from shell fragments or coral debris are common on oceanic island and tropical coasts and are also indicative of shoreward transportation. In temperate regions they are found where shelly organisms are abundant offshore, as on the Lands End peninsula, the Channel Islands, and in the machair of the Outer Hebrides, where beaches of broken shell sand are the source of coastal tracts of calcareous wind-blown sand. In Victoria, Gell (1978) found that some shelly beaches were composed of rock-dwelling species while others came from shallow sandy and muddy environments in sheltered bays and estuaries. Shelly beaches are also common on the shores of estuaries and lagoons: they are found on the shores of the Firth of Forth near Edinburgh. Beaches bordering desert coasts are often calcareous, probably because the fluvial yield of terrigenous sediment has been meagre: the Eighty Mile Beach, bordering semi-arid NW Australia, exemplifies this, and there are shelly beaches bordering the dry northern shores of Spencer Gulf near Whyalla in South Australia.

Calcareous beach and dune sands dominate the south and west coasts of Australia, whereas quartzose beach and dune sands are characteristic in the south-east. The junction between the two provinces occurs in Bass Strait, calcareous sands being dominant W of Wilsons Promontory and on the W coasts of King Island and Flinders Island, and quartzose sands to the E. The calcareous sand is largely of biogenic origin, derived from the bryozoa, molluscs and algae that live on the continental shelf south and west of Australia, swept shorewards during successive marine transgressions, whereas the quartzose sands are of granitic origin, derived by rivers draining the Eastern Highlands, and deposited at low sea level stages on the shelf area SE of Australia for subsequent shoreward delivery (Bird, 1978b). Even on the Queensland coast, behind the Great Barrier Reefs, beach sands are mainly quartzose, supplied by such rivers as the Fitzroy and the Burdekin, with relatively small admixtures of calcareous reef debris.

On volcanic islands, such as Hawaii, black sand beaches occur, consisting mainly of basaltic fragments. Volcanic pumice is a common, and often far-travelled, constituent on many Pacific coast beaches. Locally, beaches have been formed where waves have distributed sands and gravels from quarry waste dumped into the seas as at Hoed, in Denmark (Plate 34). At Workington,

34 *Prograded beach ridge plain at Hoed, Denmark, nourished by gravel waste dumped from a coastal quarry (F. Hansen)*

in NW England, beaches incorporate material derived from colliery waste and steelworks slag. Driftwood is common on many beaches. On the Westland coast, New Zealand, it consists mainly of trees washed down to river mouths, but on eroding sandy coastlines in eastern Australia undercut tea-tree litters the shore. Coasts adjacent to lumbering areas in W Canada and N Russia are piled high with sawn timber washed up on the shore, but the most unusual beach material known to this author is on Brownsea Island, in Poole Harbour (Dorset, England) where wave action has distributed the wastes of a former pipeworks to build a beach of broken subangular earthenware.

There are lateral variations in the composition of beach material, particularly in the vicinity of eroding headlands, where the proportion of locally-derived material may be high, and near river mouths, where a larger proportion of fluvial sediment is likely to be present. Chesil Beach, on the S coast of England, consists mainly of flint pebbles, but at the SE end, adjacent to cliffs of Portland and Purbeck Limestone, cobbles and pebbles of limestone (mainly from quarries) are mixed with the flint shingle. In Encounter Bay, on the South Australian coast, the beach consists almost entirely of calcareous sand towards the SE end near Kingston (almost 90 per cent calcium carbonate), the proportion of quartz sand increasing northwestwards to Goolwa at the mouth of the Murray (calcium carbonate content less than 10 per cent); a lateral variation that may reflect the former supply of terrigenous material to the coastal sector near the mouth of the Murray, diluting the calcareous sand of marine origin dominant elsewhere in this bay (Sprigg, 1959).

Wave action achieves wearing and attrition of pebble and sand grains, the pebbles tending to develop a rounded form, often slightly flattened (i.e. thinner at right-angles to the principal plane), the sand grains becoming smooth, well-rounded, and highly polished.

The process of rounding and attrition of pebbles can be studied on coasts where angular rock debris (quarry waste) is dumped on the shore, and worked by wave action as it drifts along the coast. Beaches no longer receiving fresh sediment become lower and narrower as the result of gradual attrition of pebbles to granules and sand; they are then more easily eroded by storm waves, and as their protective influence decreases, wave attack may initiate or accelerate erosion of bluffs and cliffs to their rear. Attempts have been made to distinguish between beach and dune sands in terms of the shape and roundness characteristics of the component grains (Shepard and Young, 1961; Moss, 1962–1963), and recently electron microscopy has been applied to the study of the distinctive surface textures and markings on quartz grains from beach and dune environments. These techniques can supplement statistical analyses of grain-size distributions mentioned previously in determining former shorelines at the upper limits of beach sands in stratified coastal deposits.

Lateral movements of beach material
Waves that arrive at an angle to the shore produce a transverse swash, running diagonally up the beach, and a backwash that retreats directly seaward. Sand and shingle are edged along the shore by waves that break in this manner ('beach drifting') and at the same time longshore currents developed by waves in the nearshore zone drive sand along the sea floor (Fig. 36). The combined effect of these processes is to produce 'longshore drifting', the sediment flowing first one way, then the other, according to the direction from which the waves approach. The resultant drift over a period may be negligible, or there may be a definite long-term drift in one direction rather than the other, usually indicated by the longshore growth of spits and the deflection of river mouths (Fig. 59). Optimum conditions for longshore drifting occur when wave crests approach the shore-line at an angle of 45°, the shoreline being smooth and unbroken by headlands, inlets or estuaries, the nearshore sea floor

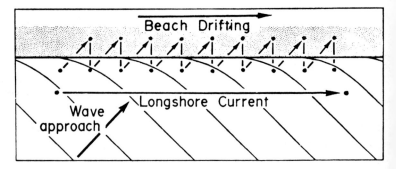

36   *Longshore drifting, the flow of coastal sediment produced by wave and current action when waves approach at an angle to the coastline*

also being smooth, and a continuous supply of sediment available.

The beaches that extend along the south coast of England include a series of 'shingle trains' moving eastward by the prevailing south-westerly wave regime, interrupted by headlands and breakwaters, and terminating either in recurved spits such as Hurst Castle (Fig. 47) or in cuspate forelands, as at Dungeness (Fig. 58). On the N Norfolk coast a predominant westward drift resulting from the prevalence of waves from the NE is indicated by the westward growth of recurved spits at Blakeney Point (Fig. 49) and Scolt Head Island (Steers, 1960). When waves arrive from the NW an eastward counter-drift is produced, and in some years the net drifting of coastal sediment has been eastward rather than westward. The evidence of spit growth, however, indicates that the long-term resultant has been westward. On coasts where the waves arriving obliquely from one side of the shore orthogonal are stronger than those arriving from the other side, more material will move in one direction than the other, and the coarser fraction of the material moved by the stronger waves may not return when the weaker waves move back the finer fraction. This is one way in which lateral sorting may develop along a beach. On such beaches it is common to find lobes of sandy sediment that migrate to and fro along the shore, or proceed intermittently downdrift until they are intercepted by a headland or breakwater, or added to the end of a spit.

On coasts exposed to ocean swell, longshore drifting is produced only if the swell is incompletely refracted so that it arrives at an angle to the beach, or if waves generated by onshore winds move at an angle through the swell to reach the shoreline obliquely. Thus south-westerly waves move sand northward along the Adelaide coast, in South Australia, to accumulate on a prograding beach at Largs Bay, where drifting is intercepted by the Outer Harbour breakwater. On the N New South Wales and S Queensland coast the predominant SE winds produce waves which set up a northward drift of sand on shore shaped by refracted ocean swell. This has led to the development of major depositional features at Moreton, Stradbroke, and Fraser Islands during Pleistocene and Recent times (see p. 189). On some coasts the pattern of beach drifting varies seasonally. Boomer Beach in California is a well known example of this, waves from the SW moving sand northward in summer and waves from the NW driving it back to the S in winter. Similar features have been noted on the beaches bordering Port Phillip Bay, where west-facing beaches show the same seasonal response to SW waves in summer and NW waves in winter (Fig. 37).

Sand can 'by-pass' the mouths of rivers and tidal entrances and be carried round headlands by longshore drifting in the nearshore zone, but large cliffed promontories that end in deep water are likely to interrupt the longshore flow and act as boundaries between distinct compartments of coastal sediment. Within such compartments, beach material moves to and fro

37   *The beach system at Black Rock, Victoria, showing typical autumn and spring beach alignments at low spring tide, and monthly onshore wind resultants which indicate a wave regime yielding southward drift of beach material from April to October and northward drift from November to March*

35 *Norman Bay, Wilsons Promontory, Victoria, showing refracted ocean swell entering the bay, parallel dunes immediately behind the beach, and older parabolic dunes farther inland*

along the shore, and backwards and forwards at an angle to the shore, but it does not pass the bordering promontories, and there can be striking differences in the nature of beaches in adjacent embayments. Examples of this are found on the coast of Cornwall, where the mineralogical composition of beach sands varies from one cove to another, and on the W coast of Wilsons Promontory (Plate 35), where three adjacent coves (Leonard Bay, Norman Bay, and Oberon Bay) have strongly quartzose, mixed quartzose/calcareous, and strongly calcareous beach sands respectively. At Wewak, on the N coast of New Guinea, uplift has led to the emergence of fringing reefs as promontories which have segregated a beach-fringed shoreline into a series of bays and cut off the former supply of eastward drifting sand derived from rivers draining to the coast farther west. Thus deprived, the bay beaches have become finer in texture, and shoreline erosion has ensued.

An understanding of patterns of longshore drifting is of great importance in the location, design, and maintenance of harbours. Sediment carried along the shore may be deposited in a harbour entrance, necessitating repeated dredging, or built up alongside breakwaters in such a way as to interrupt longshore sediment flow and lead to reduction of beaches and accelerated erosion on the downdrift shore. This problem is well known on many coasts; it has happened, for example, at Santa Barbara and Santa Monica on the Californian coast, and at the harbours of Durban, Lagos, and Madras. On the S coast of England the building of a breakwater to protect Newhaven harbour intercepted the eastward drift of shingle, depleting the beach and resulting in excessive storm damage and coast erosion at adjacent Seaford (Fig. 29). At Durban, and several American harbours, efforts are made to carry or pipe intercepted sediment past harbour entrances, depositing it to replenish the beach on the downdrift shore. At Port Hueneme, California, an offshore breakwater has been built parallel to the coast on the updrift side of the harbour entrance to create a pattern of wave refraction that concentrates sand accumulation behind the breakwater, where it is excavated at the rate of 500,000 cubic yards (about 375,000 m³) a year by a floating dredge and ferried past the entrance to replenish wasting beaches on the downdrift shore (Johnson, 1959). Where seasonal patterns of longshore drifting occur, as in Port Phillip Bay, breakwaters built to form boat harbours collect the southward drift in winter in a situation where it cannot be returned northward in summer. The harbours thus become filled with sand and the adjacent beaches erode away. This kind of problem indicates the difficulties that arise when coastal constructions interfere with patterns of longshore drifting. Knowledge of sediment source and flow patterns is essential if constructions are to be designed in such a way as to conserve the balance of erosion and deposition on adjacent shores.

Tracing sediment flow
In recent years progress has been made with methods of following the movement of sand on beaches and across the sea floor by means of tracers. A quantity of tracer material is introduced at one point, and a search is made to see where it goes. In order that it shall move in the same way as the natural sediment, the tracer particles must have a similar range of size and shape, similar hardness, and the same specific gravity as the sediment already present; they must also be identifiable after they have

moved along a beach or across the sea floor. Some tracer becomes buried, and hidden from view within a beach, and a proportion may be lost offshore.

Naturally-coloured and artificially-coloured sand have been used in simple tracer experiments, but there are difficulties in observing coloured grains when they form only a small propor-tion of the sand on a beach. These have been partly overcome by the use of sand 'labelled' with a coating of colloidal substances containing one of several commercially available fluorescent dyes (Ingle, 1966). Sand labelled in this way is dumped on the beach, and its movements can be traced by locating the dyed material subsequently. Near-ultra-violet tracer is followed by searching the beach or sea floor at night in the light of an ultra-violet lamp, or by taking samples of sand for examination by ultra-violet light in a darkroom. These fluorescent grains stand out clearly in ultra-violet light, and the method is a better means of detecting tracer at low concentrations than is a visual search for coloured grains. Russian geomorphologists who have traced sand movement on the Black Sea coast by the fluorescent tracer method have claimed that they can detect tracer at a dilution of one grain in 10 million of sand (Jolliffe, 1961).

Another method of tracing sediment flow depends on the use of radioactive tracers, which can be followed by means of a geiger counter or similar detection apparatus (Kidson and Carr, 1962). Artificial sand made from soda glass containing scandium oxide is ground down to the appropriate size and shape for use as tracer, then placed in a nuclear reactor to produce the radio-active isotope scandium 46. This has a half-life (i.e. time taken for the radioactivity to diminish to half its original strength) of eighty-five days, which means that it can still be detected three or four months after it has been dumped. Various other methods of preparing radioactive tracer have been developed, but the principle remains the same. After the tracer has been dumped, surveys are made by carrying detection apparatus over a beach, or dragging it across the sea floor mounted on a sledge. The location and intensity of radioactivity is mapped and paths of sediment flow can be deduced.

Radioactive tracers are expensive and require special prepar-ation and careful use to avoid risks to public health, but they provide a good means of tracing sand movement, for tracer can be detected even when it has been buried beneath several

inches of sand, where coloured or fluorescent tracer would not
be visible. However, fluorescent tracers have advantages of
cheapness and safety, and are often more durable in long-term
experiments; radioactive tracer permits only one experiment at
a time, but different colours of fluorescent dye can be used to
trace movement from several points at the same time.

Mineralogical methods were used to trace patterns of sediment flow in and around the harbour built at Portland, in W
Victoria, in order to test the risk of the harbour entrance becoming choked with sand (Baker, 1956). After a preliminary survey
of beach and sea-floor sands to determine the range of minerals
present, quantities of six minerals not already present were
introduced at different points, and the beaches in Portland Bay
were sampled regularly to see where the tracer minerals
appeared. It was found that the introduced grains moved across
the floor of the bay, by-passing the harbour entrance, and arriving on the beaches to the E (Fig. 38); sediment flow on this part
of the coast therefore appeared unlikely to lead to sand accumulation in the harbour entrance, and indeed has not done so.

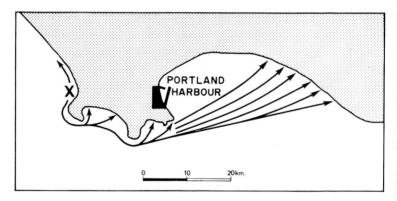

38　*Coastal sediment flow at Portland, Victoria, as determined by tracing material
dumped at X. After Baker, 1956*

The mineralogical method is laborious compared with radioactive or fluorescent tracer methods, because it depends on a
complete preliminary inventory of the minerals present. The
Portland experiment did not conform strictly with the require-
ments of a tracer experiment, for the introduced minerals were
of higher specific gravity ('heavy minerals') than the coastal

sediment, which consisted largely of quartz and shell sand. As lighter grains are moved more frequently and further than heavy grains, their long-term movement may not be in the same direction, and on some beaches, grains of different size, shape, and specific gravity are moved in different directions over a long period. Differential sediment movement is well illustrated by the concentrations of heavy minerals left behind on beaches of the E coast of Australia by waves which have carried away the lighter quartz sand. It follows that the mineralogical method of tracing sediment flow is less reliable than the fluorescent or radioactive methods, and may in certain cases give misleading results.

All the methods so far described here are qualitative, designed to show where the coastal sediment goes, but in the last few years attempts have been made to measure rates of sediment flow. Yasso (1965b) used fluorescent tracers to determine rates of sand transport on the foreshore of Sandy Hook, New Jersey. Labelled sand in four size classes was injected, and sampling on a line 100 feet downdrift indicated that the smallest particles (0.59–0.70 mm) arrived first, and the next class (0.70–0.84 mm) soon afterwards, the maximum rates of flow being 61 and 79 cm per minute respectively. Once the predominant direction of sediment flow is known, it is possible to measure the volume of sediment moved by introducing standard quantities of tracer at regular intervals at a particular 'injection point', and taking samples at another point downdrift to measure the concentration of tracer passing by. The measured concentration of tracer is proportional to the rate at which the sediment is moving, so that quantities in transit can be calculated. The principle can be explained by analogy with a stream of water into which coloured dye is poured steadily at a particular point: the extent to which the dye is diluted by the water depends on the rate of flow of the stream, so that a high concentration of dye at a point down-stream indicates a slow flow, and a low concentration a rapid flow; the volume of water moved over a particular period can be calculated from the rate of flow. The tracer concentration method has been applied successfully to the measurement of drift along shingle beaches on the S coast of England (Jolliffe, 1961), but its application to sand tracing is more difficult because of the vast number of grains involved.

An alternative approach is to calculate volumes of beach material between surveyed profiles within a beach compartment, using actual or arbitrarily-defined basal and rear planes (Fig. 39). Successive surveys can provide a basis for detecting changes in beach volume between one sector and another within a beach compartment.

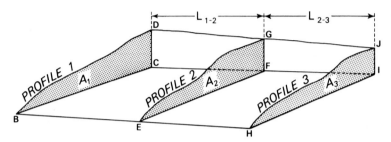

39   *Method of estimating beach volume. Cross-sectional areas are calculated on profiles 1, 2, and 3 with reference to basal (BHIC) and rear (DCIJ) planes. Volume within each sector is calculated by multiplying the average cross-sectional area at the two limits by the intervening length*

$$V_{1-2} = L_{1-2} \frac{(A_1 + A_2)}{2}; \quad V_{2-3} = L_{2-3} \frac{(A_2 + A_3)}{2}$$

Beach outlines in plan
Beaches often show smoothly-curved outlines in plan, concave seaward. It was formerly thought that these outlines were shaped by the action of strong currents sweeping sediment along the coast, but it is now realised that they are determined largely by wave action. Currents contribute to the movement of sediment to and fro along a beach, but they cannot shape depositional features built up above high tide level, and experiments in wave tanks have shown that smoothly-curved beaches can be produced by wave action alone.

On coasts exposed to waves generated by local winds but not to ocean swell, the outlines of beaches are related partly to the direction, strength, and frequency of onshore winds, partly to variations in the length of fetch or open water across which waves are generated by those winds, and partly to wave refraction. On the coasts of Denmark, Schou (1945) developed the idea that the orientation of beaches is the outcome of the long-term effects of wind-generated waves arriving from various directions. These effects he expressed as a resultant, calculated from records of the frequency and strength of winds, ignoring those of Beaufort Scale less than 4 (i.e. less than 21 km/hr) which have relatively little effect on beach outlines. A more precise relation-ship is obtained when the resultants restricted to onshore winds, which are more important in producing the waves that shape coastal outlines than offshore winds. Similar resultants are used for the analysis of coastal dune orientations (see Chapter VI), the minimum wind speed for sand drifting being slightly less than Beaufort Scale 4 (about 16 km/hr). Vectors of wind forces are obtained by multiplying the frequency of winds in each Beaufort Scale class by the cube of the mean velocity of that class, and summing the results for each wind direction. They are expressed graphically with lines of length proportional to the calculated vectors arranged in a diagram, as in Fig. 40, and from this onshore resultants can be determined for any coastline orientation.

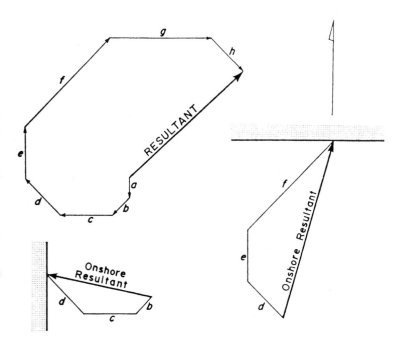

40   *Diagram to determine wind resultant (top left) from which onshore resultants are derived for an east-facing coast (bottom left) and a south-facing coast (right). a = vector line for N winds; b = vector line for NE winds, etc.*

Beaches built on coasts exempt from ocean swell, where there are no great variations in fetch, tend to be modified by erosion and accretion until they become orientated at right-angles to the onshore wind resultant. Where there are marked contrasts in fetch, however, these must be taken into account, for strong winds blowing over a short fetch may be less effective than lighter winds blowing over a long fetch. If the direction of longest fetch coincides with the onshore wind resultant, the beach becomes orientated at right-angles to this coincident line, but where they differ the beach becomes perpendicular to a line that lies between the two. On coasts of intricate configuration, fetch becomes more important than the onshore wind resultant, and beaches become orientated at right-angles to the direction of maximum fetch (Schou, 1952). Beach orientations on the coasts of the Baltic, the North Sea, and landlocked embayments or coastal lagoons, correspond well with these directional determinants. Local irregularities in the sea floor introduce a complication by refracting the waves approaching a shore so that beach outlines develop different alignments, cuspate behind offshore shoals and inset behind offshore hollows. Changes in sea-floor configuration, where currents scour out hollows or build up shoals, change the patterns of wave refraction and lead to modifications of beach outlines (Robinson, 1966). Deepening of the nearshore zone off Rhode Island during the 1976 hurricane permitted larger waves to reach the shoreline, accelerating subsequent beach erosion, whereas the shallowing of the Gulf of Bothnia has resulted in beach progradation as sea floor sand and gravel deposits are carried shoreward.

Patterns of waves and currents, and consequent sediment movement, are also modified where 'seagrass' grows on the sea floor. Submarine prairies of *Posidonia* and *Cymodocea* are extensive in shallow sea areas off South Australia, impeding sediment flow, and producing accretions of dry weed on the beaches. *Zostera* grows in bays and estuaries, producing similar 'brown hay' on the shores of Westernport Bay. In European waters the sudden decline of *Zostera* in the 1930s led to mobilisation of sediment and a phase of renewed shore accretion, notably on the Danish island of Samsø.

The shaping of beaches exposed to ocean swell is determined largely by patterns of wave refraction developed as the swell approaches the coast. Fetch is then too large to have any differential effect, and waves produced by onshore winds are of secondary importance in determining beach outlines. On calm days, a constructive swell is refracted into patterns that anticipate, then fit, the curved outlines of sandy beaches, each wave breaking synchronously along the shore (Plate 35). In Tasmania, Davies (1959) showed that southwesterly swell (wave period 14 seconds) becomes refracted to a southerly swell entering Frederick Henry Bay, and with further refraction develops outlines

41 *Refracted wave patterns in Storm Bay, Tasmania, showing how the waves anticipate, then fit, the curved outlines of bordering sandy beaches. After Davies, 1959*

42   *Modification of the outline of a bay-head beach to conform with the refracted*
      pattern of waves approaching the shore. In A, the outline of the beach is more
      sharply curved than the pattern of waves; longshore drifting (arrowed) carries
      beach material to the head of the bay until the outline of the beach has been
      adjusted to the wave pattern, as in B. After Davies, 1959

which fit the sandy beaches around that bay (Plate 2) but not the intervening sections of rocky shore (Fig. 41). Similar relationships exist between typical patterns of swell and the outlines of sandy beaches on other parts of coasts subject to ocean swell.

The effect of ocean swell is thus to modify the configuration of the coast, simplifying the irregular outlines produced by marine submergence into a succession of curved sandy shores between protruding rocky headlands, as on the coast of New South Wales (Fig. 70). If the shoreline is less sharply curved than the approaching swell, lateral currents are generated which move sand to the centre of the bay, prograding it until it fits the outline of the arriving swell (Fig. 42). It is a process of mutual adjustment, for, as the sea floor is smoothed by erosion and deposition, wave refraction becomes less intense, and the outlines of beaches correspondingly less sharply curved. Convergent longshore drifting in Byobugaura Bay, near Tokyo, has prograded the central sector at Katakai in this way, with sediment derived from the erosion of the northern and southern parts.

Davies (1972) distinguished *swash alignments*, where beaches are built parallel to incoming wave crests and net longshore sediment movement is minimal, from *drift alignments*, where beaches run parallel to the line of maximum longshore flow generated by waves arriving at an angle of 40° to 50°. Bay beaches (Fig. 45) are typically built on swash alignments, but spits (Fig. 47) are usually on drift alignments. In general, swash alignments are smoother in outline than drift alignments, which are typically sinuous, with intermittent migrating lobes or slightly divergent longshore spit and bar formations.

Attempts have been made to express the plan geometry of beach outlines mathematically. Yasso (1965a) examined the curvature of a number of North American beaches developed adjacent to headlands and subjected to a predominant direction of wave approach, and noted that the radius of curvature increased away from the headland in a curve reminiscent of the logarithmic spiral

$$r = e^{\theta cot\alpha}$$

where r is the length of a radius vector from a log-spiral centre, θ is the compass bearing and α the constant-spiral angle between the radius vector and the tangent to the curve at a particular point. Computers were used to generate best-fitting log-spirals to mapped coastline curves, and close relationships were obtained. Such a quantitative establishment of geometrical forms may permit a distinction between simple systems, where shoreline curvature is related to a predominant wave refraction pattern, and complex systems, where the outline is related to composite wave patterns or where other complicating factors exist. The notion that development of a beach outline that fits the pattern of dominant refracted waves marks the attainment of coastline stability is clearly erroneous, for onshore–offshore movements of sediments can continue, prograding or retrograding such a coastline on parallel alignments (Plate 36).

Beach outlines in profile
The profile or cross-section of a beach at any time is determined largely by wave conditions during the preceding period, and the effects of a severe storm may still be visible several months later. In calm weather, low waves form 'spilling' breakers with a constructive swash which moves sand or shingle on to a beach to build up a ridge or 'berm' parallel to the shoreline. In rough weather, higher and steeper waves form 'plunging' breakers, with collapsing crests which produce less swash, and a more destructive backwash which scours sediment away from the beach. According to Johnson (1956) waves with deep-water steepness (H_0:L_0) exceeding 0.025 are destructive, and those with smaller ratios constructive. The alternation of scour by storm waves and berm-building in calm weather is known as 'cut and fill'. Many sandy beaches show an eroded profile after storms, and a berm built up along the shore when calmer weather

36 *On the seaward margin of reclaimed land in Singapore intermittent sea walls were designed to permit beaches to attain an asymmetrical curvature in the expectation that this would become a stable coastline. However, erosion is continuing in the asymmetrical bays (Wong Poh Poh)*

prevails (Davies, 1957). The effects of winter storms on a sandy beach at Apollo Bay, in Victoria, are shown by the successive profiles given in Fig. 43.

The vertical section subject to removal and replacement is termed the sweep zone. Measurements on the Ninety Mile

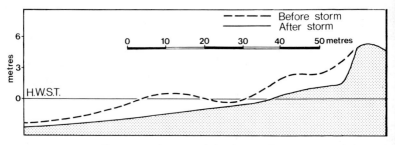

43 *Successive profiles measured on a sandy beach at Apollo Bay, Victoria, before and after a storm. The first profile showed a broad foredune and a beach berm, but in the second the foredune had been trimmed back and the beach had been lowered. This is typical of the alternation of cut and fill on sandy beaches: the zone between the pecked and the solid line is the sweep zone. H.W.S.T. = high water spring tides*

Beach have shown that the seasonal sweep zone has a mean cross-sectional area of 42 m², indicating a loss of 6 million m³ of sand from this beach during stormy phases, which are most frequent in winter, and equivalent replacements during fine weather. Such a beach may be said to be in equilibrium in the sense that its profile variations are cyclically restored by natural processes over periods of time. Whether waves of a particular form will push sediment up on to a beach or withdraw it from the beach face depends also on the pre-existing transverse profile of the shore and the grain size characteristics of shore sediments. As these features are also partly related to wave dimensions the wave-beach system is one with interactions between interdependent variables.

Attempts have been made to refine the description of this interactive relationship between beach profiles and wave conditions on the New South Wales coast, where fine-to-medium sandy beaches occupy asymmetrical embayments in a microtidal moderate-to-high wave energy environment (Wright *et al.*, 1979, 1982). A distinction has been made between steep reflective beach sectors, which can be cut by moderate wave action,

37   *Constructive waves washing sand and shelly material on to the beaches of Encounter Bay, South Australia. In the absence of a retaining vegetation, sand is blown inland as transgressive dunes.*

and flatter dissipative beaches, which are scoured only when swash levels are augmented by storm surges, exceptionally high tides, or surf beat (see p. 19). Reflective beaches face relatively deep water close inshore, whereas dissipative beaches are fronted by nearshore sand bars and wide surf zones (Plate 37).

Beach profiles can also be modified by wind action, when sand is blown along or across the beach, lowering some parts and building up others: beach barchans may form, and migrate down-wind. Sand winnowed from the beach face by onshore winds is carried inland, whereas offshore winds sweep it into the sea. Runoff during heavy rains may also wash beach sand into the sea.

Beach profiles are modified by changes in the relative levels of land and sea. Other things being equal, submergence leads to recession of the beach and emergence to progradation, but it is necessary to take account of other factors, including variations in the incidence of cut and fill and the availability of beach sediment. A beach receiving abundant sediment may prograde even during a phase of submergence, while a beach that is losing sediment offshore or alongshore may be cut back even during a phase of emergence. Bruun (1962) suggested that if a beach profile has attained an equilibrium in relation to the processes at work on it, a relative rise of sea level will cause erosion of the upper beach and deposition in the nearshore zone in such a way as to displace the original profile landward. Schwartz (1967) has confirmed this, both from laboratory model experiments and from careful surveys of beaches near Cape Cod during the period from one neap low tide to the next spring low tide, during which there is a successive raising of the high-tide swash zone, which can be taken as simulating a short-term sea level rise. It was found that the beach profile was displaced landward, erosion of the upper beach being compensated by nearshore deposition in such a way as to maintain the water depth adjacent to the shore (Fig. 44). By contrast, active emergence promotes shoreward drifting of sea floor sand on to accreting beaches, as in the Gulf of Bothnia, where wave action is re-working drowned eskers in a shallowing sea, and around the emerging Caspian coasts. This reverses the sequence shown in Fig. 44.

Sand removed during storms is often retained as bars, awash at low tide, in the nearshore zone. These are concentrations of

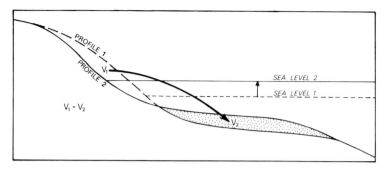

44   *Response of a beach profile to a sea level rise: the 'Bruun Rule'*

sand where the waves break, sand carried shorewards by the
waves meeting sand withdrawn from the beach by the backwash. This effect has been reproduced in wave tanks, where it
can be shown that the size of 'break-point bars' and their distance from the shore for a given calibre of sediments are related
to the dimensions of waves: bigger waves build larger bars
farther offshore. In calm weather, when constructive swash is
more effective, bars move closer to the shore, and become
swash bars, flatter in profile. Bars of this type are well developed
off the Ninety Mile Beach, in Victoria, and at low tide the swell
breaking on them forms a strong surf. They are interrupted by
transverse channels formed and maintained by rip current systems, carrying the backwash seaward through the surf zone
(Chapter II). Transverse, or finger, bars usually orientated at
right-angles to the shoreline, are common off sandy beaches on
low to moderate wave energy coasts, as in Florida and parts of
North Queensland. Their mode of origin is obscure, but once
established they are in dynamic equilibrium with the nearshore
water circulation, being maintained by the currents generated
by wave refraction (Niedoroda and Tanner, 1970).

The alternation of cut and fill on a shore receiving plenty of
sand may produce a succession of parallel ridges (Plate 38). Once
a berm survives a storm, a new one is built up in front of it as
sand is supplied to the beach during a succeeding phase of calm
weather. Prograded sandy beaches may show a series of parallel
ridges, often surmounted by dunes built up in the manner
described in the next chapter. At Woy Woy, to the north of
Broken Bay, a large number of parallel ridges has been built up
where cut and fill has influenced the mode of deposition of sand

accumulating in a coastal embayment. The successive formation of ridges is marked by a sequence of soil and vegetation features, the most deeply-leached sand and the most advanced stage in vegetation succession being found on the inner ridges on the landward side, with a progression to little-leached soils and pioneer dune vegetation on the youngest ridges, towards the sea. Sandy ridges of this kind have also been described by Nossin (1965) from the E coast of Malaya, and similar features exist on St Vincent Island in Florida.

Parallel sandy ridges can also be formed by the successive addition of spits growing parallel to the shoreline. Successive maps of South Haven Peninsula on the Dorset coast indicate a historical evolution of this kind (Robinson, 1955), and a similar sequence can be seen on the W coast of the Falsterbo peninsula, in SW Sweden, and on the coastline of the Burdekin delta (Fig. 114, p. 243).

The profiles of shingle (gravel) beaches differ in some ways from those of sandy beaches. This is partly because storm waves can have a slightly different effect: in addition to scouring shingle away from the beach face, the breaking waves throw some of it forward to build a ridge higher up the beach. In this way, a storm phase leads to the steepening of the beach profile. Subsequently, in calm weather, shingle returns to the beach face, restoring a gentler profile. Ridges on prograded shingle beaches are the outcome of successive storms, each of which threw up a ridge of shingle parallel to the shoreline.

It appears that shingle, and possibly also coarse sand, can be built into berms by storm wave action which is purely destructive on beaches of finer sand. On the N Norfolk coast, the storm surge of 1953 scoured away sandy beaches, but built up the crests of adjacent shingle beaches, sectors of which were rolled landward. When the offshore profile is gentle, storm waves may break constructively, producing a strong swash, instead of plunging as they do on steeper shores. Under these conditions sand ridges can be built up along the shore by storm swash. Psuty (1965) has described parallel sand ridge formation by this process on the shores of the deltaic coast of Tabasco, Mexico, where fluvially-supplied summer sand accretion is built into ridges by winter storm swash.

The height and spacing of parallel sand or shingle ridges are influenced by a number of factors, including the rate of supply

38   *Prograded sandy beach ridge plain near Robe, South Australia*

39   *Ridge and runnel foreshore near Bowen on the Queensland coast*

of sand or shingle to the shore, the incidence of cut and fill, and changes in the relative levels of land and sea. A series of ridges showing an overall seaward descent in the levels of crests and swales may indicate progradation on an emerging coast, but the other factors must also be taken into account. Johnson (1919) discussed some of the difficulties encountered in attempting to use parallel ridge crest and swale levels as evidence of submergence or emergence of a coast.

On sandy shores where the tide range is sufficient to expose a broad foreshore at low tide, systems of ridges and troughs are found parallel, or at a slight angle, to the coastline (Plate 39). These are essentially flattened bars, formed where wave action is relatively weak. They are known as 'low-and-ball' or 'ridge-and-runnel' in Britain where Gresswell (1953) has described them from tidal flats on the Lancashire coast. Their amplitude rarely exceeds 1 m, and the ridges are often as much as 100 m apart. As the tide falls the troughs may be temporarily occupied by lagoons, but these drain out by way of transverse channels as the ebb continues. Once established, these features persist through many tidal cycles; they are associated with wave action as the tide rises and falls, for when the waves have been arriving at an angle to the shore the ridge pattern also runs obliquely. The transverse channels are related to rip currents in the nearshore zone. On the Australian coast these features occur where the tide range is large, particularly where the effects of ocean swell are weak or excluded: the author has observed them at low tide on the shores of Westernport Bay in Victoria, and on the shores bordering Gulf St Vincent, in South Australia, and similar features have been described by Russell and McIntire (1966) from tidal flats in the Darwin area and the coast near Port Hedland in N Australia.

On a smaller scale, a variety of rippled surfaces may develop on the lower beach or foreshore exposed at low tide, produced by bottom currents associated with wind, wave, and tidal action. Simple transverse current ripples are typically asymmetrical, with a steeper face away from the current, and associations of cross-currents, generated by winds, waves, and tides, can produce intricate networks of transverse current ripples. In addition, there are longitudinal ripples, aligned parallel to a strong unidirectional current, and these also can be complicated by interfering wave motion and cross-current patterns (Van

Straaten, 1953). Tanner (1963) devised mechanical methods of simulating ripple-producing bottom-shear, and found that eddy currents are important in steepening and sharpening sub-aqueous ripples to produce the forms observed on tidal fore-shores.

Features related to sorting
Sorting of sediment on the beach by wave action takes several forms. Concentrations of heavy minerals are often found at the back of a beach after storms when waves have carried away the lighter sand grains, and seams of heavy minerals deposited in this way may afterwards be discovered beneath dunes built up behind the beach. Stratified layers of finer and coarser sediment within a beach record alternations of stronger and weaker wave action. Superficial sorting often produces zones of shingle and coarse and fine sand parallel to the shoreline, sometimes with a steeper upper beach separated by a break of slope, often a seepage line, from a flatter lower beach exposed as the tide recedes (Plate 40). On the English coast the upper beach is often of shingle, clearly demarcated from the lower beach of sand, the

40 *Coarse sand upper beach sharply demarcated from fine sand lower beach on the North Queensland coast near Mossman*

contrast probably reflecting the different response of shingle and sand to storm wave action, which tends to pile up a shingle ridge and to withdraw the sand. Within each stratified layer or beach face zone the distinctive sediment is well sorted, being related to a particular phase of deposition or reworking by waves.

Lateral gradation in mean particle size is also common along beaches, notably on Chesil Beach, which grades from granules and coarse sand on the beach towards the W end near Bridport through to pebbles and cobbles on the higher (12 m above high tide level) beach towards the E end near Portland Bill (Fig. 45). This gradation may be related to a lateral increase in wave energy, with higher waves coming in through deeper water to

45 *Chesil Beach, a shingle barrier on the Dorset coast and (inset) the shingle barrier and lagoon at Slapton, in Devonshire, England*

46   *On the shores of Hawke Bay, New Zealand, beach sediments derived from Mohaka River show a lateral gradation (modal size) from pebbles through granules to very coarse, coarse and medium sand eastward from the river mouth, due to a combination of sorting and attrition*

build a higher and coarser beach at the more exposed SE end. Bascom (1951) related a similar gradation in beach sand particle size at Half Moon Bay, California, to variation in degree of exposure to refracted ocean swell coming in from the NW, coarse sand on the exposed sector grading to fine sand in the lee of a headland at the northern end. Lateral gradation of particle size may alternatively be the outcome of wearing, attrition, and selective sorting of shingle derived from a particular sector of the coast as longshore drifting carries it away from the source area. This may explain the graded beach that extends between Nice and Antibes in France and the similar one on the shores of Hawke Bay, New Zealand (Fig. 46), in a sector fed by gravels drifting from the mouth of Mohaka River. Landon (1930) described how angular gravel from a cliff on the W coast of Lake Michigan becomes rounded and reduced in size as it drifts southward along the shore. Variations in beach particle size and sorting around Tasmania have been correlated with variations in wave energy, the coarser and better sorted beaches occurring on coasts exposed to strong oceanic waves (Davies, 1978), but clearly variations in the calibre of material supplied to a coastline can complicate such sorting.

A different kind of sorting produces *beach cusps* in the swash zone on sand and shingle beaches (Russell and McIntire, 1965a). These consist of regular successions of half-saucer depressions, up to 1 m deep between cusps of slightly coarser material up to 30 m apart. They are ephemeral features, but once formed they influence the patterns of swash as the waves break; it has been shown that larger waves build bigger cusps, and they are most frequently found where the waves arrive parallel to the shore-line, rather than obliquely. They are also best developed where there is a less permeable layer beneath the superficial beach deposits (Longuet-Higgins and Parkin, 1962). In Australia they frequently form on steep coarse sandy beaches as in the bays of the Sydney coast and also on the sandy shores of landlocked embayments, such as Botany Bay. Recent work has correlated beach cusps with the swash salients developed by the combination of waves arriving parallel to the shoreline and orthogonal edge waves (p. 19) (Guza and Inman, 1975); it is not yet clear whether the beach cusps are a cause or a consequence of edge waves. Cuspate re-entrants also develop on beaches behind the heads of rip currents, where larger waves move in through water deepened by outflow scour.

Wave-built beach forms are essentially similar on coasts in various climatic environments, except in high latitudes where cold conditions introduce important modifications. When the sea is frozen, wave and nearshore processes are halted, but when storm waves break up a winter ice fringe and drive it on to the shore, ice-pushed mounds and ridges are formed. These have been described from Arctic coast beaches in Alaska, N Canada, and Siberia, and from beaches in Antarctica, where ice-rafted erratic rock fragments and the debris yield of coastal glaciers are added to the beach, and summer melt-water cuts channels across the backshore. Beach gravels are less well rounded than on shingle beaches in warmer regions, the addition of frost-shattered and solifluction gravel out-weighing the rounding and smoothing effects of summer wave action. The beaches are also less well sorted and often include muddy zones. Freeze-and-thaw processes form cracks and mounds and produce stone polygons on the poorly sorted beach material. Yet the characteristic beach forms, including beach ridges, spits, and tombolos, have developed on the N and W coasts of Alaska, and have been described from the ice-free shores of McMurdo Sound in Antarctica.

Beach rock

Beach rock is formed where a layer of beach sand becomes consolidated by secondary deposition of calcium carbonate at about the level of the water-table (Russell, 1962). The cementing material is precipitated from ground water in the zone between high and low tide level, which is subject to repeated wetting and drying as the water-table rises and falls with the tide, or during and after wet weather. Some believe that precipitation of calcium carbonate is aided or brought about by the action of micro-organisms, such as bacteria, which inhabit the beach close to the water-table. Often the cementing material is aragonite, probably derived from sea water, rather than calcite, derived from ground water (Stoddart and Cann, 1965). Where the cemented material is gravel rather than sand, the resulting formation may be termed a beach conglomerate (rounded gravels) or beach breccia (angular gravels). Cementation can proceed rapidly, for artefacts such as bottles have been found incorporated in beach rock.

Beach rock has been found on the shores of the Caribbean Sea, around the Mediterranean, the Red Sea, and the Arabian Gulf, and on the coasts of Brazil, South Africa, and Australia; it is commonly found on sand cays built up on reefs off tropical coasts (Plate 64). Its restriction to warm environments has been attributed to a requirement that interstitial water should have a temperature exceeding 20°C for at least half the year in order to produce cementing of the beach sediment (Russell and McIntire, 1965b). As it forms at a definite horizon in relation to sea level, the occurrence of beach rock above this level is a good indication that emergence has taken place. Relatively resistant, beach rock may impede shoreline erosion; it often persists in patterns which commemorate the former outlines of beaches and cays that have since been eroded away.

Material similar to beach rock has been found on shores backed by cliffs of limestone or calcareous sandstone, from which seepage rich in dissolved carbonates has become a source of cement which binds talus or beach material on the backshore. These cemented materials are not related to water-table horizons within a beach and are not confined to warm environments; on the calcarenite coasts of southern Australia they are associated with spring deposits as a form of shore tufa.

Spits

Spits are depositional features built up above high tide level in such a way as to diverge from the coast, usually ending in one or more landward hooks or recurves (Schwartz, 1972). Gulliver (1899) ascribed spit growth to current action, but although currents may contribute sediment to them, they grow in the predominant direction of longshore sediment flow caused by waves, and their outlines are shaped largely by wave action. The recurves are formed either by the interplay of sets of waves arriving from different directions (Fig. 47), or by wave refraction around their distal ends. Traces of older recurves on the landward side mark former terminations of a spit prolonged intermittently, a feature well shown by Cape Bowling Green (Fig. 114) on the N Queensland coast (Plate 41). Salt marshes often develop on the sheltered landward side of spits, notably

47   *The shaping of a recurved spit (based on the outline of Hurst Castle Spit, S England): waves from A, arriving at an angle to the shore, set up longshore drifting which supplies sediment to the spit; waves from B and C determine the orientation of its seaward margin and recurved laterals respectively*

48 *Coastal landforms in North Norfolk, England*

49   *Blakeney Point, a recurved spit on the N Norfolk coast (for location see Fig. 48).*
Successive recurves mark stages in the intermittent growth of the spit to the
WNW, culminating in Far Point (cf. Fig. 50); intervening areas are occupied
by salt marshes. Deflected westwards, the Blakeney Channel opens to a tidal
estuary, south of which are more salt marshes, backed by an earlier coastline

between recurves, as on Blakeney Point (Fig. 49) and Scolt Head
Island in Norfolk (Figs. 48, 49, 50). Here spits built of sand and
gravel derived from glacial drift deposits have been driven landward athwart the salt marshes in successive storm surges (e.g.
1953, 1976, 1978), so that salt marshes outcrop on the seaward
side (Fig. 51). Other spits have been widened by the addition of
successive ridges on the seaward side, and stages in their evolution can be deduced from the pattern of beach ridges, as on the
spit in Carrickfergus Bay, on the E coast of Tasmania (Fig. 52).
Sand eroded from cliffs of glacial drift on the Cape Cod peninsula has been built into a spit, prograded on the seaward side,
at Provincetown (Fig. 53). As Davis (1896) showed, the fulcrum
of this spit has migrated up the coast so that part of the formerly
prograded sector has now been truncated by marine erosion.
The recurved spit at Sandy Hook, New Jersey, originated in a
similar way. The evolution of spits such as Blakeney Point and
Orford Ness on the East Anglian coast can sometimes be traced
from old maps showing earlier stages in their growth, bearing

in mind the limitations of historical cartographic accuracy noted by Carr (1962). The shingle spit extending from Orford Ness has deflected the mouth of the River Alde about 18 km south, and maps made since about A.D. 1530 suggest that it has grown about 6 km during the past four centuries (Steers, 1953). De Boer (1964) has traced the history of Spurn Head (Yorkshire) since the 14th century, and detected cycles of growth and decay. This kind of information is rarely available outside W Europe and North America, but eventually it will be possible to use successive

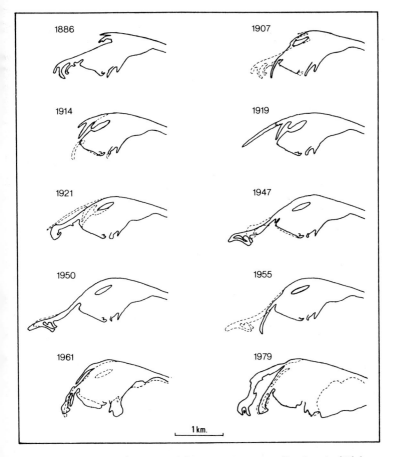

50   *Changes in the configuration of the western extremity (Far Point) of Blakeney Point, Norfolk (cf. Fig. 49) between 1886 and 1979 (from an unpublished thesis by Juliet Bird)*

41 *Recurved sand spit near Mackay, Queensland, with mangroves and salt marsh between recurves on landward side*

42 *The dune-covered sandy isthmus linking North and South Bruny Islands, Tasmania, forms a tombolo or tie-barrier. Its eastern shores (left), exposed to ocean swell, are smoother in profile and in plan than the more sheltered western shores, which are bordered by extensive sand bars and rippled topography.*

surveys and series of dated aerial photographs to trace the evolution of spits. Carr (1965) used this kind of evidence to analyse short-term changes at the S end of the Orford Ness spit over the period 1945–62.

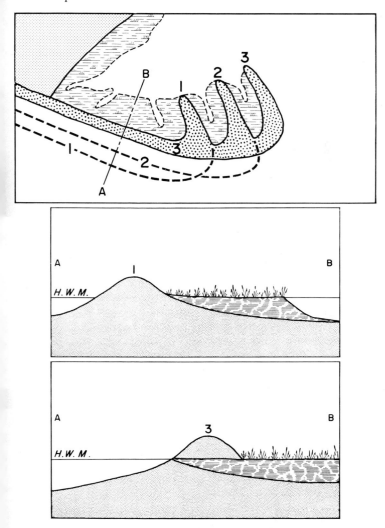

51   *Stages in the evolution of a recurved spit. The upper diagram shows three stages in development, with successive terminal recurves, and marshland formed on the sheltered side. The middle and lower diagrams are sections along AB at the first and third stages, showing how the main bank had been driven landward over the marshland until marsh deposits outcrop on the seaward side*

52 *The recurved spit in Carrickfergus Bay, Tasmania. Selected beach ridges (I-VI) show former outlines of the shore, stages IV, V and VI having been added after an earlier spit (stages I-III) had been truncated by erosion. After Davies, 1959*

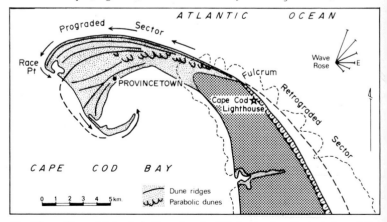

53 *The outline of Cape Cod, Massachusetts, U.S.A., showing the evolution of the Provincetown spit by accumulation of sand and gravel drifting from the retro-grading cliffs south of the lighthouse. Pecked lines show earlier configurations. The wave rose indicates relative frequency of waves reaching the outer coastline*

King and McCullach (1971) developed a computer model to simulate the processes responsible for the shaping of Hurst Castle spit (Fig. 47). They were able to examine the relative significance of waves approaching from various directions, the effects of wave refraction, and the influence of submarine topography, and to trace probable stages in its evolution to the present outline. When the simulation was extrapolated into the future it generated an additional elongated recurve extending north-westwards, but this is not likely to develop because of the presence of marshland in that direction, a constraint that had been omitted from the simulation model. The shape of a growing spit can also be influenced by the space available for its growth, and by the adjacent sea floor topography: spits grow more rapidly across shallow areas than into deep water, and their configuration may be related to variations in exposure to wave action determined by nearby headlands, islands or reefs. The evolution of many spits has been modified, even halted, by the addition of artificial structures. Dawlish Warren in Devonshire and Sandy Hook, New Jersey, are two examples of spits

54   *Spits on the shore of the Gippsland Lakes, coastal lagoons in SE Australia (cf. Fig. 69). The recurved spit at Butlers Point has been shaped by waves arriving from three directions (cf. Fig. 47) and the cuspate spit at Harrington Point and the arrow-spit at Metung mark a sector of convergence of longshore drifting of sand and shingle*

with complex histories that have been 'armoured' by the building of sea walls intended to stabilise their present configuration.

Some of the best examples of spits are found on the shores
of landlocked seas, lakes, and coastal lagoons, where sand and
shingle carried along the shoreline are deposited as spits where
the orientation of the shoreline changes, in forms related to
prevailing wave conditions. Examples of this are found in the
Gippsland Lakes (Fig. 54). These spits show on a small scale
forms comparable with the sand spits in the Danish archipelago
(Schou, 1945), Puget Sound, and the New England coast; in each
case, cliffing of glacial drift has yielded sand and gravel for
longshore transport to nourish nearby spit structures. Arrow-
spits also develop in the lee of islands, as in the 'comet-tails' off
the Brittany coast, and the various 'trailing spits' described by
Hopley (1971) from high islands off the North Queensland coast.
In cases where the island has subsequently been eroded away
the depositional trail may persist as a 'flying spit', either elongated in the direction of sediment flow or aligned at right-angles
to the predominant waves, with terminal recurves at each end.
Examples of these forms occur off the Boston coast and in the
Strait of Georgia, W Canada, in both cases derived from islands
of glacial drift.

Other depositional forms include tombolos, which are spits
linking an island to the mainland. The term comes from Italy,
where these features are well developed at Orbetello, and Johnson (1919) has described examples from Nantucket, New England. In Australia the Yanakie isthmus which ties the granitic
upland of Wilsons Promontory to the coast of Victoria, is a
tombolo, as is the sand isthmus at Palm Beach, linking Barrenjoey to the mainland (Fig. 55). Cuspate spits form in the lee of
shoals or close-in islands, and are shaped by waves refracted
round the island; they may eventually grow into tombolos linking the island, as at Cape Verde on the Senegal coast, or tie-
barriers between islands (Plate 42). Alternatively, the breaching
of a tombolo may leave residual cuspate spits (Gabo I., Fig. 56). A
tombolo that is partly or wholly submerged by the sea at high
tide is known as tombolino, or tie-bar. Cuspate spits also form
on the shores of lagoons and narrow straits, where waves
approaching from each diagonal are stronger and more frequent than those coming directly onshore, so that, at points of
convergence of longshore drift, sediment is built up from two

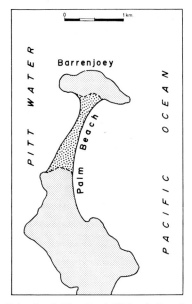

55   *The tombolo at Palm Beach, New South Wales, linking Barrenjoey Island to the mainland*

56   *Cuspate sandy foreland in the lee of an offshore island around which waves are refracted (Gabo Island, SE Australia). Historical maps show that this became a tombolo, attaching Gabo Island to the mainland, but it was breached about a century ago*

directions (see p. 231). Similar features may develop where currents converge, or in relation to an eddy in a longshore current: a possible explanation for Cape Hatteras and the other cuspate spits on the E coast of the United States, although it has been suggested alternatively that these relate to wave refraction by offshore shoals (Russell, 1958). Cuspate forelands are spits that have been enlarged by the accretion of ridges parallel to their shores, and stages in their evolution may often be deduced from the patterns of these ridges. Some have remained stationary, and developed symmetrically, while others have migrated, so that one set of ridges has been truncated, and is bordered by the other set (Fig. 57). Dungeness, a cuspate shingle foreland on the Channel coast of England (Fig. 58) has a ridge pattern indicative of eastward migration during its accretion (Lewis, 1932). Cape Kennedy and the Darss peninsula on the Baltic coast of East Germany are other examples of cuspate sandy forelands of complex origin (Johnson, 1919) while on the Gulf Coast in Florida Cape San Blas is a major foreland related to, and nourished from, sand shoals derived ultimately from the Apalachicola River.

River mouths and lagoon entrances are often deflected by the growth of spits, prolonged in the direction of longshore drifting (Fig. 59). As the spit grows, the transverse ebb and flow of tidal currents is impacted against the farther shore which is cut back by current scour. Some deflected entrances become sealed off altogether, leaving a channel that formerly led to an outlet.

57 *Cuspate forelands on a lagoon shore. Beach ridge patterns indicate that A has grown symmetrically, remaining in position as accretion of sediment took place, whereas B has migrated along the shore, one set of ridges being truncated by the other*

Migrating entrances of this kind punctuate the sandy outer
barrier on the Atlantic coast of the United States: the Outer
Banks of North Carolina have had a long history of entrance
deflection, migration, and closure (Dunbar, 1956). Non-
migrating entrances are often bordered by paired spits, with
outlines influenced by patterns of waves, refracted as they enter.
These may indicate the constriction of a tidal entrance by convergent longshore drifting (Fig. 60), but they can also develop

58   *Dungeness is a cuspate shingle-foreland in SE England, built out in front of a
former cliffed embayment now occupied by reclaimed marshland. Pecked lines
indicate stages in evolution. After Lewis, 1932*

59   *Deflection and closure of lagoon outlets in response to longshore drifting*

60   *In Drakes Bay, California, sand eroded from cliffs and washed in from the sea floor has been built by convergent drifting into paired spits on either side of the entrance to Drakes Estero, a tidal inlet formed by marine submergence of an incised valley system. By contrast the more exposed ocean coast has a long surf beach backed by parabolic dunes north of the rocky Point Reyes peninsula*

61   *South-west of the Ninety Mile Beach (cf. Fig. 62) sand deposition has formed a chain of barrier islands east of Corner Inlet. Progradation continues on Snake Island as sand is washed in from shoals east of Wilsons Promontory*

alongside an entrance breached through a coastal barrier. Spits
of this kind border the entrances to estuarine harbours on the
S coast of England at Poole, Christchurch, and Pagham (Robinson, 1955), and are well developed on the flanks of the entrances
to Corner Inlet, in Victoria (Fig. 61). Longshore growth of a spit
in front of a former coastline is one way in which a coastal
barrier can develop.

Barrier beaches and related forms
The deposition of beach material offshore, or across the mouths
of inlets or embayments, in such a way as to form barriers
extending above the normal level of highest tides and partly or
wholly enclosing lagoons, is a widely-distributed phenomenon
which has received considerable attention in recent years. Barriers, thus defined, are distinct from bars, which are submerged
for at least part of the tidal cycle, and from reefs of biogenic

62   *The coastal barriers of East Gippsland, Victoria. Erosion is predominant along the*
      Ninety Mile Beach except in the sectors adjacent to the artificial entrance (inset:
      cf. Fig. 75) to the Gippsland Lakes (cf. Fig. 69)

origin, built by coral and associated organisms (Chapter IX). They show a variety of forms. *Barrier beaches* are narrow strips of low-lying depositional land consisting entirely of beach sediment, without surmounting dunes or associated swamps. Many barriers do have these additional features, and some attain widths of several kilometres, with crests of dunes sometimes rising more than a hundred metres above sea level. The term *bay barrier* describes a feature built up across an embayment, and *barrier island* indicates a discrete segment, often recurved at both ends. Figs. 61 and 62 show barrier islands and the spit at the SW end of the Ninety Mile Beach, and Fig. 63 shows part of the Frisian Islands, a barrier island chain with intervening tidal entrances on the German North Sea coast. Chains of barrier islands separated by tidal entrances are also well developed on the Gulf and Atlantic coasts of the United States, and in NW Australia, as well as on a smaller scale elsewhere. It is clear from recent work that barriers have originated in a variety of ways, and that no single explanation will account for all these depositional features (Schwartz, 1973).

The two main modes of barrier origin are by the longshore growth of spits (Fig. 64) and by development of emergent bars as beaches offshore during a phase of sea level lowering, and by the partial submergence of a pre-existing coastal sand ridge during a phase of sea level rise. Many barriers have had a composite origin. On the West African coast, Guilcher and Nicolas (1954) have described elongated barrier spits such as the Langue de Barbarie extending as the result of southward longshore drifting, in such a way as to deflect estuaries, notably the mouth of the Senegal. On the other hand, the barrier islands bordering the Texas coast have the appearance of features that were initiated offshore and parallel to the coastline. Johnson concluded that such barriers formed on coasts bordered by shallow seas as the result of a relatively sudden emergence, when reduction of water depth offshore caused waves to break farther out, building a bar which emerged as it was driven shoreward. It is possible to generate this sequence of events experimentally in a wave tank, but it is doubtful if it applies to many actual barriers, for the majority of these came into existence during the episode of submergence marked by the Holocene marine transgression (Russell, 1958), and many of them are the outcome of shoreward sweeping of sediment during, and

63   *East Frisian Islands, a barrier island chain on the German North Sea coast*

64   *Stages in the evolution of a barrier to enclose a lagoon: by prolongation of a spit (above) or by shoreward migration of a barrier that originated offshore (below)*

perhaps also since, this marine transgression. Some may be the outcome of reworking of deposits that were stranded on the emerging sea floor during the preceding marine regression, collected and built up as the sea rose again. Such collecting and shoreward drifting of sediment may have been facilitated by minor emergences during the oscillating Holocene marine transgression, the accumulated material being subsequently built up and driven landward as the sea resumed its upward movement. Hoyt (1967) proposed that the transgressive sand barriers on the south-east coast of the United States were initiated when the sea rose to partially submerge a previously-built coastal dune ridge, penetrating lower land to the rear to form lagoons behind a chain of barrier islands.

The shingle barrier at Chesil Beach, on the English coast stands in front of a lagoon (the Fleet), and an embayed mainland coast which has escaped marine cliffing (Fig. 45). The barrier must therefore have been driven shoreward during the Holocene marine transgression in such a way as to protect the submerging land margin from the waves of the open sea. Carr and Blackley (1973) have shown that the beach is underlain by a bedrock surface that descends from the hinterland slopes to flatten at about 15 metres below sea level, the cross-section being much as in Fig. 65, except that Chesil Beach is a single ridge. Steers (1953) suggested that it developed during the early stages of the Holocene transgression, when the rising sea collected gravels that had previously been strewn across the emerged sea floor, and swept them shoreward. The origin of such an emerged feature during a marine transgression presents a problem. It is possible that it first developed as an emerged feature during one of the sea level regressions that occurred during the oscillating Holocene transgression, and was thereafter driven shoreward as a barrier. Chesil Beach is still moving shoreward intermittently, for vigorous storms sweep shingle over the crest and down into the waters of the Fleet. Eventually it will come to rest against the mainland coast, which will thereafter be cut back as marine cliffs by storm wave activity: this is already happening near Bridport at the western end, and rejuvenation of the coastal slopes is spreading gradually eastwards. Zenkovich (1967) has invoked a similar sequence of events to explain the barriers of sand and shingle that have developed in front of uncliffed mainland coasts in Siberia, and

Le Bourdiec (1958) reached the same conclusion for barriers on the Ivory Coast. It has also been suggested that shoreward sweeping of sediment during the Holocene marine transgression initiated the barrier island system which borders the Gulf coast of the United States (Shepard, 1963). In each case the barrier formations rest upon an older (Pleistocene) land surface submerged by the Holocene transgression (Fig. 65).

65   *Section through a barrier enclosing a lagoon*

The supply of sediment for the building of barrier systems raises the same problems as were previously considered in relation to beach nourishment. Chesil Beach is apparently receiving little new shingle either from onshore or longshore drifting at the present time, and experiments with radioactive pebbles dumped on the sea floor failed to show any clear evidence of shoreward drifting to Scolt Head Island, a barrier island on the N Norfolk coast, under present conditions. These features are evidently relict formations, a legacy of the Holocene marine transgression.

Other barrier systems are still receiving sediment derived from adjacent cliffed coasts, river discharge, and possibly shoreward drifting. The barriers which extend across embayments on the New England coast, enclosing lagoons or ponds, are built of sediment derived from adjacent cliffs cut in glacial outwash material. They are well developed on the S shores of Martha's Vineyard (Fig. 66) and Nantucket Islands off the Massachusetts coast, and on the S shores of Cape Cod (Johnson, 1925). The barrier spits termed *nehrungen* on the S Baltic coast are similarly derived from glacial deposits eroded by the sea and carried along the shore to enclose embayments as lagoons, and Vladimirov (1961) described barriers and spits derived from intervening cliffs of Tertiary sediment on the coast of Sakhalin. Predominantly fluvial nourishment is indicated for barriers in S Iceland built by the constructive action of Atlantic swell working

66   *Barriers and lagoons at Marthas Vineyard Island, Massachusetts, U.S.A. (after Johnson, 1925). The upper diagram indicates the probable configuration of the coast prior to truncation of promontories by marine erosion, yielding sediment for the building of the barrier which now encloses the lagoons*

on the superabundant sediment, chiefly sand, recurrently supplied to the coast by glacifluvial streams. The sand and shingle barrier enclosing Lake Ellesmere on the New Zealand coast (Fig. 67) is built largely of reworked glacifluvial material derived from partially submerged late Quaternary outwash plains.

On the Australian coast there are sectors with multiple barrier systems and intervening tracts of lagoon and swamp (Bird, 1973). The inner barriers are generally of Pleistocene age, having been dissected by stream incision during the Last Glacial low sea level phases, whereas the outer barrier is often of Holocene age, having come into existence during and since the ensuing Holocene marine transgression (Fig. 71). There are many complications, for barriers have been built, then dissected or destroyed, and subsequently rebuilt, sometimes in overlapping

alignments, during the Quaternary episodes of sea level oscillation. Complex barrier systems investigated on the Victorian
coast (Bird, 1978a) (Fig. 69) and on the coast of New South Wales
(Fig. 70) have developed in predominantly quartzose sand, and
have not become lithified in the manner of the calcereous sand
barriers of S and W Australia, which are commonly preserved
as relatively durable calcarenite. In the SE of South Australia
there are numerous parallel ridges of calcarenite which formed
as successive barriers during Pleistocene times (Fig. 12) and are
indicative of intermittent coastal emergence, due in part to
tectonic uplift accompanying eustatic changes. The intervening
tracts are corridors of swamp land, developed in former
lagoons. The Coorong, behind the outer barrier on the shores
of Encounter Bay, is the last in the sequence of inter-barrier
lagoons, not yet filled by swamp deposits. Complexity of barrier

67   *Lake Ellesmere, a coastal lagoon near Banks Peninsula, South Island, New Zea-*
       land, enclosed by a shingle barrier: the outlet varies in dimensions, and is
       sometimes sealed off by beach deposition

68 *Coastal lagoons between Robe and Beachport, South Australia, between an inner barrier of calcarenite and a similar outer barrier which is undergoing dissection and denudation on the seaward side*

evolution is illustrated farther south, between Robe and Beachport (Fig. 68), where the coast consists of a cliffed and dissected
ridge of Pleistocene calcarenite, there being no Holocene outer
barrier of unconsolidated sand here.

The sandy barriers on the SE coast of Australia have their
counterparts on similarly-oriented coasts in SE Africa (Natal) and
SE South America (between Rio and Cabo Frio). In each case
there has been widening by progradation in Holocene times.
Such barriers are not migrating shoreward in the manner of the
shingle barrier, Chesil Beach, except to a local and limited
extent where winds or storm waves carry sand over into the
lagoon. Many of these barriers have been prograded by the
addition of successive parallel beach ridges on alignments
which, like the curved outline of the present beach, result from
the refracted patterns of dominant swell approaching the coast.
Often the beach ridges are surmounted by parallel dunes, developed successively during progradation. The pattern of beach
ridges and dunes can be used to decipher the history of barrier
evolution, particularly where there are relics of former recurves
indicative of stages in longshore growth. The outer barrier on
the E Gippsland coast (Fig. 69) originated as a chain of barrier
islands which were extended both NE and SW by longshore
drifting, deflecting outlets from coastal lagoons and in some
cases sealing off the deflected channels (cf. Fig. 59). Subsequently, this barrier was widened by progradation, with successive parallel ridges added on the seaward side to take up the
alignment of the Ninety Mile Beach along the present coast
(Bird, 1978a). Radiocarbon dating of samples obtained from
drilling in sand barriers on the NSW coast has been used by
Thom *et al.* (1981) to establish the Holocene progradation history of these features, most of which have been truncated along
their seaward margins by ensuing marine erosion. By contrast,
the Outer Banks of Carolina north of Cape Hatteras have been
migrating landward as the result of spillover dunes and wash-
over sand invading Pamlico Sound and gradual recession, rather
than progradation, of the seaward margin (Leatherman, 1981).
Transgressive barrier formations result in complex patterns of
overlapping stratigraphy on the Dutch coast (Van Straaten,
1965).

Barriers are best developed where the tide range is relatively
small, as on the SE coasts of Australia. A large tide range generates strong ebb and flow currents which maintain gaps through

69 *The Gippsland Lakes, a group of coastal lagoons in SE Australia enclosed within a former embayment by a series of coastal barriers*

barriers and prevent wave action from depositing sand or shingle to seal them off. On the E Gippsland coast the spring tide range increases from about 1 m at the NE end, where there are no natural tidal entrances, to 2.5 m at the SW end, where tidal currents have maintained channels between a chain of barrier islands at the entrance to Corner Inlet. As a result, the Gippsland Lakes (Fig. 69) were almost completely sealed off from the sea at the eastern end while Corner Inlet, a similar embayment, has an incomplete barrier system (Fig. 61). A similar contrast exists between the relatively unbroken *nehrungen* on the almost tideless S coast of the Baltic Sea and the chain of barrier islands with intervening tidal entrances on the strongly tidal S coast of the North Sea (Fig. 63).

Beach erosion
Beach erosion is in progress on many coasts. Seaside resorts such as Deauville in France, Miami in Florida and Surfers Paradise in Australia are among those that have suffered when

70   *Coastal features near Newcastle, New South Wales, where inner and outer barriers have developed successively in a coastal embayment. After Thom, 1974*

43 *An advancing sandy coastline at Waratah Bay, Victoria*

44 *A receding sandy coastline at Leonard Bay, Wilson's Promontory, Victoria*

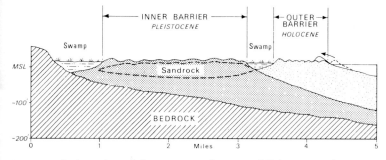

71　*Typical relationships of Pleistocene inner barriers and Holocene outer barriers on the Australian coast (cf. Fig. 70)*

storms have removed the beaches that attracted their visitors. In such cases 'cut' has exceeded 'fill', only part of the sand removed by storm wave scour being returned to the beach by natural processes in calmer weather. Sandy coastlines in many parts of the world have been retreating during the past century, and possibly for a longer period (Russell, 1967; Thom, 1974). Recession is in progress even on the shores of barriers that were previously prograded by deposition, for example along the Ninety Mile Beach in SE Australia (Figs. 62 and 73), where progradation during the past century has been confined to sectors on either side of the Lakes Entrance harbour jetties (Fig. 75). It is quite difficult to find sectors of naturally prograding sandy beach (Plate 43), whereas receding sandy shorelines are extensive (Plate 44). In 1972 the International Geographical Union set up a Working Group to investigate these changes on the world scale, and this work has continued as part of the program of the Commission on the Coastal Environment which succeeded this Working Group in 1976 (Bird and Koike, 1981; Paskoff, 1981). Factors that have contributed to the modern prevalence of erosion on sandy coastlines include reductions in sediment yield from rivers, especially where dams have been built to impound reservoirs (e.g. S California); a diminution in sand supplies from the sea floor (Davies, 1974); the response to a possible rise in sea level relative to the land (Bruun, 1962); and the possibility of increased storminess in coastal waters (Thom, 1974). These factors vary in relative importance from sector to sector along sandy coastlines. In some cases the erosion has a local explanation: the reduction of sand supply from eroding cliffs or spilling dunes (Plate 33), the interception of longshore drift by artificial structures such as breakwaters, or increased scour following beach or nearshore quarrying or wave reflection from sea walls. An analysis of erosion on sandy barriers in Rhode Island, U.S.A., led Fisher (1980) to propose the budget of sand loss shown in Fig. 72.

72 *Budget of changes on sandy barrier island coast of Rhode Island, U.S.A. Coastline recession of 0.2 metres per year is due partly (15%) to the effects of a rising sea level, partly (26%) to overwash processes, partly (35%) to losses into tidal inlets, and partly (24%) to removal of sand to the sea floor (cf. Fig. 44). After Fisher, 1980*

The response to beach erosion has often been the construction, elaboration and extension of artificial structures designed to protect the coastline. In Japan long sectors of the cyclone-prone east coast of Honshu are now protected by large sea walls and concrete tetrapods weighing up to 50 tonnes each (Plate 67), while much of the Italian resort coast between Venice and Rimini has beaches lined by offshore breakwaters built of limestone brought from the hinterland.

Alternatively, eroded beaches (especially in resort areas) have been replenished artificially by pumping or dumping sand taken from the sea floor or from coastal or inland quarries on to the foreshore. Miami Beach is one of several United States beaches restored in this way, while in Britain the beach at Bournemouth, depleted after sea wall construction cut off its sand supply from nearby cliffs, has been replenished with sediment pumped in from the sea floor. In a similar way, sand from the floor of Port Phillip Bay has been piped onshore to restore eroded beaches on the Melbourne coast (Bird, 1979). It is necessary in such cases to ensure that the sediment supplied to the artificial beach is at least as coarse in texture as that which existed naturally, and to take care that sea floor excavations do not cause significant deepening of nearshore areas and consequent increases in wave energy, initiating or accelerating coastal erosion.

Beach systems are thus dynamic interactions between shore processes and coastal sedimentation (Komar, 1976). An understanding of these interactions is a necessary prelude to beach management.

VI

COASTAL DUNES

Coastal dunes are formed where sand deposited on the shore dries out and is blown to the back of the beach. Where the tide range is large, as on the Atlantic coast of Devon and Cornwall, sand blown from broad foreshores exposed at low tide is built up as dune topography extending inland from high tide mark, as at Braunton Burrows, Perran Sands, and Gwithian Sands. Dunes are similarly derived from broad inter-tidal foreshores on the North Sea coasts of Belgium, Holland, Germany, and Denmark. On coasts where the tide range is small, sand delivered to the beach by wave action may have provided the material for dune construction, as on the W and SE coasts of Australia, the W coast of Africa, and sectors of the Atlantic and Pacific coasts of the United States. On arid zone coasts bordering the Sahara and in NW Australia desert dunes may adjoin and mix with dunes derived from beach sands.

On some coasts wind-blown sand has been accumulating during and since Pleistocene times, producing extensive and complicated sequences of dune topography. Where the parent sands are calcareous, as on the W coast of Australia, the older dunes have been lithified by internal deposition of calcium carbonate from percolating water, forming dune limestone, an aeolian calcarenite which preserves the dune topography in solid rock, but where the parent sands are quartzose, as on Australia's SE coast, this kind of lithification has not taken place, and the dunes remain unconsolidated—either active and mobile, or retained by a vegetation cover. In South Australia there is a lateral transition in the composition of dune sands SE of the Lower Murray, the proportion of terrigenous quartzose sand diminishing as the proportion of marine calcareous sand increases southeastwards (see p. 121). The strongly calcareous dune ridges to the SE are preserved in solid calcarenite, but they grade northwestwards into more irregular and disrupted dune topography, lithification diminishing as the sand becomes less calcareous. On the E Mediterranean coast there is a similar transition, the calcarenite dune topography of the Israel coast passing southward into more irregular, mobile dunes on the

176

coast of the Gaza Strip, where the sands have an increasing content of terrigenous (Nile-derived) quartzose sediment.

Coastal dunes are best developed on coasts in the temperate and arid tropical zones: in the humid tropics they are of limited and local extent, sandy coastal topography consisting of low beach ridges with little transgressive dune development. It has been suggested that the prevailing dampness of beach sands on humid tropical coasts impedes deflation and backshore dune development, particularly on microtidal sectors where the beaches are narrow. This may be a contributory factor, but observations on temperate coasts indicate that strong onshore winds can dry off a beach surface and blow away sand even when it is actually raining. Another suggestion is that rapid colonisation of coastal sand accumulations by luxuriant vegetation prevents dune development in the humid tropics, but it is doubtful if the vegetation has much effect: if aeolian sand were arriving at the backshore, dense vegetation would simply trap it and facilitate the building of a high foredune. It seems to be a question of a relatively meagre sand supply to the backshore, largely because winds strong enough to deflate beach sand and build up dunes are rare in the humid tropics in comparison with other climatic zones. The occasional violence of winds in tropical cyclones is usually accompanied by torrential rainfall which saturates the beach surface and impedes sand transportation by the temporarily strong wind action. Nevertheless, dunes are found on humid tropical coasts where there is a sustained sand supply and prevailing onshore winds, as at Parangtritis in southern Java, and locally on the E Malaysian and Sri Lankan coasts (Swan, 1979).

Characteristics of dune topography have been studied in various parts of the world. The following account is mainly in terms of the Australian coast, with incidental references to other areas.

Foredunes

Foredunes are built up at the back of a beach or on the crest of a beach ridge of sand or shingle where dune grasses colonise and start to trap blown sand (Plate 45). They become higher and wider as accretion continues. There are regional variations in the grass species which act as pioneer colonists and foredune-builders. In the British Isles and W Europe the typical pioneer dune plant is marram grass (*Ammophila arenaria*), a species that has been introduced to many other parts of the world, including Australia, as a dune stabiliser; lyme grass (*Elymus arenarius*) and the sea wheat grass (*Agropyron junceum*) are also common dune pioneers in Europe, the latter extending around the Mediterranean and Black Seas. In Australia and New Zealand the native dune pioneers are coast fescue (*Festuca littoralis*) and sand spinifex (*Spinifex hirsutus*). In the United States another form of marram grass, *Ammophila brevigulata*, is a common pioneer species. Marram grass is the most vigorous of the dune-building plants, thriving on cool, wet coasts where it is able to trap blown sand, and capable of adding up to 2 metres of sand to an accreting foredune in the course of a single year. However, where sand accretion is slow, marram grass grows poorly, and other grasses often take its place. On sandy coasts in tropical regions the vegetation is generally sparser, and dominated by creeping vines such as *Ipomoea* and *Canavalia*, rather than tussocky grasses (Ranwell, 1972). On arid coasts (as in Baja California and at the head of the Great Australian Bight) vegetation may be too sparse to trap sand blown from beach to backshore, and dunes move on inland. Even on humid coasts the available vegetation

45   *Foredune built by sand accretion in marram grass at San Remo, Victoria, with incipient foredune developing on beach berm (right)*

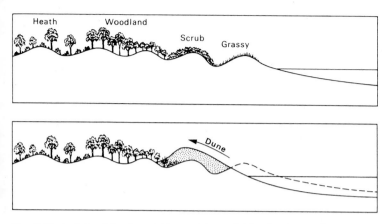

73　*Typical relationships of vegetation and prograded beach ridges, and more recent development of dunes moving landward behind the beach on Holocene outer barriers in Australia*

may prove inadequate for the trapping of sand, either because of a superabundant sand supply blown from a rapidly accreting beach (Sandy Cape, Queensland) or because the onshore winds are exceptionally strong (possibly the case on the NW Tasmanian coast).

On some coasts a single foredune persists, cut back from time to time by storm waves on its seaward side but restored subsequently by accretion of wind-blown sand in recolonising vegetation. A dune of this kind borders the NE coast of Norfolk in the vicinity of Sea Palling, where it has revived after severe damage and breaching during the 1953 storm surge. But many coasts have dunes arranged in patterns of ridges parallel to the coastline, formed by the development of successive foredunes on a prograding sandy shore. These are particularly well developed in SE Australia, notably on the coastal barriers of E Gippsland, but there are similar features on many other coasts, including parts of the E coast of Britain, at Tentsmuir in Scotland, and Winterton Ness in East Anglia. The Australian examples are believed to result from an extension of the cut and fill process described in the previous chapter, when the resulting beach ridges become the foundations for successive foredune development (Fig. 74). As has been noted (p. 173), the seaward margins of such parallel sand ridge terrain have generally been truncated during the more recent phase when erosion has prevailed on sandy coastlines (Fig. 73).

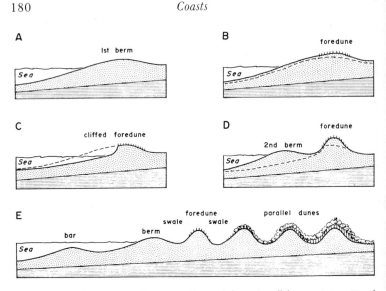

74   *Stages in the successive formation of coastal dunes parallel to an intermittently prograded coastline*

Parallel dunes

When the seaward margin of a foredune is trimmed back by waves during a storm, a crumbling cliff of sand is exposed (Fig. 74C). Subsequently, during calmer weather, waves build up a new beach ridge in front of, and parallel to, the trimmed margin of the foredune, separated from it by a low-lying trough or swale (Fig. 74D). Dune grasses tend to colonise the new beach ridge first, leaving the swale unvegetated, so that sand accretion is concentrated along the line of the beach ridge, and a new foredune is built up. Continued growth of the new foredune gradually cuts off the supply of sand to its predecessor, which becomes relatively stable, and the dune grasses are then invaded and replaced by scrub vegetation, which in SE Australia is dominated by the coast tea-tree (*Leptospermum laevigatum*), and in Britain by a rose and bramble thicket with buckthorn scrub (*Hippophae rhamnoides*).

If shoreline progradation continues, alternating episodes of cut and fill lead to the formation of a series of parallel dunes, separated by swales (Fig. 74E), and as each foredune is built upon a beach ridge formed by constructive waves the alignment of the parallel dunes is determined indirectly by the characteristic patterns of refracted ocean swell (Plate 35). The process of dune formation parallel to the coastline is well illustrated at Lakes Entrance, in Victoria, where sandy forelands have developed as the result of accretion of sand on either side of jetties built beside the entrance seventy-five years ago (Fig. 75). The pattern of accretion has been determined by ocean swell, refracted on encountering a sand bar offshore, so that the coastline of each foreland is cuspate in form. Three beach ridges have formed parallel to this prograding coastline, and each has been colonised by dune grasses, which have contributed to the building of roughly symmetrical foredunes, each about 3 m high. The innermost now receives little sand, and here the dune grasses are being invaded by scrub.

75 *Landforms at the entrance to the Gippsland Lakes, Australia (cf. Fig. 69), an artificial entrance cut in 1889 and maintained by current scour (maximum depth of entrance channel more than 20 m). Sandy forelands have developed on either side of the breakwaters that flank the entrance, and these show stages in parallel dune formation*

The height and spacing of such dunes is a function of the rate of sand supply to the shore, the history of cut and fill and the effectiveness of vegetation in binding sand and building the dunes. Where sand supply has been rapid on a prograding shore subject to frequent storms, a large number of low, closely-spaced parallel dunes are formed, but on a similar shore less exposed to storms the effects of 'cut', which is responsible for the separation of the dunes into parallel ridges, are less frequent, and there are fewer, but larger, parallel dunes. In the absence of episodes of 'cut', a foredune becomes broadened as a coastal terrace of vegetated sand, advancing as the beach prograde. Where sand supply has been slow, parallel ridges are unlikely to form on a stormy shore, but a few low dunes might be formed parallel to more sheltered sections of the coast. Attempts have been made to deduce former sea levels from the heights of successive parallel dunes, an overall seaward descent of crests of swales being claimed as evidence of coastal emergence during their formation. Olson (1958) related alternating phases of backshore dune development and shoreline recession to historical fluctuations in the level of Lake Michigan. This kind of pattern could also be produced by diminishing sand supply or increasing storm frequency, without any change in the relative levels of land and sea, and so it cannot be accepted as conclusive evidence for coastal emergence.

A succession of stable parallel dunes usually shows a sequence of vegetation types from grasses on the seaward side, through scrub to woodland or heath, accompanied by the development of successively deeper soil profiles. On quartzose dunes, pedogenesis (soil formation) leads to the development of podzols: the upper layers are leached of shell material by percolating rainwater which also removes the yellow stain of iron oxides from the sand grains, leaving the surface sand grey or white in colour, while the lower layers are enriched by the deposition of iron oxides, together with downwashed organic matter, to form a slightly-cemented red-brown sand horizon, often known as 'coffee rock'. The oldest dune ridges on the landward side show the most advanced stages in vegetation succession, often with heath or heathy woodland on sand that has been deeply leached.

Many coastal dune systems do not show regular patterns of dunes parallel to the shoreline. Some show traces of a former parallel pattern that has been interrupted by the formation of blowouts and parabolic dunes (see p. 186), but others are quite irregular, and have not necessarily originated from dunes built in parallel lines. There are good examples on the Atlantic coast of Europe and the Pacific coast of North America. The development of a large, irregular coastal dune topography can result from a rapid supply of sand to the shore, without the separation of deposited successive foredunes by cut and fill alternations in the manner described above, or from the delivery of sand blown from the emerged sea floor during glacial phases of the Pleistocene period, when sea level was lower (Fig. 76). This latter hypothesis may account for the submerged dune topography off the S and W coasts of Australia, where aeolian calcarenite passes beneath present sea level, and dunes must have formed when the sea was lower, relative to the land, before a phase of coastal

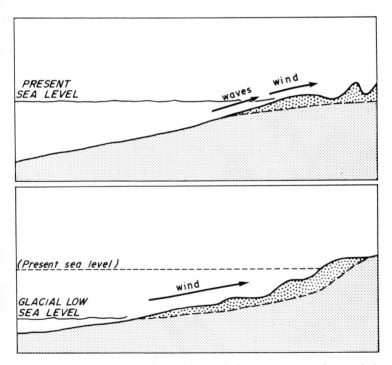

76   *Two possible mechanisms for the delivery of sediment to a coast. Above, with the sea at its present level, sand is being carried from the sea floor and delivered to the beach, where wind moves it inland; below, with sea level low during a glacial phase in Pleistocene times, sand is winnowed from the emerged sea floor and deposited in the coastal region*

77 *Calcareous sand deposition on the South Australian coast. After Bauer, 1961*

subsidence or sea level rise. The fringe of dune limestone plastered on to much of the coast of South Australia (Fig. 77) and Western Australia has been regarded as an accumulation of sand blown from the emerged sea floor during Pleistocene phases of glacio-eustatically lowered sea level; it pre-dates the Holocene marine transgression, and has usually been trimmed back on the present coast by marine denudation, forming rugged cliffs bordered by shore platforms (Plate 28). Strongly-cemented layers, often associated with buried soil horizons, form prominent ledges in cliff profiles. Bauer (1961) has described how the calcarenite formed on Kangaroo Island, off the coast of South Australia, partly obscures the evidence of Pleistocene coastal terraces cut in bedrock.

The submergence and dissection of coastal dune limestone topography is well shown on the coast of Western Australia, where the Holocene marine transgression isolated Rottnest Island and Garden Island as it invaded Cockburn Sound and drowned the lower part of the Swan River valley (Fig. 78) (Churchill, 1959). The drowned ridges have generally been planed off by wave action on the sea floor, but detailed soundings have shown that parts of a submerged dune topography survive. Similar calcarenite topography is found on the S and E shores of the Mediterranean, on the Red Sea coast, around the Caribbean, on the Brazilian coast, and in South Africa.

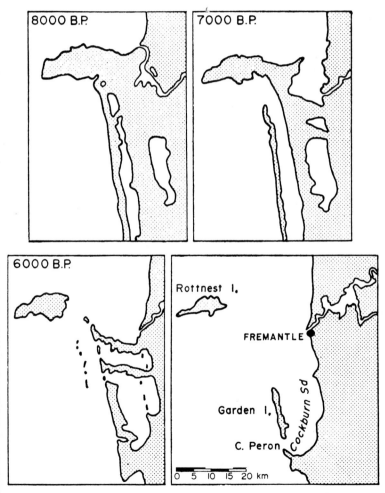

78   *Stages in coastal submergence in the Fremantle district. After Churchill, 1959*

Blowouts and parabolic dunes

Blowouts develop where the vegetation cover of unconsolidated coastal dunes is destroyed or removed, so that sand is no longer held in position. They are often initiated by intensive and localised human activity, where footpaths are worn over the dunes by people walking to a beach, or where trackways are made over the dunes for vehicles to reach the shore. Burning of coastal vegetation and excessive grazing by rabbits, sheep, cattle, or goats can destroy the vegetation cover and initiate blowouts, the effect of rabbits being accentuated where they have burrowed in the dunes. During a phase of aridity, weakening of the vegetation cover may lead to the formation of blow-

79   *Above, diagram of a parabolic dune. Below, blowouts and parabolic dunes interrupting parallel dunes, and showing axes aligned with the onshore wind resultant (cf. Fig. 40). Parabolic dunes may coalesce into transgressive dunes that spill landward behind a sinuous dune front*

outs, and may mobilise dunes that had been fixed by vegetation under preceding humid conditions. Blowouts may also be initiated when the outer margin of a foredune is cut away by the sea during a storm, leaving an unvegetated cliff of loose sand. On a prograding shore the rebuilding of the beach, with new berms developing into newer foredunes, prevents much erosion, but if the shoreline is gradually receding, and the beach is not fully replaced, blowouts will continue to develop.

The evolution of blowouts is related to onshore winds and is most rapid on sections of the coast exposed to strong winds. A blowout that becomes enlarged begins to migrate through coastal dunes, with an advancing nose of loose sand (sloping at 30°–33°) and trailing arms of partly-fixed sparsely-vegetated sand; in this way it develops into a parabolic or U-dune (Plate 46). Dunes of this type are often found disrupting a pattern of parallel dunes (Fig. 79). In some areas they have been halted and fixed by vegetation in parabolic forms within an older system of parallel dunes. Active parabolic dunes, moving landward across a coastal dune fringe, are common on the SE coasts of

80   *Relationship between the mean directions of blowout axes and onshore wind resultants on three sectors of the Ninety Mile Beach, Victoria*

46 Parabolic dunes advancing inland from the Queensland coast near Cape Flattery

47 The dune of Pyla, in south-west France advancing inland and invading the Landes
    Forest (cf. Fig. 83)

Australia, and have been described in detail by Jennings (1957) from King Island. Their movement is a response to the direction, frequency, and strength of onshore winds, the axis of each parabolic dune, defined as the line bisecting the angle between the trailing arms and directed towards the advancing nose (Fig. 79), being parallel to the resultant of onshore winds of Beaufort Scale 3 and over (Chapter V). This was demonstrated by Jennings on King Island where the parabolic dunes on the W coast are moving eastwards while those on the E coast are moving westwards. The axial directions of parabolic dunes behind the Ninety Mile Beach change as the orientation of the coast changes bringing in different component groups of onshore winds with different angles of onshore resultant (Fig. 80). The dunes retain their parabolic form as long as they remain partly vegetated, so that the trailing arms are held back by vegetation, but on parts of the Australian coast, overgrazing and fires have so reduced the dune vegetation that in places parabolic dunes have given place to masses of mobile, unvegetated sand, which show forms similar to dunes in arid regions, their profile at any time being a response to preceding wind conditions: a strong wind in one direction drives the crest of the dune one way, but subsequent winds from other directions modify the outline.

It is sometimes possible to distinguish successive waves of dunes which have migrated inland from a shore. On parts of the Australian coast, dunes have been banked against, or have climbed over, coastal cliffs, so that their crests reach altitudes hundreds of metres above sea level. Dunes have migrated up and over rocky promontories on the Victorian coast, notably Cape Bridgewater and Cape Paterson, and in some cases there are relict cliff-top dunes (Fig. 81) no longer linked with a source area of blown sand on adjacent beaches (Jennings, 1967). The very high dunes of the coast of S Queensland, on Stradbroke Island, Moreton Island (where at one point they exceed 275 m above sea level) and Fraser Island are not piled on to rocky foundations: above sea level they consist entirely of windblown sand, and borings have shown similar aeolian sand extending well below sea level. On Stradbroke Island there are several sets of transgressive frontal dunes, arranged in sequence parallel to the ocean coast, each partly overlapping its predecessor (Fig. 82). These have clearly advanced away from the shore during episodes of dune migration, but they are now stabilised beneath a

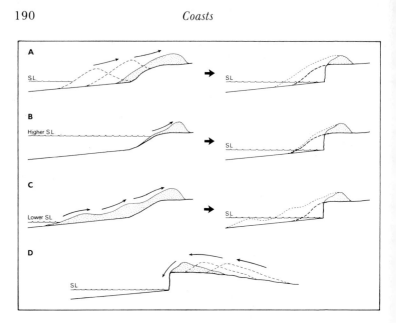

81   *Various ways in which cliff-top dunes may be formed. A, a transgressive dune truncated by cliff recession. B, a dune formed at a higher sea level stranded by cliff recession after emergence. C, a dune formed during a lower sea level truncated by cliff recession after emergence. D, a dune that has advanced from inland to the cliff crest. After Jennings, 1967*

cover of scrub and forest. On the New South Wales coast there are several sectors where a transgressive dune of mobile, unvegetated sand is migrating inland and burying older dune topography with its scrub or forest cover. Some of these dunes have been initiated by human activities, notably the grazing of stock and the burning of vegetation, liberating unconsolidated dune sand on the coastal margin. Residual hummocks, crowned by vegetation, are relics of the former stabilised dune topography. Some originated prior to European colonisation, for Captain Cook observed active dunes on Fraser Island in 1770. Aboriginal activities may have initiated these, or they may result from natural processes. A rapidly rising sea can trim back the margins of older dune topography, initiating transgressive dune development, but it is also possible that a rapidly receding sea could expose sandy deposits to be built into dunes and driven inland by onshore winds.

  Similar sequences of transgressive dunes have been studied on the W coast of Auckland, New Zealand (Schofield, 1975), on the Pacific coasts of Oregon and Washington (Cooper, 1958) and on the Atlantic coasts of France and Britain. In Spain, successive waves of transgressive dunes are being driven inland by the prevailing SW winds on the shores of the Gulf of Cadiz (Vanney *et al.*, 1979). The Pyla dune, in SW France is a huge mass of sand moving from the eroding shore S of the Arcachon estuary and spilling inland over the Landes pine forests (Plate 47). It was initiated during the eighteenth century, and has now attained a crest altitude of more than 100 m, with a steep wall (32°) of sand advancing inland at an average rate of 1 m a year. It appears that tidal scour on the estuary shore, resulting from deflection of the ebb channel by the southward growth of Cap Ferret spit, maintains the sand supply to the migrating dune (Fig. 83). New-borough Warren, on the coast of Anglesey, consists of three

82   *Transgressive frontal dunes (I-V) on Stradbroke Island, Queensland. The diagram-matic cross-section shows their transgressive relationship*

83   *The Bassin d'Arcachon and the Dune of Pyla (Plate 47), SW France*

transgressive dunes which have migrated inland from the sandy shore of Caernarvon Bay, and the Culbin Sands on the Scottish coast were formerly similar transgressive dunes until afforestation halted them. Measurements of dune movement have indicated that dune fronts 10 to 20 m high typically advance inland at rates of 1 to 10 m per year, but at Cronulla, S of Sydney, a dune 20 m high advanced 19 m, and smaller dunes as much as 50 m, in a year.

Relative age of dune development

Some parts of the Australian coast show evidence of several phases of coastal dune accumulation, with older dunes on the landward side and newer dunes bordering the coast. Where the dunes are built of quartzose sand, there are marked contrasts between the topography, soils, and vegetation of older and newer dunes. Older dunes have a comparatively subdued topo-graphy, and have been leached of shells and iron oxides by percolating rainwater to a depth of several feet, underlain by indurated horizons of 'coffee rock', formed by deposition of downwashed iron oxides and organic matter. Their vegetation consists of heath, or heathy woodland. Newer dunes, forming a coastal fringe, are more continuous, with bolder outlines, and accretion of sand often still continuing. They are fixed by grasses or scrub, except where blowouts and parabolic dunes are deve-loping, or where large transgressive masses of mobile sand are advancing inland. The sand is fresh and yellow in colour, and has not yet been leached of its small shell content or of the iron oxides which stain the sand grains. On the coast of King Island the older dunes on the landward side are thought to be of Pleistocene age, and the coastal fringe of newer dunes is the product of sand accretion during Holocene times (Jennings, 1957). The junction between the two is well marked, particularly where the newer dunes are transgressive, advancing across the more subdued older dune topography. The distinction between older and newer dunes is sometimes demonstrable on calcar-eous dunes, where older dune forms are preserved in aeolian calcarenite, and newer dunes remain unconsolidated, but the contrasts in vegetation are less marked, and the older dunes have only a superficial layer of sand decalcified by percolating rainwater.

Coastal sandrock

Horizons of cemented sand, termed sandrock, occur in quart-zose dunes on the E coast of Australia, and are sometimes exposed as ledges of slightly more resistant rock where the dunes have been dissected by wind action or eroded by the sea (Coaldrake, 1962). One type of sandrock is podzolic 'coffee rock', which is formed where iron oxides and organic matter have been washed down through the dune by percolating rainwater and deposited in a layer at, or slightly above, the water-table. Deposition of leached material at this level may be a conse-quence of repeated wetting and drying in the zone between the high-level water-table of the wet season and the low-level water-table of the dry season. Another type of sandrock has formed

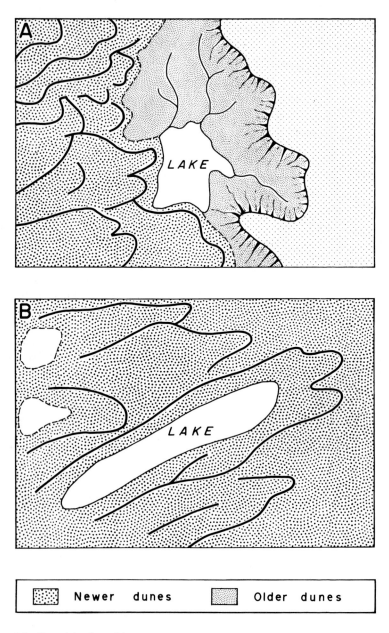

Newer dunes   Older dunes

84   *Dune lakes formed by*
     A   *The impounding of a drainage system*
     B   *The flooding of a hollow formed previously by deflation*

where sandy swamps or peaty sand in low-lying seasonally or permanently waterlogged sites have been overrun and compressed beneath advancing dunes. This type often contains compressed plant remains, which are not found in 'coffee rock'.

Dune lakes

Hollows in dune topography that pass beneath the level of the water-table are occupied by dune lakes, which may be intermittent, forming only when the water-table rises after heavy rains and drying out subsequently. In seasonally dry areas the shrinkage of dune lakes may expose sand for deflation and construction of active and migrating dune forms moving away from the lake basin. Some lakes have been impounded where dunes have been built across the mouth of a valley, ponding back the stream (Fig. 84A), and lakes occupying hollows excavated by deflation during dry weather (particularly between the trailing arms of parabolic dunes) (Fig. 84B). On Fraser Island there are dune lakes at various levels in hollows where the presence of underlying impermeable sandrock prevents the water draining away. Several have been impounded in hollows in the older dune topography enclosed by the advance of transgressive newer dunes. Infilling of dune lakes may produce flat-floored enclaves within a stabilised dune topography.

VII

ESTUARIES AND LAGOONS

The marine transgression that took place during Holocene times produced inlets at valley mouths and embayments on the sites of submerged coastal lowlands. The branched inlets formed by partial submergence of river valleys have been termed *rias*, and are well exemplified by Port Jackson (Sydney Harbour) and other inlets of similar configuration on the coast of New South Wales (Fig. 85). As Cotton (1956) pointed out, these do not conform with Richthofen's original definition of a ria, which is restricted to drowned valleys aligned with a geological strike transverse to the coast, as in Bantry Bay and adjacent areas on the SW coast of Ireland. Even the rias of NW Spain, from which the term originated, are not rias in this strict sense, and the term has come to be used as a synonym for drowned valley mouths remaining open to the sea: it overlaps broadly with the concept of an estuary (see below, p. 200). The drowned valley mouths which form branched inlets in SW England are

85   *Port Jackson, New South Wales, a valley system partly drowned by marine submergence*

86   *Carrick Roads, an extensive ria in Cornwall, SW England*

rias in this wider sense. On the N coast of Cornwall they have been largely filled by sand washed in from the Atlantic Ocean, as at Padstow, but on the Channel coast they generally remain as relatively deep inlets, like Carrick Roads (Fig. 86), often with a threshold sand bar at the entrance, as at Salcombe. In California, Drakes Estero is a fine example of a drowned river valley, a branching inlet incised into the hilly country of the Point Reyes peninsula, its mouth bordered by sand spits (Fig. 60).

Inlets at the mouths of formerly glaciated valleys on steep coasts are known as *fiords*, and are exemplified on the coasts of British Columbia and Alaska, Greenland, Norway, around the margins of the Arctic Ocean, and in W Siberia. The sea lochs of W Scotland are essentially fiords. In the southern hemisphere there are fiords on the S coast of Chile, on the W coast of South

87   *The outline of the fiord coast bordering the mountains of Southland, New Zealand*

Island, New Zealand, where Milford Sound is a fine example (Fig. 87), and on the margins of Antarctica and outlying islands. The chief characteristics of fiords are inherited from prior glaciation. The glacial troughs were scoured out by ice action well below the low sea levels of Pleistocene glacial phases, and submerged by the sea as the ice melted away. Depths of more than 1,300 m have been recorded in Scoresby Sound, a fiord on the E Greenland coast, and Sogne Fiord in Norway attains a depth of 1,244 m. These inlets are steep-sided, narrow, and relatively straight compared with drowned river valleys, and they have the classic 'U-shaped' cross-profile of glaciated troughs, together with hanging tributary valleys which may also have been partly submerged by the sea. Near the seaward end there is often a shallower threshold, which may be either a rocky feature or a drowned morainic bar: the threshold at the entrance to Milford Sound is evidently a broad rocky sill. It has been suggested that thinner ice towards the mouths of these glaciated troughs scoured less deeply, leaving a threshold on the seaward side of an excavated basin. Some thresholds are less than 100 m deep, and were probably land areas separating the sea from a lake in the glaciated trough until submerged by the sea during the later stages of the Holocene marine transgression.

Inlets formed by marine submergence of valleys and depressions in low-lying glaciated rocky terrain are known as *fiards* in SW Sweden, and similar inlets in coastal plains of glacial deposition are termed *förden* on the German Baltic coasts. The elongated firths of E Scotland appear to be a closely related category of drowned valley in formerly glaciated lowlands. Beyond the limits of past glaciation, many drowned valley mouths have marginal features related to past periglaciation, as in SW England, where the rias are bordered by slopes covered with solifluction deposits (known locally as Head) exposed in fringing cliffs (see p. 77). The drowned mouths of deeply-incised river valleys beyond the limits of past glaciation may resemble fiords: Bathurst Channel, opening into Port Davey, in SW Tasmania (Fig. 88) is a steep-sided inlet that was formerly thought to be a fiord, but it has no evidence of glaciation at or below present sea level, and none of the features of glacial sculpture that distinguish true fiords.

On the Red Sea coast, marine inlets termed sharms have developed where wadis or valleys cut by streams in wetter low

88   *The configuration of Port Davey, Tasmania. Bathurst Channel, formerly regarded as a fiord, is now considered to be a drowned river valley*

sea level episodes have been invaded by the Holocene marine transgression; their entrances are constricted, and in some cases blocked, by fringing coral reefs. An example is Abhur Creek, just N of Jeddah in Saudi Arabia.

Estuaries

Estuaries are the mouths of rivers, widening as they enter the sea (Emery and Stevenson, 1957; Lauff, 1967). There is considerable overlap between the concept of an estuary and the various kinds of rias and fiords described above. Some rias and fiords are valleys that have been almost completely drowned by marine submergence, receiving so little drainage from the land that they are essentially arms of the sea, but most are fed by rivers, the mouths of which can be described as estuarine. Some have attempted to distinguish rias as features formed by the partial submergence of valleys incised into coastal uplands, restricting the term estuary to the mouths of valleys on low-lying coasts, but this is not always satisfactory: Broken Bay, at the mouth of Hawkesbury River in New South Wales, has many of the characteristics of an estuary, although it is steep-sided and bordered by high plateau country.

Alternatively, an estuary may be defined in terms of tidal conditions, as the lower reaches of a river subject to tidal fluctuations, or in terms of salinity, as the area where fresh river water meets and mixes with salt water from the sea. The ideal estuary is funnel-shaped, opening seawards, subject to tidal fluctuations, and influenced by the salinity of the sea (Fig. 89), a form that is best developed on coasts with a relatively large tide range. In Britain the Thames, the Humber, and the Severn show this form; in W Europe the Rhine, the rivers of NW Germany, the Seine, the Loire, the Gironde, and the Tagus; and in Australia the rivers draining into the macrotidal northern gulfs: the Fitzroy (King Sound), the Ord and the Victoria (Joseph Bonaparte Gulf), and the Daly.

At low tide in such estuaries, there are often a number of channels leading from the river to the sea, between banks of sand, silt, and clay. These are shaped largely by tidal currents. Some are predominantly ebb channels, with a residual outflow

89 *Diagram of an estuary, showing zones related to salinity and tidal conditions*

of water and sediment; others predominantly flood channels, with a residual flow into the estuary. The ebb channels become shallower towards the sea; the flood channels are deeper at the seaward end. Up to half an hour after low tide it is possible to find outflow continuing in ebb channels when the tide has begun to move up the flood channels (Robinson, 1960). The currents tend to change the position and dimensions of channels, cutting away sediment in one place and building it up in another, so that estuaries on which ports are sited often require dredging to maintain the depth and alignment of navigable approach channels. A knowledge of the characteristic patterns of erosion and deposition is necessary to ensure that dredged material is not dumped in such a place that it gets washed straight back into the channel required for navigation, and in recent years use has been made of radioactive tracers to determine paths of sediment flow in the Thames estuary to ensure access to the port of London. Banks of sand, silt, or clay exposed at low tide in estuaries are subject to rapid changes in configuration; they often bear superficial ripple patterns, produced by the action of waves and currents on the estuary floor as the tide rises and falls. Ahnert (1960) has drawn attention to the meanders that develop in estuarine channels, as in Chesapeake Bay, related to the patterns of strong ebb and flood currents at mid-tide level. They are best developed in tidal marshland areas, the more intricate meandering of fluvial channels giving place to elongated pools with alternating cuspate bank projections and deposition of bars in the intervening calmer zones (Fig. 90). Usually there is an accompanying 'flaring' of the estuarine channel related to the rapidly increasing volume of ebb-augmented discharge towards the river mouth. Examples of these features

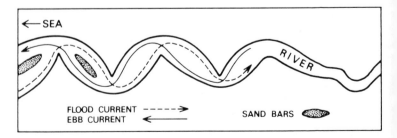

90   *Estuarine meanders (cf. Plate 48)*

are found in the rivers that drain into Joseph Bonaparte Gulf, in N Australia (Plate 48).

Estuaries are typically areas of active sedimentation, the area drowned by Recent submergence being progressively infilled, contracting in volume, depth, and surface area until the river winds to the sea through a depositional plain. It is possible to find every stage between the deep, branching estuary, little modified by sedimentation (e.g. Port Jackson), through to former estuaries that have been completely filled in, and with deltas developing beyond the former coastline (Chapter VIII). The chief factors are the original area and volume of the drowned valley mouth and the rate of sediment inflow from various sources. Enclosure by spits and barriers will tend to accelerate the natural reclamation of an estuary, whereas coastal subsidence will tend to postpone it.

Sediment is carried in by rivers, washed in from the sea, and derived from erosion of bordering slopes and shorelines. Rivers draining catchments where argillaceous formations outcrop, or where superficial weathering has yielded fine-grained material, are sources of estuarine muds. Many of the rivers of S and E England have derived muddy sediment from extensive clay lowlands for deposition in their estuaries: the London Clay has been a major source of Thames estuary muds, and the Mesozoic clay formations of the English Midlands have yielded muds to the estuaries of the Severn, the Humber, and the rivers draining into the Wash. The muds of the Wadden Sea are derived, at least in part, from the N German rivers, laden with silt and clay derived from loess and argillaceous outcrops. It is more difficult to account for the muds found in the rias of Devon and Cornwall, where the rivers drain mainly granite and Palaeozoic metasediment outcrops, but the source appears to be fine-grained material washed out of the Head deposits, the Pleistocene periglacial drifts which mantle hillsides in the SW peninsula, and are eroded as low cliffs bordering the rias. The same drifts mantle coastal slopes, but the fine-grained sediment is generally dispersed by the open sea, except in low wave energy sectors, as at Penzance and Newlyn on the W side of Mounts Bay, in the lee of the Lands End peninsula.

The rate of sediment yield from a river catchment is a function of lithology, weathering, and runoff conditions. It can be accelerated either naturally by uplift, volcanic activity, or a climatic change in the hinterland, or by man's impact, through

48　*Estuarine meanders near the Ord River mouth, Western Australia*

49　*Tidal channels persist in parallel alignments between mangrove-covered mudflats in Missionary Bay, Hinchinbrook Island, North Queensland*

deforestation, overgrazing, or unwise cultivation of erodible lands within the catchment. Stronger runoff then augments the sediment supply to rivers, estuaries, and adjacent coasts. There are examples of this from many parts of the world. Rapid infilling of estuaries following soil erosion has influenced Chesapeake Bay on the E coast and several Oregon estuaries on the W coast of the United States. Soil erosion from deeply-weathered catchments in the humid tropics has delivered vast masses of mud to estuaries and coastal embayments, accelerating the progradation of mudflats and the spread of mangrove swamps as in Jakarta Bay (Verstappen, 1953), and on the W coast of New Caledonia, where estuaries are being rapidly infilled. On Mediterranean shores, shrinkage of estuaries since classical times is related to widespread soil erosion following the impoverishment of vegetation by overgrazing and unwise land use, notably in Greece. Mining operations can also accelerate sediment yield to rivers, as in Cornwall, where the wastes from tin, copper, and kaolin mining have been washed into the rivers and carried down to fill their estuaries. The River Fal is white with suspended kaolin derived from the St Austell claypits, which is being deposited in rapidly accreting marshlands at its entry to Carrick Roads (Fig. 86).

Deposition of marine sediment in the entrances to estuaries takes a variety of forms. The growth of spits and barriers across the mouths of estuaries has already been discussed (Chapter V). In open, funnel-shaped estuaries with a large tide range, marine sediment interdigitates with fluvial sediment in the zone traversed by ebb and flow channel systems as previously described. Where the entrance to the estuary is narrow, because of constriction by bedrock promontories or the growth of paired spits (p. 159), marine sediment is deposited in the form of a tidal delta, submerged at least at high tide, and having a pattern of diverging channels both on the landward and the seaward side. Double tidal deltas of this kind are found between barrier islands on the Gulf coast of the United States, for example at Pass Abel, one of the entrances to Barataria Bay in Louisiana. On the Atlantic coast, where wave energy is greater, tidal deltas are developed only on the landward side of such entrances, as at Moriches Inlet on Long Island. Lucke (1934) described a similar feature at Barnegat Inlet, New Jersey, but this has since been modified by dredging.

Where the tide range is small, and wave action strong, the tidal delta becomes a wider threshold, usually with a single channel winding over a broad sandy flat exposed at low tide, a smooth and gentle seaward slope and a steep inner slope, where sand is advancing into the estuary from the sea. Thresholds of this kind are found in the entrances to estuarine inlets on the New South Wales coast (Bird, 1967), notably at Narooma (Fig. 101).

The configuration of an estuary can also be changed by wave and current action around its shores, particularly at high tide, when the sectors more exposed to strong wind and wave action tend to be eroded, and the material deposited on other parts of the shoreline, or on the estuary floor, in the manner described from Poole Harbour, an estuary in S England, by Bird and Ranwell (1964). Berthois has made detailed studies of erosion and sedimentation patterns at the mouth of the Loire (Guilcher, 1956), where much of the fluvial sediment is eventually deposited near high tide mark after circulating within the estuary.

Physiographic features in estuaries are much influenced by climatic factors. In cold environments (St Lawrence) estuarine waters freeze in winter; in temperate environments there are bordering salt marshes and in the tropics, mangrove fringes (Guilcher, 1979).

Salt marshes and mangrove swamps

Vegetation plays an important part in the shaping of depositional forms within estuaries and on tidal shores where estuarine conditions are found. Carpets of algae, such as *Enteromorpha*, and marine grass wrack (*Zostera*), partially stabilise the surface of tidal flats, and salt-tolerant (halophytic) plants colonise the margins of an estuary and spread forward across the inter-tidal zone as *salt marshes* (Chapman, 1960). These often show a well-defined zonation parallel to the shoreline, with plants such as *Spartina* or *Salicornia* dominating the outermost zone which is most frequently submerged by the tide, and the shore rush, *Juncus maritimus*, with other salt marsh communities, occupying higher zones that are less frequently submerged. In Europe a high salt marsh with perennial vegetation is often bordered seaward by low salt marsh which carries *Salicornia* only in summer (Fig. 94).

In tropical regions, and in many Australian and South African estuaries, mangroves form the pioneer community, spreading

50   *Mangroves advancing on to tidal mudflats in Westernport Bay, Victoria*

51   *Zoned mangroves advancing on to tidal mudflats in Cairns Bay, North Queensland*

from the shores of estuaries and colonising mudbanks exposed at low tide (Plate 49). Drainage from the swamp becomes confined to definite channels, often forming a reticulated creek network as in the tidal estuarine sectors of the Nigerian coast (Allen, 1965), or a dendritic pattern, as in many Australian mangrove swamps. The extent to which mangroves promote accretion of mud is uncertain, but where mud is being deposited mangroves spread on to it and create a sheltered environment, enabling other salt marsh plants to colonise when the mud surface has built up to a suitable level. Mangrove encroachment is impeded by strong wave action or tidal scour, so that mangrove swamps become most extensive in sheltered areas, and only reach the sea on low wave energy sectors of the coast (Plates 50 and 51). An advancing mangrove fringe is indicated by an abundance of seedlings and young shrubs with an unbroken rising canopy as the trees increase in age and size landward. Recession is indicated where a sharp margin exposes trunks of mature mangroves, undermined and falling on the shore. Zonation of mangrove species may result from a vegetation succession accompanying shore accretion, or indeed promoting it; but on some coasts the zonation may simply reflect existing habitat conditions.

Sediment carried into salt marsh communities by the rising tide is filtered out by the vegetation and retained as the tide ebbs. In this way, the level of the land is gradually built up, and vegetated marshland encroaches on the estuary. Broad intertidal land has developed around the shores of gulfs and estuaries in N Australia, where the tide range is large (e.g. Port Darwin, Fig. 91), and wide tracts of mangrove swamp are backed by saline flats flooded during exceptionally high tides. Rates of accretion of sediment in tidal marshlands can be measured by laying down identifiable layers of coloured sand, coal dust, or similar material on the marsh surface, and returning later to put down borings and measure the thickness of sediment added. Measurements made in this way by Steers and others on salt marshes in Britain have shown that accretion is relatively slow at the upper and lower limits of a marsh, and more rapid in the intervening zone, where salt marsh vegetation forms a relatively dense sediment-trapping cover and is repeatedly invaded by sediment-laden tidal water (Steers, 1960). In section, salt marshes build up in the form of a wedge (Fig. 92), and, as they

91   *Port Darwin, in N Australia, showing the extent of inter-tidal land in a gulf where the spring tide range is large (5.5 m at Darwin)*

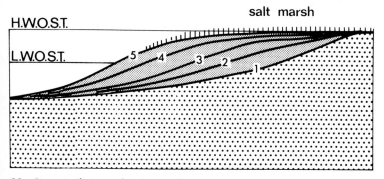

92   *Stages in the upward and outward growth of a salt marsh, showing levels of high and low water at ordinary spring tides*

develop, the ebb tide maintains a system of creeks, by which water flows off the marsh (Plate 49). The margins of these may be built up as levees by accretion in a fringing shrub community, such as the *Halimione* which borders Norfolk salt marsh creeks. There may also be residual enclosed depressions, known as *pans*, which remain unvegetated and retain water after the tide has fallen. In arid regions high evaporation makes these hypersaline (more saline than the sea), or dries them out as salt flats. As the marshland surface is built upwards and outwards, a vegetation succession may take place, one salt marsh community giving place to another, until the land is built up to a level at which high tide flooding becomes rare. Sedimentation then proceeds very slowly, and if rain and runoff leach out the superficial salt, the marshland may be invaded by reed-swamp communities, dominated by such species as the common reed, *Phragmites communis*, and eventually by swamp scrub, or even woodland vegetation.

Similar sequences occur where the pioneer vegetation is mangroves, as on the shores of Westernport Bay in SE Australia (Fig. 93) and Cairns Bay in Queensland. It is more difficult to measure rates of sedimentation in mangrove areas because burrowing crabs churn up marker layers placed on the substrate, but monitoring of changes on implanted stakes indicates sustained accretion in mangrove areas in contrast with vertical fluctuations on adjacent mudflats, and there is little doubt that root structures, especially prop roots and projecting pneumatophores (breathing-tubes), form an environment which aids accretion of sediment and locally-generated organic matter; indeed, the microtopography usually shows slight rises correlative with the density of these structures.

The zonation bordering Westernport Bay in SE Australia is shown in Fig. 93.

93   *Zonation of mangroves and salt marsh in Westernport Bay, Victoria, in relation to tidal levels*

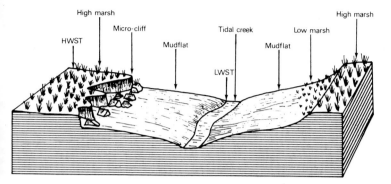

94   *Tidal creek bordered by high and low salt marsh and tidal mudflats (after Guilcher, 1979). On the left the outer edge of the salt marsh is cliffed; on the right the low marsh is advancing*

The outward spread of salt marsh or mangroves into an estuary slows down as tidal waters become confined to a central channel, in which ebb and flow currents are relatively strong. The outer edge of the marshland may then oscillate, advancing during phases of local accretion, and receding during episodes of tidal scour, in relation to a dynamic equilibrium between channel dimensions and the volumes of tidal ebb and flow (Figs. 94 and 95). Møller (1963) has reported detailed measurements of changes in marshland topography on the Danish coast, based on maps prepared in 1941 and 1959–62 on a scale of 1 : 10,000 with marshland surfaces contoured at 5 cm intervals. Patterns of vertical and lateral erosion and accretion can thus be located. Guilcher and Berthois (1957) measured sedimentation over a five-year period and recognised cyclic patterns of marginal erosion and accretion in the salt marshes bordering estuaries in Brittany. Salt marshes on the southern shores of the macrotidal Bay of St Michel are undergoing dissection by ebb run-off and rapid erosion along their seaward margins (Plate 52). Erosion of the seaward edge of a salt marsh can be due to several factors: current scour alongside a laterally migrating tidal channel, stronger wave action following deepening of the lower intertidal zone in consequence of progressive entrapment of sediment in the upper vegetated area, or continuing submergence of the coast. In New England, Redfield (1972) has illustrated salt marsh development on a coast subject to continuing subsidence, with stages from the seeding of bare sand flats through inter-

52 *Dissection of seaward margins of a salt marsh on the southern shores of the Baie de Saint Michel, France*

53 *Depositional terrace built by introduced* Spartina anglica *on an estuarine shore near Invercargill, New Zealand*

tidal marshland to the formation of high marsh underlain by peat deposits more than 6 m deep. On the shores of the St Lawrence estuary, Dionne (1972) has described the effects on salt marshes of winter snow cover and ice action. Ice-rafted debris, including rocks, beach materials, dislodged marsh fragments, and driftwood, are left behind on the salt marshes after the spring melt, and when the air trapped under winter ice on

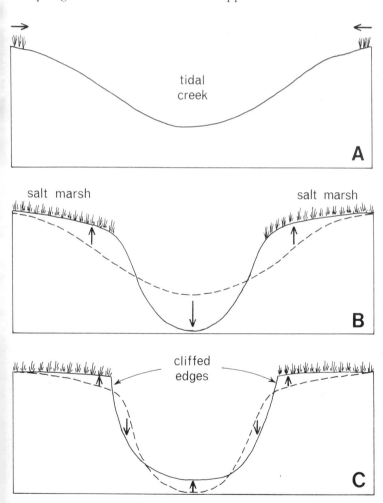

95   *Stages in the evolution of a tidal creek as salt marsh encroachment takes place, forming terraces on either side of a deepening channel (B), the sides of which eventually become unstable (C)*

mudflats finally escapes with the thaw the surface develops small mamillated mud-domes, termed *monroes*.

The influence of vegetation on estuarine sedimentation has been dramatically displayed in many estuaries in Britain since the arrival, or introduction, of the vigorous hybrid, *Spartina anglica* (Plate 53), a grass which evidently originated as a cross between native and American species of *Spartina* in Southampton Water in the 1870s (Hubbard, 1965). It spreads across tidal flats of silt and clay, builds up marshland at a rapid rate, and has been used as a method of stabilising and reclaiming tidal flats in estuaries in various parts of the world, including the Netherlands, Denmark, New Zealand, and the Tamar estuary in Tasmania. It is spreading rapidly on tidal mudflats in Anderson's Inlet, Victoria. In Britain some of the older *Spartina* marshes

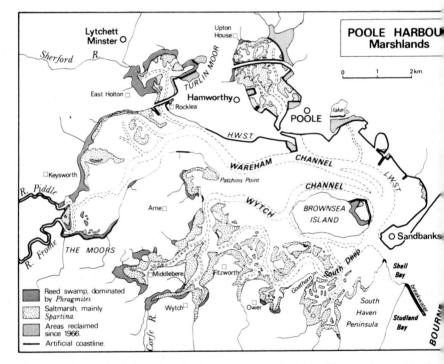

96　*Poole Harbour, S England, is an estuarine inlet bordered by extensive marshlands, especially* Spartina anglica *salt marsh which has developed here since 1899. This is backed in the upper reaches by* Phragmites communis *reedswamp where salinity is reduced by fresh-water inflow. Land reclamation has proceeded, especially on the urbanised northern fringes (supplied by V.J. May in 1980)*

97   *The inter-tidal zone in Westernport Bay, Victoria, showing the tidal watershed that is exposed at low tide north-east of French Island*

show evidence of die-back, especially around pans and along their seaward margins, but the ecological reasons for this are not fully understood. At the seaward margins where the sward dies and sediment previously trapped is released and the marshland erodes away the erosion is a sequel to die-back which must be due to some kind of adverse ecological condition. The process may be cyclic in the sense that released mud is deposited in new or reviving *Spartina* marshes elsewhere. Within Poole Harbour there are sectors where *Spartina* is still advancing, mainly in the upper estuary, as well as sectors of die-back and erosion of the marshland (Fig. 96). Salt marshes in the Venice lagoon, where mean sea level rose 22 cm between 1908 and 1980, also show marginal die-back and erosion.

The tidal areas which lie behind barrier islands and spits on the N Norfolk coast and on the North Sea coasts of Holland, Germany, and Denmark have estuarine characteristics. There are banks and shoals of sand and mud, with marshland developed where vegetation has colonised the upper inter-tidal zone, and intricate and variable patterns of intersecting creeks out of which the ebb tide drains. Ripples (see also Chapter V) develop

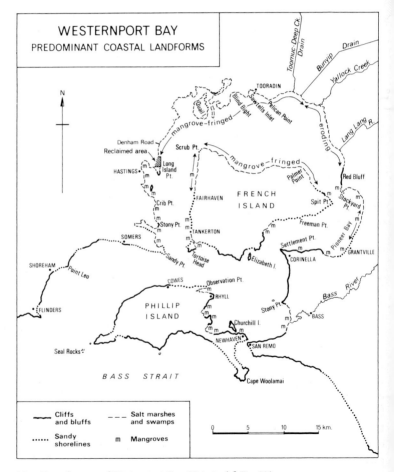

98   *Shore features of Westernport Bay, Victoria (cf. Fig. 97)*

99   *Segara Anakan, an estuarine embayment in S Java, bordered by mangroves which are spreading rapidly on to tidal mudflats built up by sedimentation, mainly from the Citanduy River, the yield from which has been increased in recent decades following soil erosion due to deforestation and cultivation of its steep upper catchment*

on the surface, especially in sandy areas, where they may attain a relief of more than 1 m, usually aligned at right-angles to the tidal flow and migrating in the direction of the current (Van Straaten, 1953). Gierloff-Emden (1961) has published a series of aerial photographs illustrating features of the morphology of tidal shores in the Wadden Sea, on Germany's North Sea coast.

Westernport Bay (Fig. 97), in SE Australia, is a landlocked embayment with some estuarine features (Marsden, 1979). Tide range increases from two entrances either side of Phillip Island northward to more than 3 m north-east of French Island. As the tide falls, the waters divide on either side of a tidal watershed, and extensive inter-tidal mudflats are exposed. The shoreline is intricate, partly cliffed, partly sandy, and extensively mangrove-fringed (Fig. 98). Within historical times the mangrove fringe has been reduced by clearing, reclamation, and local die-back, especially where fine sand has accreted, burying the *Avicennia* pneumatophores (Bird and Barson, 1975). By contrast, the Segara Anakan embayment in Indonesia has shown rapid advance of the mangrove fringe on to accreting mudflats in the past few decades (Fig. 99).

The mouths of many Australian estuaries are partly blocked by spits and barrier islands, built up by strong wave action on high wave energy coasts. Some are sealed off completely in the dry season, when river flow is unable to maintain an outlet, but after heavy rain the rivers flood, and water level builds up until it spills out, reopening the entrance (Jennings and Bird, 1967). Such estuaries are known as 'blind estuaries' in South Africa, and are in fact estuarine lagoons.

Coastal lagoons

Coastal lagoons are areas of relatively shallow water that have been partly or wholly sealed off from the sea by the formation of depositional barriers. There are good examples on the Gulf and Atlantic coasts of the United States; in Mexico and southern Brazil; in SW Iceland and on the southern coasts of the Baltic Sea. They occur around the Mediterranean, notably between Perpignan and Marseilles in France, in E Corsica, the northern Adriatic, Egypt, and the NW Black Sea, including the Sea of Azov. An intermittent chain of barrier-enclosed lagoons extends from the Ivory Coast to the Cameroons in W Africa, and lagoons are also present in Natal, on the Indian and Sri Lankan coasts, on the north coast of Hokkaido, and eastern Sakhalin. In the arctic they are well developed on the coasts of Alaska and NE Siberia. In France a lagoon is termed an étang, in Germany a haff, in Portugal an estero, on the Russian Black Sea coast a liman, and in New England a pond. On the south coast of Britain there are a number of small lagoons impounded behind shingle barriers, notably at Porthleven in Cornwall, Slapton in Devon, and Chesil Beach in Dorset. On the Australian coast, lagoons are best developed behind sandy barriers on the coast of Western Australia S of Perth, and on the coast of SE Australia from the mouth of the Murray around to S Queensland (Bird, 1967). New Zealand has lagoons on the shores of the Bay of Plenty in the North Island, and in the South Island Lake Ellesmere, the Southland lakes east of Bluff, and Okarito Lagoon on the west coast.

Lagoons have thus formed where inlets or embayments produced or revived by Holocene marine submergence have become enclosed by depositional barriers. They are best developed on low coasts behind shallow coastal seas: as a rule they have not formed on steep or fiord coasts, and have disappeared from receding cliffed coasts, or where rapid fluvial deposition has filled them. It is necessary to decide how enclosed an inlet or embayment must be to qualify as a coastal lagoon: in general the combined width of entrances from the sea should be less than one-fifth of the length of enclosing spits and barriers, but where the gaps are wider (e.g. between Frisian Islands fronting the Wadden Sea) the term 'open lagoon' may be applied.

Coastal lagoons show a wide variety of geomorphological and ecological features, but their essential characteristics can be summarised as in Fig. 100. There are often three zones: a freshwater zone close to the mouths of rivers, a salt-water tidal zone close to the entrance, and an intervening transitional zone of brackish (moderately saline) but relatively tideless water. The proportions of each zone vary from one system to another: the Myall Lakes, on the New South Wales coast, consist largely of

100 *Diagram of a coastal lagoon, showing variations in tidal levels and seasonal salinity conditions*

54   The coastal lagoon at Slapton Ley, Devonshire, England, with bordering reed-swamp and an enclosing barrier of fine shingle (cf. Fig. 45)

55   The artificial entrance to the Gippsland Lakes, Victoria, cut through the dune-covered coastal barrier (see Plate 58) (N. Rosengren)

the fresh-water zone; Lake Illawarra consists largely of the intermediate zone, and Wagonga Inlet (Fig. 101) largely of the salt-
water tidal zone. The extent of each zone depends largely on the
proportion of fresh-water inflow to the lagoon system, lagoons
tending to be more brackish in relatively arid regions, and on
the nature and dimensions of the entrance from the sea.
Lagoons completely cut off from the sea, like those on the
Landes coast N and S of Arcachon, are essentially fresh-water
lakes. In S England the Fleet is a typical estuarine lagoon with
salinity augmented by percolation of sea water in through the
shingle barrier, and Slapton Ley an almost fresh coastal lake
(Fig. 45 and Plate 54).

Lagoon entrances
The configuration of lagoon entrances is the outcome of a
contest between the currents that flow through them and the
effects of onshore and longshore drifting of sand or shingle
which tend to seal them off (Bruun, 1967). Currents are generated through entrances in several ways. There are tidal currents
produced by tides entering and leaving the lagoon, their
strength increasing with tide range; there are currents due to
·outflow from rivers, particularly after heavy rain when floods
build up the level of the lagoon so that water pours out through
the entrance; and there are currents generated by wind action,
onshore winds driving sea water into the lagoon and offshore
winds driving lagoon water out to sea. Strong currents tend to
maintain the dimensions of lagoon entrances. An entrance cut
entirely in unconsolidated sediment has a cross-sectional area
which varies in relation to the volume of water passing through,
being widened or deepened during episodes of floodwater discharge. When the outflow is weak the entrance may be
deflected by the longshore movement of sand caused by waves
and wave-induced currents in the nearshore zone. Waves that
arrive parallel to the coast move sand from the sea floor shorewards on to beaches and into lagoon entrances, and waves that
reach the shore at an angle cause longshore drifting of sand,
which deflects lagoon entrances and may seal them off
altogether.

The position and dimensions of lagoon entrances change
frequently in response to variations in the processes at work,
and some have been stabilised by the construction of bordering
breakwaters. When explorers arrived at the Gippsland Lakes, in

Coasts

WAGONGA INLET

0   1   2 km.

Alluvium
Sand above H.W.S.T.
Sand below H.W.S.T.
Beach dunes
Depth contours in feet

Kianga Point
Wagonga Head
NAROOMA

Cross section at AB
Dunes on barrier
H.W.S.T.
L.W.S.T.
15 metres
Sand spit
Longitudinal section
River sediments

101   *Wagonga Inlet, New South Wales, an estuary with a well developed in-washed sandy threshold*

Victoria, in the 1840s they found a small natural outlet at Cunninghame Arm, near the E end of the lagoon system, which was sealed in calm weather when onshore and longshore drifting of sand overcame the effects of transverse currents, and remained closed until heavy rains flooded the rivers and raised the level of the lagoons so that water spilled out over the barrier. The difficulties of navigating such an unreliable passage led to a local demand for an artificial entrance, and in 1889 a gap was cut through the enclosing barrier at what is now Lakes Entrance (Plate 55). This gap, bordered by stone jetties, has become a permanent artificial entrance, maintained by currents which have scoured a channel to a maximum depth of more than 20 m, and with a looped sand bar offshore testifying to the efforts of wave action to drive sand into the entrance and seal it off (Fig. 75). The natural entrance has fallen into disuse, and is now permanently sealed (Bird, 1978a). In a similar way the previously migrating entrance to Ringkøbing Fiord (Fig. 102) on the W coast of Denmark, has been stabilised by bordering breakwaters and a sluice at Hvidesande. Sand accumulating on the N side of the breakwaters is indicative of the southward drift which formerly diverted the lagoon entrance. Artificially stabilised entrances are also found between barrier islands on the east coast of the United States, as at Jacksonville in Florida, but many of these entrances remain unmodified, variable in dimensions, sometimes migratory, and occasionally sealed off completely (Shepard and Wanless, 1972).

Lagoon entrances are often located on sections of the coastline where wave action is relatively weak, and the action of inflowing and outflowing currents therefore more effective. On wave refraction diagrams, such sections occur where there is a marked divergence of wave orthogonals, as at the head of the embayment in Fig. 7B. Many lagoon entrances on the New South Wales coast are situated at the S ends of sandy bays and close to rocky headlands, in positions where the dominant SE swell is intensely refracted, and therefore weakened (Bascom, 1954). Other lagoon entrances are 'rock-defended'—close to offshore reefs or foreshore rock outcrops which break up constructive waves and prevent them completing the barrier at a particular point: the entrance to Lake Illawarra is protected by Windang Island, immediately offshore (Fig. 105).

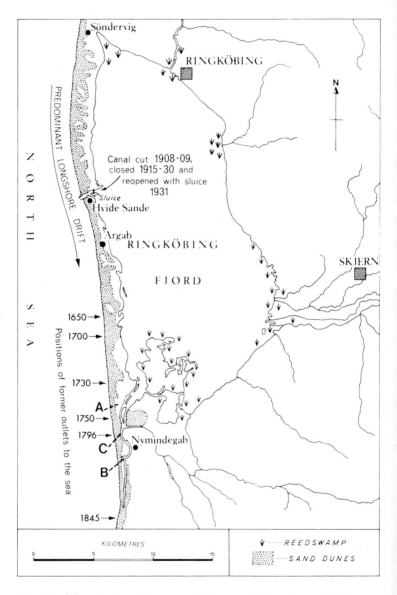

102 *Ringköbing Fjord, on the west coast of Denmark (where the term fjord includes coastal lagoons) had a variable, migrating outlet to the sea, and in the nineteenth century unsuccessful attempts were made (A, B, C) to stabilise it. The present artificial entrance at Hvide Sande contains a sluice to prevent inflow of sea water*

The dimensions of lagoon entrances influence the extent to which tides invade a lagoon (tidal ventilation), the tide range diminishing rapidly inside the entrance. The more remote parts of large lagoon systems are unaffected by marine tides, but are subject to irregular changes of level from heavy rain, river flooding, or the action of strong winds. Winds blowing over a lagoon lower the level at the windward end and build it up to leeward; when the wind drops, the normal level is restored, often by way of a succession of oscillations of diminishing amplitude termed seiches.

Entrance dimensions also influence the pattern of salinity in a coastal lagoon. Salinity is determined by the meeting and mixing of fresh water from rain and rivers and salt water from the sea: it generally diminishes from the lagoon entrance towards the mouths of the rivers. In regions with seasonal variations of precipitation the salinity regime is also seasonal, for in the dry season sea water flows in through the entrance to compensate for the diminished river flow and the loss of fresh water by evaporation, but in the wet season evaporation losses are reduced and the lagoon is freshened by rain and rivers. In arid regions lagoons may become hypersaline, because the inflow of sea water is insufficient to prevent the development of high concentrations of salt as water evaporates from the lagoon. During the summer months, hypersaline conditions develop in enclosed lagoons such as Lake Eliza and Lake St Clair (Fig. 68), on the coast of South Australia, and also at the S end of the Coorong, away from the lagoon entrance, where tidal ventilation is too weak to prevent the development of high salinity in the evaporating water. Locally, saline evaporite deposits have formed where lagoons have dried out completely. Such deposits are typical of enclosed lagoons on arid coasts. On the shores of the Arabian Gulf salt-encrusted areas of this kind, often partly enclosed by sandy spits and barriers, are known as *sebkhas*: for example at Abu Dhabi, where the sebkha is invaded by the sea only during storm surges. Similar features are seen in inter-dune swales bordering King Sound in NW Australia (Plate 56).

Salinity conditions influence modes of sedimentation. Clay carried in suspension in fresh water is flocculated and precipitated by the electrolytic effect of sodium chloride in solution when saline water is encountered. Salinity is also of ecological importance, affecting the development and distribution of shore

56   *A sebkha on the west coast of King Sound, Western Australia*

57   *Reed-swamp encroachment on the shores of the Gippsland Lakes, Victoria.* **Phragmites** *and* **Typha** *are spreading into the lake, followed by swamp scrub vegetation on newly-formed sedimentary land*

vegetation around lagoons and thus influencing patterns of sedimentation in encroaching swamps.

Swamp encroachment
In the vicinity of tidal entrances to lagoons salinity conditions are essentially similar to those in estuaries. Banks of sediment are exposed at low tide, and the shores may be bordered by encroaching salt marshes and mangrove swamps. Away from the entrance, where the water is brackish and tidal fluctuations diminish, encroachment by salt marsh or mangrove swamp is much reduced; mangroves, in particular, are halophytic com- munities which require regular tidal inundation, and are best developed on the margins of tidal creeks (Gierloff-Emden, 1961). Lagoon shores in this intermediate zone may be bordered by a narrow fringe of salt marsh vegetation, but more often they are unvegetated and bordered by beaches of sand or gravel derived

103   *Reed-swamp encroachment (above) promotes sedimentation and may initiate a vegetation succession to swamp scrub. If ecological conditions become unfavour- able for reed growth (below), die-back occurs, and the swamp land that had previously been built up is likely to be eroded*

from erosion of the shores. Towards the mouths of rivers, where the water is relatively fresh, reed-swamp communities dominated by species of *Phragmites*, *Scirpus*, and *Typha* may colonise the shore, and where these communities are spreading into the lagoon, they influence the pattern of sedimentation, trapping silt and floating debris and contributing organic matter so that new land is built up.

This process of swamp encroachment has greatly reduced the area of relatively fresh lagoons, such as Lake Wellington, one of the Gippsland Lakes (Fig. 69), which is bordered by extensive swamp land on its S and W shores (Plate 57). Reed-swamp was formerly more widespread on the shores of the Gippsland Lakes, but increased salinity since the opening of the artificial entrance at Lakes Entrance has killed the reed vegetation and resulted in the erosion of land that had formerly been built up by sedimentation (Fig. 103) (Bird, 1978a). On the other hand, freshening of lagoons that have become more completely sealed off from the sea, either naturally by the development of barriers or artificially by the insertion of weirs and barrages, can

104   *Coastal lagoons at the mouth of the Murray River, S Australia. Barrages completed in 1940 close gaps between barrier islands and prevent the inflow of sea water, so that these lagoons have become almost fresh water systems*

stimulate the spread of reed-swamp around their shores and initiate new patterns of sedimentation in the encroaching swamps. This has happened in the Murray-mouth lakes (Fig. 104), following the completion in 1940 of barrages built to exclude sea water, and in the Étang de Vaccarès, a lagoon on the Rhône delta in the Camargue region of S France, where sluices now exclude sea water and freshening has followed the inflow of runoff from irrigated ricefields. Lymarev (1958) has described extensive *Phragmites* encroachment on the shores of the Aral Sea, drawing attention to the part played by swamp encroachment in promoting shoreline progradation there, and similar conditions are found on parts of the Baltic coast, notably in S Finland.

Configuration of lagoons

The initial form of a coastal lagoon depends on the shape of the inlet or embayment enclosed and the configuration of the barriers that enclose it. Some lagoons were originally broad embayments (Lake Illawarra, Fig. 105); others show the much-branched form of submerged valley systems (Lake Macquarie, Fig. 106); and in some the enclosing barriers incorporate islands (Tuggerah Lakes, Fig. 107). The inner shores of the enclosing

105   *Lake Illawarra, New South Wales, a broad embayment almost cut off from the sea by sandy coastal barriers, with a tidal entrance situated in the lee of Windang Island. The Macquarie Rivulet delta is shown in Plate 62*

106   *Lake Macquarie, New South Wales, an embayment of intricate configuration almost enclosed by sandy coastal barriers*

107   *The Tuggerah Lakes, a system of lagoons on the coast of New South Wales with an enclosing barrier which incorporates former offshore islands*

barriers are usually simple in outline. There may be relics of recurved ridges, which marked stages in the prolongation of a spit which became a barrier enclosing an inlet or embayment; or there may be promontories formed where sand has blown over as an advancing dune, or washed over through low-lying sections of the barrier by storm waves or exceptionally high tides. Deposition is also common in the zones behind barrier islands where tides flowing in from entrances meet, as in the Wadden Sea (Fig. 63) and on the S side of Scolt Head Island. The tidal watershed may become a marshland area.

As a barrier develops to enclose a lagoon, sea waves are excluded and the estuarine effects of marine salinity and tidal changes of level are reduced. Winds blowing over the lagoon cause waves and currents which are related to their direction and strength, and the lengths of fetch across which these winds are effective. Long, narrow lagoons have the strongest wave action in diagonal directions, along the maximum fetch. If the shores are not protected by vegetation, waves coming in at an angle move sediment to and fro along the beaches, eroding embayments and building up spits, cusps, and cuspate forelands which may grow to such an extent that the lagoon becomes divided into a series of small, round, or oval lagoons, linked by narrow straits, or sealed off completely (Fig. 108). This process has been called *segmentation* by Price (1947), who described it from lagoons on the Texas coast, and Zenkovich (1959) has described a similar process at work in some Russian coastal lagoons. Segmentation is essentially an adjustment of lagoon form to patterns more closely related to waves and currents generated within the lagoon. Currents play a part in smoothing the curved outlines of the shore in the later stages of segmentation and may also maintain the connecting straits between segmented lagoons. But strong tidal currents deflect spit growth and inhibit the segmentation process.

In the Gippsland Lakes, Cunninghame Arm (Fig. 108) shows a series of cuspate spits (Plate 58) which, towards the E end, have grown to such an extent that they have almost cut off a chain of shallow pools, the Warm Holes. Small connecting creeks are

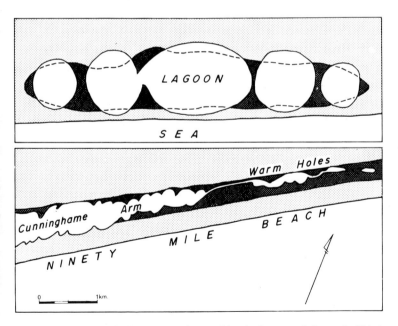

108   *Segmentation of a long narrow lagoon (above), the original shape of which is indicated by the pecked line (after Zenkovich, 1959). The lower diagram shows segmentation in progress in the Cunninghame Arm, a branch of the Gippsland Lakes, Victoria (cf. Fig. 69)*

maintained by wind-driven and tidal currents. On the South Australian coast, the lagoons between Robe and Beachport (Lake Eliza, Lake St Clair, and Lake George) (Fig. 68) have been formed by the segmentation of a long narrow lagoon, originally similar to the Coorong, farther north. Many lagoons are bordered by growing spits and scoured embayments indicating incipient segmentation. The Lagoa de Araruama, near Cabo Frio in Brazil, has cuspate spits that have been enlarged as a result of coastal emergence, which shallows lagoons and hastens segmentation.

The sheltered waters of coastal lagoons are also favourable for the development of deltas at the mouths of rivers. In the Gippsland Lakes, small deltas have been built by the Latrobe and Avon Rivers entering Lake Wellington, and the Tambo and Mitchell Rivers entering Lake King. These and other deltas in coastal lagoons will be discussed further in the next chapter.

The patterns of sedimentation in lagoons are complex, and related to the characteristic patterns of waves and currents, as well as to the influence of shoreline vegetation. Comparison of

58   *The coastal barrier at Lakes Entrance, Victoria, showing cuspate sandspits on the shore of Cunninghame Arm, scrub vegetation on the dunes and the Ninety Mile Beach (left). (N. Rosengren)*

the geomorphological features of lagoons on the Australian coast indicates that those bordered by encroaching reed-swamp contract in area until they are completely occupied by swamp land, whereas those without shoreline vegetation are reshaped by waves and currents as segmentation proceeds. Eventually, after many changes in configuration, coastal lagoons receiving sediment are replaced by coastal plains, across which rivers and residual creeks wind, uniting to pass out to sea through the tidal entrance. Close examination of patterns of sediment on coastal plains sometimes reveals the outlines of former lagoon systems that have been extinguished by deposition of sediment. Alternatively, renewed erosion may remove the barrier, opening up the lagoon as a coastal embayment. It is likely that Guichen Bay, at Robe, on the South Australian coast (Fig. 68) and Rivoli Bay, at Beachport, farther south, were at one stage enclosed lagoons, comparable with Lake Eliza, Lake St Clair, and Lake George, which lie behind a barrier of calcarenite on the intervening coast. Reefs and islands of calcarenite in Guichen Bay and Rivoli Bay indicate the former extension of this barrier northward and southward, and it is inferred that these sections have been removed by marine erosion. Fig. 78 traces the breaching of similar calcarenite barriers on the coast of Western Australia to form Cockburn Sound, and lunate embayments of similar origin have also developed on the calcarenite coast of Israel near Nahsolim, and on the N coast of Puerto Rico (Kaye, 1959).

Detailed studies of the geomorphology and ecology of coastal lagoons include Webb's (1958) work on Lagos lagoon, Stevenson and Emery (1958) on Newport Bay, California, and Fisk (1958) on the Laguna Madre, a hypersaline Texas coast lagoon. In terms of the geological time scale, coastal lagoons are ephemeral features, likely to be replaced by depositional plains or reopened as coastal embayments, depending on the subsequent evolution of the coastal region in which they have developed.

VIII

DELTAS

Deltaic forms and structures

Deltas are built where sediment brought down by rivers has filled in the mouths of valleys drowned by Holocene marine submergence to form a depositional feature protruding from the general outline of the coast (Coleman and Wright, 1977). A delta will only be built if the sediment accumulating at the river mouth exceeds that carried away by waves and currents. Delta progradation above high tide level depends on swash deposition along the delta margins and vertical accretion alongside river channels of sediment delivered by floodwaters. Most deltas also incorporate sediment of marine origin, brought alongshore or from the sea floor. Small rivers may build deltas on the sheltered shores of lakes or tideless seas, but on coasts dominated by strong wave action and tidal scour, protruding deltas are built only by large rivers draining catchments that yield an abundance of sediment. Sectors of formerly submerged valley mouths reclaimed by fluvial deposition are essentially deltaic, even if they do not protrude from the general outline of the coast. The Rhine, Guadalquivir, Senegal, Colorado, and Amazon all have features of this kind, and it is convenient to include them as deltas, even though they lack the characteristic shape that led Herodotus to apply the Greek letter as a geomorphological term.

The classic example of a delta to which Herodotus referred is that of the Nile, built into the Mediterranean Sea on a coast where the tide range is less than 1 m (Fig. 109). Other examples of protruding deltas built into relatively tideless seas include the Ebro, the Rhône, and the Tiber deltas built into the Mediterranean, the Po delta in the Adriatic Sea, the Danube delta in the Black Sea, and the Volga delta in the Caspian. Extensive deltas have been built out into microtidal Indonesian waters by the several large rivers that flow northward across Java (Plate 59). Microtidal conditions are not essential for delta development, however: the Irrawaddy delta region has a tide range of 5.5 m and the Ganges 4.5 m. Both are on coasts where the wave energy is relatively low, because of broad shallow areas offshore

234

109 *The Nile delta, Egypt. The black triangles point to rapidly-eroding sectors, and the arrows indicate the longshore drift pattern. After Orlova and Zenkovich, 1974*

which diminish wave action. The Mississippi delta has been built in a microtidal and generally low wave energy environment, subject to occasional hurricanes.

Deltas are rare on high wave energy coasts, where sediment delivered by rivers is dispersed by strong wave action, the coarse fraction (sand and gravel) being deposited in beach and barrier formations on the coast, and the finer material settling on the sea floor or carried away in suspension by the sea. However, on the west coast of South Island, New Zealand, rivers such as the Taramakau, the Arahura, and the Haast have brought down sufficient gravelly material from mountainous glaciated catchments to build slightly protruding, blunted deltas on a high wave energy coast. Protruding deltas have generally not developed on the ocean coasts of Australia because of high wave energy conditions and because fluvial discharge is relatively small: an exception is the De Grey delta, on a sector of the NW coast where wave energy is moderate because the continental shelf is

59　The Cimanuk delta, northern Java, showing active growth of distributary lobe (A). The line between B and C is a beach-ridge zone which formed the coastline in 1947 (N. Rosengren)

60　Reed-swamp (roseau) growing in shallow water outlines the pattern of digitate growth of the South Pass, Mississippi delta, into the Gulf of Mexico (cf. Fig. 111) broad and the coastal waters macrotidal. Many Australian rivers have a marked seasonal regime, with reduced flow and reduced sediment yield in the dry season, and several valley mouths drowned by Holocene submergence have not yet been filled in by sediment. The Murray-Darling system has a catchment basin of more than one million sq. km, but in its lower reaches the Murray flows through a semi-arid region and loses so much water by evaporation that it has not been able to carry sufficient sediment to fill the lagoons (Lakes Albert and Alexandrina) that remain at its mouth (Fig. 104). In SE Australia many submerged valley mouths remain as inlets or lagoons enclosed by spits or barriers, but larger rivers such as the Snowy and the Shoalhaven have brought down more sediment, and reclaimed their drowned valleys as depositional plains. These deltaic plains do not protrude from the general alignment of the coast; their

110   *The Shoalhaven delta, New South Wales. Strong ocean swell from the South Pacific has prevented the formation of a protruding delta, but there is a small submerged sandy delta off the river mouth*

seaward shores have smoothly-curved outlines shaped by ocean swell (Fig. 110). On low wave energy sectors of the Queensland coast, sheltered from ocean swell by the Great Barrier Reefs, rivers that have reclaimed their drowned mouths are building protruding deltas (e.g. Burdekin, Fig. 114).

The shape of a delta is determined partly by the interaction between fluvial deposition at and around a river mouth and the effects of waves and currents, tending to disperse the sediment and smooth the coastline. Wave action is modified by the submarine profile off the delta, attenuation being greater when fluvial deposition has built a broad shallow nearshore platform, and less where nearshore waters remain deep. At one extreme is the Mississippi delta, where an abundant fluvial sediment supply is delivered through branching distributary channels to a coastal sector where wave energy has been reduced by passage through shallowed nearshore waters: the result is a series

111   *Configurations of deltas; digitate (Mississippi), cuspate (Ebro), lobate (Niger) and blunt (São Francisco, Brazil). After Wright and Coleman, 1972*

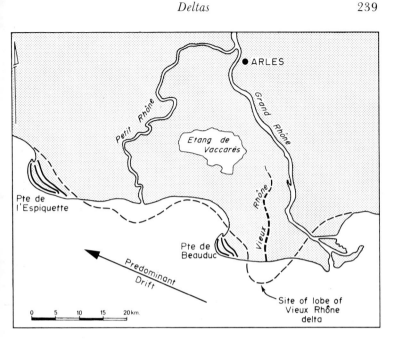

112   *The Rhône delta, France*

of *digitate* deltas, where narrow levees have been prolonged seaward by deposition at distributary mouths during floods. The delta shoreline is indented and marshy, with only minor sandy beaches and spits. With slightly stronger wave action the Ebro delta also protrudes, with a *cuspate* outline and a generally sandy shoreline, with beaches prolonged as spits. Next in sequence of increasing wave energy are the *lobate* delta of the Niger, and the *blunt* delta of the São Francisco, both exposed to ocean swell from the South Atlantic (Fig. 111). Finally, in a high wave energy environment the Senegal River opens on a sandy Atlantic Ocean shoreline that is straight rather than protruding, the river mouth having been deflected southwards by longshore spit growth (Wright and Coleman, 1972). Some deltas consist only of a single river channel which is flanked by depositional land while others have wandering and intermittent outlets, as in the Rhône delta, where the old main outlet is now the relatively unimportant Petit Rhône and the present river discharges through the larger Grand Rhône channel farther east (Fig. 112). Others have a river branching into several distributaries, as in the Nile delta, where all but two of the outflow channels are now defunct (Fig. 109). Distributaries are common on deltas where the accumulation of sediment in river channels tends to lift the river to the surface, so that it spills out in various directions. Some distributaries originate where new outlets are scoured during floods; others where a river mouth is blocked by deposition or split into two or more channels by the formation of shoals and islands. Tidal ebb and flow tends to maintain distributary mouths, whereas longshore drifting tends to divert them or seal them off altogether. Where the tide range is large delta distributaries widen seawards to funnel-shaped estuarine outlets (e.g. Rhine, De Grey). River outlets may change during floods. The Mississippi has had a long history of distributary development, with successive formation of subdelta lobes (Fig. 113). As a lobe extends, channel gradients in the river are reduced, and the outflow diminishes. Bordering levees may then be breached during floods to form crevasses, giving a shorter and steeper outflow channel, which then develops a new distributary lobe, producing eventually the branched form shown in Fig. 111. Confinement of the Lower Mississippi

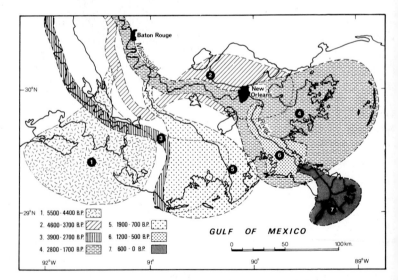

113   Outlines of seven successive sub-deltas of the Mississippi. Stages 1 to 5 are now partly submerged and dissected as the result of isostatic subsidence and marine incursion, the most recent growth (stages 6 and 7) being SE from New Orleans (cf. Fig. 111). After Kolb and Van Lopik, 1966

between artificial levees during the past 250 years has intensi-
fied its outflow to the Gulf and increased the sediment supply
to the mouths of its distributaries. The pattern of digitate extension has been much influenced by the growth of reed-swamp
('roseau') vegetation, which intercepts sediment alongside river
channels (Plate 60), and around each distributary mouth there is
deposited shoal topography with local upwellings known as
mudlumps, extrusions of prodelta marine clays as the result of
sediment loading.

Beaches, spits, and barriers built by marine processes on the
shores of a delta often enclose lagoons and swamps, and are
sometimes themselves incorporated as the delta grows larger.
The Burdekin River has built a large protruding delta (Fig. 114)
filling a former embayment and enclosing a number of high
islands that formerly lay offshore. The river divides into distributaries in the delta region, some of which are former outlets,
partly sealed, or carrying water only during floods. A number
of spits have been built northwards, deflecting outlets from
former distributaries, and the growth of a long recurved spit,
terminating in Cape Bowling Green, also testifies to a northward longshore drift resulting from the prevalence of waves
generated by the SE trade winds: a pattern seen also on the
Kakinada spit, growing on the Godavari delta in eastern India.
In N Italy the Tagliamento delta has a series of symmetrical
parallel sandy beach ridges marking stages in the progradation
of a cuspate delta shoreline (Fig. 115). The *cheniers* of the
Louisiana coastal plain are of different origin, being long,
narrow, low-lying strips of sand deposited on pre-existing
swamps and alluvial flats, and marked out by contrasts in the
vegetation pattern. Similar features are found in Surinam on the
coast of South America, where several sand ridges have been
emplaced on broad swampy deltaic plains adjacent to the
Amazon and the Orinoco. It is probable that these were
deposited during occasional high tides or storm surges when
sand was carried inland on coasts where wave energy is normally low. An example from a similar environment in N Australia is shown in Plate 61.

Delta coastlines continue to prograde as long as the supply of
sediment, mainly from the river, exceeds removal by wave and
current action. Progradation can be spectacular in shallow seas,
especially on parts of tropical deltas: progradation of over 200 m

61 *Sandy cheniers intersected by tidal creeks on the coastal plain south of the mangrove-fringed shoreline of Van Diemen Gulf, N Australia*

per year has been recorded on some Javanese deltas. Accelerated delta growth can result from increased sediment yield due to deforestation, overgrazing or unwise cultivation leading to rapid soil erosion in the river catchments.

Delta growth is slower if deep water, or a submarine canyon, exists offshore: off the Ganges delta, sediment is lost to the sea floor and delta growth may be relatively slow. Sectors of a delta

114   *The Burdekin delta, Queensland, showing offset spits that have grown successively northward from river mouths (cf. Hopley, 1979)*

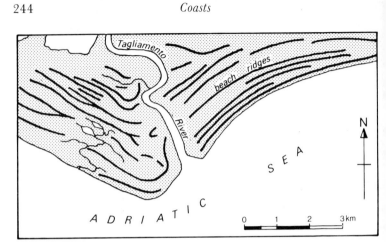

115   *Beach ridge patterns indicate symmetrical growth of the Tagliamento delta, Italy*

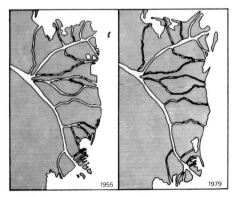

116   *Historical stages in the growth of the Kilia lobe of the Danube delta, Romania
        (based on data provided by Y. Shuisky, 1980)*

shoreline no longer receiving fluvial sediment may start to be eroded, as on the Rhône delta, following the decay of the Vieux Rhône and diminishing outflow from the Petit Rhône (Fig. 112). Lobes of sediment which had been built by these distributaries have been consumed by marine erosion, and the dominant SE waves have transported derived sandy material westwards to be built into depositional forelands at Pointe de Beauduc and Pointe de l'Espiguette respectively. Changes in delta configuration can sometimes be traced from successive maps and air photographs. Such evidence was used in the compilation of Fig. 116, which shows stages in the growth of the Danube delta since 1830. Nossin (1965) used cartographic records to reconstruct the evolution of the North Padang delta in Malaya since the early seventeenth century.

Erosion has been prevalent on the shores of the Nile delta since the beginning of the present century, and in recent decades it has been locally rapid, attaining 30 to 40 m per year near the Damietta mouth. This coastline was previously prograded by the recurrent delivery of Nile sediment to the coast by floodwaters, but the building of the dam at Aswan in 1902 and its subsequent enlargement in 1920 reduced runoff and sediment yield, and the addition of the high dam in 1964 has further depleted the supply of Nile sediment to the delta coastline. Erosion has thus been initiated (Orlova and Zenkovich, 1974), and protection works have become necessary (Khafagy and Manohar, 1979).

The modern Po delta has grown after a new outlet was cut in the late sixteenth century to divert the river away from the Venice region, where it threatened siltation of the lagoon. The Po branches into distributaries, and the seaward fringes of swampy deltaic islands are lined by transgressive sandy barriers; in recent decades, delta enlargement has ceased because of a diminishing sediment yield due to river impoundments and soil conservation works upstream. Growth has almost ceased on the Rhône delta, where dam construction upriver has reduced fluvial sediment yield from 11 to less than 5 million tonnes annually (Paskoff, 1981). On the other hand, the deltas on the north coast of Turkey are still receiving a large sediment yield, and are growing rapidly into the Black Sea.

The simplest deltas are those built by rivers entering tideless lakes. Where the lake level has fallen, and bordering deltas have emerged, it is possible to examine their sedimentary structure. The emerged delta that bordered the ancient 'Lake Bonneville'* consists of almost horizontal bottomset beds, which were laid down on the lake floor, inclined foreset beds (10°–25°), consisting of layers of sediment that were delivered progressively as the delta advanced, and horizontal topset beds, which form the upper surface (Gilbert, 1890). Deltas built up on sea coasts during and since Holocene marine submergence are more complicated than this and may not include foreset beds. Their sedimentary structures, inferred from borings, show intercalations of marine sediment deposited during episodes of marine transgression (Fig. 117). Such a delta has been built forward during phases of

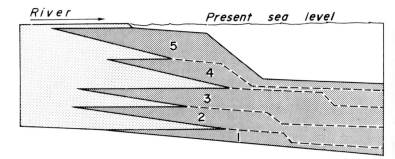

117   *The stratigraphy of a delta that has been subject to five successive marine transgressions, each marked by an intercalation of marine sediment. Renewed growth of the delta after each transgression has produced a wedge of fluvial sediment*

stillstand of sea level (or during episodes when sea level was falling), but at other times it has been submerged by a rising sea. Much of our knowledge of the oscillating transgression of the sea in late Pleistocene and Holocene times has been obtained from the stratigraphic evidence yielded by borings in deltas and coastal plains formed by deposition, notably on the Gulf Coast of the United States and in the Rhine delta region. In dealing with this kind of evidence, it is necessary to remember that the level of stratigraphic horizons within a delta may have been lowered, relative to present sea level, by compaction of under-lying sediments (especially peat and clay) and by the crustal

---

* Lake Bonneville is the name given to an extensive lake that existed in W Utah (U.S.A.) during Pleistocene times. This region has since become more arid and the lake is now represented by scattered remnants of which Great Salt Lake is the largest.

subsidence which has taken place in many deltaic regions. The stratigraphy of the Mississippi delta, for example, shows plunging formations equivalent to deposits on river terraces which border the valley upstream (Fig. 118), and sectors of this delta where continuing subsidence is not compensated by sedimentation become lagoon depressions, or are invaded by the sea. On the Niger delta a sequence of dead coralline banks, partly obscured by sediment on the sea floor, indicate stages in subsidence and lateral tilting during the past four thousand years (Allen and Wells, 1962). Subsidence along the northern flank of the Sepik delta in New Guinea has widened and deepened an old meandering channel to form the chain of lagoons known as the Murik Lakes. The volume of sediment deposited in these deltas in Holocene times is enormous: 2,800 km³ in the Mississippi delta, and 1,400 km³ in the lobate delta of the Niger.

118   *Plunging terraces traced into a delta, where borings have indicated deposits equivalent to those on the 1st and 2nd terraces upstream (based on Russell's interpretation of the Mississippi delta)*

The valley floors built up by deposition of sediment in drowned valley mouths are typically underlain by a deltaic stratigraphy, with interdigitation of fluvial, estuarine, and marine sediments. The sedimentary fill normally occupies a valley that was excavated by the river when it flowed out to lower sea levels during glacial phases of the Pleistocene period, and may include relics of materials deposited in these valleys during interglacial phases of high sea level, as well as the sediment deposited during and since the Holocene sea level rise.

It is not easy to discover how far the sea penetrated into river valleys during the Holocene marine submergence. Stratigraphic evidence, where available, is the most reliable indication, the extent of marine deposits beneath the valley floor marking the maximum extent of submergence. These deposits are overlain by fluvial sediments deposited by the river since the submergence came to an end. Often horizons of marine deposits pass laterally into estuarine, then fluvial deposits, and the limit reached by the sea can rarely be determined accurately. Where the valley sides have been cliffed, and are bordered by beach deposits containing marine fossils, it is evident that open water existed for a sufficient period for waves to attack the margins of a drowned valley, before river deposition built up the flood plains and deltas. In some valleys the maximum extent of submergence may be indicated by the form of the meandering river channel: upstream, where the valley floor was never submerged by the sea, meandering is often more intricate than in the lower reaches, where broad, sweeping channels wind across a valley floor that is strictly of deltaic origin.

Natural levees

Landforms of deltaic regions may include natural levees bordering river channels and backed by low-lying, often swampy or flooded depressions in the lower parts of river valleys. This topography is the outcome of an unequal building up (aggradation) of the flood plain, whereby sediment is deposited more rapidly in the zone immediately adjacent to the river channel than in the zone beyond. When a river rises and overflows its banks, the flow of water is most rapid along the line of the river channel and much slower on either side so that the coarser load of sand and silt carried by floodwaters is relinquished at the borders of the channel where water velocity diminishes, and only the finer clay particles are carried into the calmer water beyond. As natural levees are built up along the sides of the river channel, they develop gentle outward slopes, passing down to lateral depressions, known as levee-flank, backplain, or backswamp depressions in the Mississippi valley. After floods have occurred, water may persist in these depressions for a long time, particularly if the levees impinge locally on the valley side and enclose them, completely preventing down-valley drainage. The depressions are floored by clay deposits which settle from floodwaters, and are often occupied by swamp vegetation, which may build up peat deposits. Similar valley-floor features are found in

62   *The delta built by Macquarie Rivulet into Lake Illawarra, New South Wales (cf.
Fig. 105)*

SE Australia, where the rivers have regimes with marked seasonal variation and flooding occurs almost every year. In dry
years, repeated evaporation of water from enclosed backswamp
depressions leads to a concentration of salt, increasing soil salinity so that some of these backswamp depressions are occupied
by salt marshes, or even unvegetated saline flats. Deflation from
these dry depressions may lead to the building of silt or clay
dunes, as on the Senegal delta (Tricart, 1956), and seasonally dry
distributaries yield sand for local dune development.
   The process of deposition which produces natural levees
along the sides of a river channel also prolongs them at the
mouth of the river, providing wave and current scour does not
prevent this. In New South Wales, sedimentary jetties have

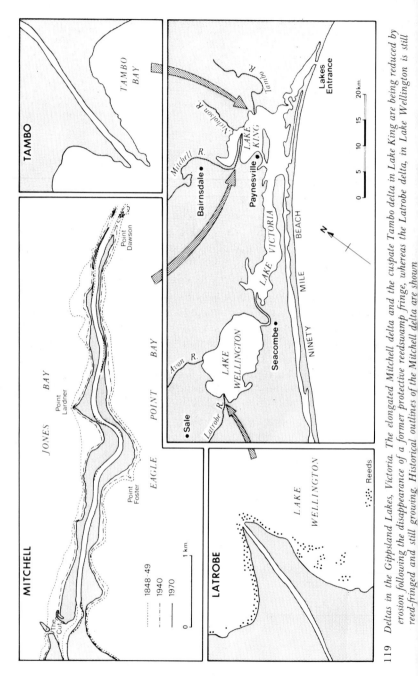

119 Deltas in the Gippsland Lakes, Victoria. The elongated Mitchell delta and the cuspate Tambo delta in Lake King are being reduced by erosion following the disappearance of a former protective reedswamp fringe, whereas the Latrobe delta, in Lake Wellington is still reed-fringed and still growing. Historical outlines of the Mitchell delta are shown

formed at the mouths of creeks opening into coastal lagoons. The delta of Macquarie Rivulet, in Lake Illawarra (Fig. 105), is curved and elongated, with a branched outlet (Plate 62), and similar features have developed at the mouths of Dora Creek in Lake Macquarie (Fig. 106) and Ourimbah Creek in the Tuggerah Lakes (Fig. 107). In the Gippsland Lakes (Fig. 119) the Latrobe delta is lobate, the Tambo delta cuspate, and the Mitchell delta consists of long silt jetties. The growth of these deltas has been assisted by the presence of shoreline reed-swamp, which traps and retains sediment deposited at the mouths of rivers during floods. Where the reed-swamp fringe has disappeared as the result of salinity increase, the deltaic sediment is no longer retained by shoreline vegetation, and waves are attacking the unprotected shores of the silt jetties, eroding their margins and dissecting them into a chain of islands. The Tambo delta and the Mitchell delta in Lake King show advanced stages in dissection, but the Latrobe and Avon deltas, in Lake Wellington, are still reed-fringed and still growing. Evidently the presence of reed-swamp influenced the pattern of sedimentation so that deltas were built at these river mouths, but when the reed fringe disappeared, the deltas were no longer stable, and erosion began to consume them (Bird, 1978a). Fig. 119 uses outlines from historical maps and early air photographs to trace stages in the shrinkage of this deltaic feature. This is clearly a special case. In general, abundance of sediment and absence of excessive wave and current scour are sufficient to ensure the formation of a delta.

IX

CORAL REEFS AND ATOLLS

Reefs built by coral and associated organisms occur extensively in tropical waters, and are widespread between latitudes 30°N and 30°S in the W parts of the Pacific, Indian, and Atlantic oceans. They are well developed in the Caribbean Sea, the Red Sea, and Indonesia. In this account, examples are drawn mainly from the reefs and atolls of the SW Pacific area, and around the coasts of Australia (Fig. 120) particularly off the E coast of Queensland where the Great Barrier Reefs extend from Torres Strait in the N to the Bunker and Capricorn groups in the S (latitude 24°S). Outlying reefs extend farther south, to the Middleton and Elizabeth atolls (29°-30°S) and the W coast of Lord Howe Island (32°S). There are scattered reefs off the N coast of Australia, and off the W coast of the continent they extend as far south as Houtman Abrolhos, in latitude 29°S (Fairbridge, 1967). Where reefs border the coast they are termed *fringing reefs*; where they lie offshore, enclosing a lagoon, they are known as *barrier reefs*; and where they encircle a lagoon, they are called *atolls* (Fig. 121). In addition there are isolated reef platforms of various shapes and sizes which do not fit any of these categories.

Reefs are mainly of biological origin, built by coral polyps, small marine organisms that take up calcium carbonate from sea water and grow into a variety of skeletal structures. Closely associated with these are small plants, the calcareous algae, which grow in and around the coral structures. Each set of organisms assists the other, the algae utilising much of the carbon dioxide released into the sea by coral respiration in the manufacture of food by plant photosynthesis; this in turn replenishes the oxygen dissolved in sea water, and thus helps to maintain a supply of oxygen for coral respiration. While coral is essential for reef-building, it generally forms only a small proportion of reef material. Algae, together with foraminifera, molluscs, other shelly organisms, and sedimentary fragments of shell and coral, fill in the skeletal coral structures to form a calcareous mass, which eventually, with partial solution and re-precipitation of calcium carbonate, becomes a massive reef limestone. There are also extensive sediments derived from

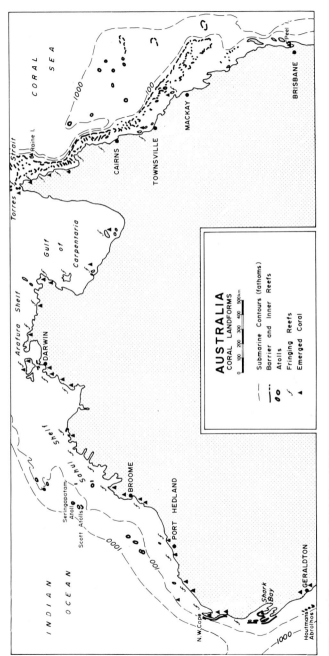

120 *Australian reefs. After Fairbridge, 1950*

AUSTRALIA
CORAL LANDFORMS

0   100   200   300   400   500 km

--- Submarine Contours (fathoms)
·ı· Barrier and Inner Reefs
ᴔ Atolls
ʃ Fringing Reefs
▲ Emerged Coral

121   *Reef landform types*

reef erosion banked against the flanks of the massive reef (Jones and Endean, 1977).

In addition to coral reefs there are various other organic reefs, notably the extensive oyster reefs built up by *Crassostrea virginica* off parts of the Gulf and Atlantic coasts of the United States, the small structures built by bryozoans, serpulids, and mussels on rocky or sandy foundations, and algal reefs associated with rocky shores. Protruding inter-tidal ledges built by algae in association with marine invertebrates are known as 'trottoirs' in the Mediterranean region.

Factors influencing reef development
Reef-building takes place in ocean areas where free-floating planktonic coral larvae are distributed by ocean currents and where ecological conditions permit the establishment and growth of coral and associated algae. An adequate supply of sunlight is essential for algal photosynthesis, and growth of coral is best in clear, warm water. Intensity of sunlight diminishes downwards into the sea, and although live corals have been found in exceptionally clear water at depths as great as 100 m, the maximum depth at which reefs are being built is rarely more than 50 m. In coastal waters, increased cloudiness due to land-derived sediment (chiefly silt and clay) in suspension reduces penetration by sunlight and impedes growth of reef-building organisms. Off river mouths, this cloudiness, together with the blanketing effects of deposits of inorganic sediment, often prevents the growth of reef-building organisms and breaks the continuity of fringing reefs. Corals can dispose of small accessions of sediment, but are choked by continued deposition of large quantities of detritus, or by heavy loads of sediment dumped suddenly from discharging flood waters. Some species are tolerant of muddy water: in Fiji a reef dominated by *Porites* spp. is still living off the mouth of the Mba River, Viti Levu, despite the recurrent outpouring of muddy floodwaters

after heavy rainfall in successive cyclones. In Indonesia, reefs are missing from coasts subject to repeated accessions of lava or ash from volcanic eruptions.

Coral growth is confined to warm seas, where the mean temperature of the coldest month (generally August in Austra- lia) does not fall below 18°C. Salinity must be within the range 27–38 parts per thousand, dilution by fresh water off river mouths contributing to the persistence of gaps in bordering reefs. Excessive salinity may explain why reefs are absent from certain parts of the coast such as Hamelin Pool, in Shark Bay (Western Australia), where salinity is up to 48 parts per thousand in summer. Where ecological conditions are favourable and there is an adequate supply of mineral nutrients in the sea water, reefs grow upwards until they form platforms that are exposed at low tide, but the corals cannot survive prolonged exposure to the atmosphere and they die off when the reef platform attains a level just above low water spring tide level. Algae (chiefly *Lithothamnion*) may then build up a slightly higher reef crest, awash at high tide (Stoddart, 1969). Reefs along the southern coasts of the Indonesian archipelago, exposed to rela- tively strong oceanic waves, have higher and wider algal rims than those in the more sheltered waters of the Java and Flores Seas.

Coral growth remains vigorous on the steep bordering slopes of reefs below low tide level. The best growth is where sea water is being circulated sufficiently to renew the supply of plankton, on which the coral polyps feed, and to maintain the supply of oxygen, particularly at night, when it is no longer replenished by algal photosynthesis. Where the slopes of reefs are exposed to strong wave action, as on the seaward flank of a barrier reef or the outward slope of an atoll, there is adequate circulation of sea water for vigorous coral growth, but the impact of waves tends to break off, or inhibit the formation of, the more intricate skeletal forms of coral, so that the seaward slopes often consist of a more compact mass of growing coral. On the leeward side, in more sheltered waters, a greater variety of growth forms is found, and some of these broken off during occasional storms are cast up on to the reef platform as sand and gravel fragments, and occasionally the large round boulders that Matthew Flind- ers termed 'negro-heads'. Blocks measuring several cubic metres thrown up on to the Great Barrier Reef during storm surges may persist for decades, even centuries; they are gradually undermined by notches formed by solution, and dissected karstically by rain water and sea spray. Great quantities of broken reef material are banked up as sedimentary deposits on reef flanks and on lagoon floors, and some of this material is deposited as a veneer on the platform exposed at low tide, and may be built up by waves to form islands surmounting the reef and extending above high tide level. Off the Queensland coast these

63   *Snapper Island, a high, reef-fringed island off Port Douglas, Queensland*

are known as 'low islands' to distinguish them from the 'high islands' of non-coralline rock that are also present (Plate 63). 'Low islands' will be discussed later.

During the past two decades, the crown-of-thorns sea-star (*Acanthaster planci*) has developed in plague proportions on parts of the Great Barrier Reef, and has extensively killed the coral. Broken coralline debris is unusually abundant on and around the reefs affected, and it is possible that such biological changes may occasionally generate large amounts of broken reef material for local deposition. The crown-of-thorns outbreak now appears to be a cyclic phenomenon that will eventually fade away, allowing the reef-building corals to revive and resume their former role.

Fringing reefs

The simplest reef landforms are fringing reefs, built upwards and outwards in the shallow seas that border continental or island shores. These consist of a platform at low tide level which is similar in many ways to the low tide shore platforms found on cliffed limestone coasts (Chapter IV), except that fringing reefs have been built up, rather than cut down, to this level. The comparison is even closer when coastal emergence has exposed a fringing reef into which a shore platform has been cut. Fringing reefs are usually thin, resting on a rocky foundation, and are generally being widened by the continuing growth of coral at their seaward margins. They have developed during the present stillstand of sea level on coastal sectors ecologically suitable for colonisation by reef-building coral communities: where conditions have become adverse they are dead and disintegrating, but incipient fringing reefs are rare, presumably because ecological transitions from adverse to suitable conditions for coral establishment have been exceptional within the past few centuries.

Some fringing reefs, especially in East Africa, have a higher outer segment backed by a 'boat channel' a few hundred metres wide and up to 10 m deep. At low tide the outer segment is exposed, and the boat channel becomes a lagoon; at high tide the whole area is submerged, and oceanic waves wash through to the coastline. There is greater vigour of coral and algal growth at the outer margins of such a reef, but this cannot explain the boat channel unless there has also been a relative rise of sea level.

An intermittent fringing reef extends along the coast of Queensland, N of Cairns. The reef platform adjoining the coast is generally strewn with sand, partly of terrigenous origin, and there are patches of mangrove swamp bordering the shoreline near high tide mark. Live coral is confined to the outer edge which is briefly exposed at low tide. In some cases the fringing reef was formerly a nearshore reef, which became attached to the coast as the result of depositional progradation of the adjacent coastline.

Several of the high islands off the Queensland coast also have fringing reefs (Plate 63). They are present on the shores of Lizard Island, on the islands of the Flinders Group, and on several of the islands in the Whitsunday Group, notably Hayman Island. Fringing reefs also occur on the N coast of Australia, notably on the shores of Arnhem Land, around Darwin, and between Port Hedland and North West Cape. They are missing from swampy sections of the shores of the Gulf of Carpentaria and other northern gulfs which are receiving deposits of land-derived sediment. In these sectors they give place to tidal flats of the kind described by Russell and McIntire (1966).

Offshore reefs

Reefs that lie offshore pose other problems. They include atolls, barrier reefs (roughly parallel to the coastline and separated from it by a relatively shallow lagoon), and isolated reef platforms. Each type is represented in Australian coastal waters. The Great Barrier Reefs extend for about 2,000 km from N to S off the Queensland coast. In the north they consist of an outer barrier reef (a chain of elongated or crescentic reefs with intervening gaps, generally about a kilometre wide) in the N, lying about 130 km off the tip of Cape York Peninsula, about 50 km off Port Stewart, less than 15 km off Cape Melville, and about 56 km seaward from Cooktown. Off Cairns there is a broad transverse passage known as Trinity Opening, which allows ocean waves to penetrate to the mainland coast but the outer barrier reef reappears farther south, diverging from the mainland coast until it lies about 100 km off Rockhampton. At the southern end it breaks up into the scattered reef platforms of the Capricorn and Bunker groups, with Lady Elliot Island the southernmost reef, just S of latitude 24°S. It is not clear whether the southern limit of reef building in these coastal waters is determined by the temperature of the sea or by the inhibiting effects on coral growth of the sand that drifts northwards across the sea floor from Fraser Island.

The outer barrier plunges steeply (40°–50°) on its seaward side to water more than 1,800 m deep off the northern section, shallowing to about 180 m S of the Trinity Opening. Coral is growing to a depth of about 45 m on this seaward slope, which is marked by patterns of grooves and spurs (buttresses) aligned at right angles to the reef edge. These serrations are common on reef margins exposed to strong wave action, but their mode of formation is not clearly understood. The grooves often show evidence of scouring by swash and backwash, and abrasion by waves armed with reef debris, and the spurs are crowned by a rich compact coral and algal growth, but the differentiating mechanism is obscure: the problem is analogous to that of explaining other rhythmic shore forms, such as beach cusps (p. 146). At low tide the outer barrier reef is exposed as a chain of elongated platforms, up to 25 km long and up to a kilometre wide, typically with an outer rim on which the surf breaks, a shallow moat, and an algal crest, beyond which the reef slopes gently (5°–10°) into the quieter waters of the lagoon. Yonge Reef (Fig. 127) is a typical outer barrier segment, crescentic in form, with recurves at the N and S ends bordering gaps in the reef. The recurved form is evidently analogous to the recurved spits that border gaps in between barrier islands of sand or shingle, with outlines determined by refraction of waves that enter the gap (Chapter V). The gaps may commemorate the sites of river outlets at low sea level stages. They persist because the rising and falling tides create a strong scouring current which prevents them from being sealed off by coral growth and reef sedimentation.

In one section, SE of Cape Melville, there is a double barrier, with parallel reefs separated by a lagoon about 8 km wide. The inner barrier is less regular in form than the chain of outer barrier reefs, and may be a relic of an earlier barrier reef outflanked by the enlargement of a younger outer reef.

The lagoon between the outer barrier reef and the mainland coast of Queensland is generally between 18 and 45 m deep, with a somewhat featureless floor, because the deposition of land-derived sediment washed in by rivers and reef-derived sediment washed in by the sea has smoothed over any inequalities. Lagoon-floor sediments behind such reefs show a high proportion of calcareous organic sediment (typically 80 to 90 per cent) with land-derived sediment mainly confined to the zone close to the shore. The width of a lagoon behind a barrier reef is related to the pre-existing sea floor topography and the rate and pattern of upward growth of the reef during Holocene submergence. Coral is growing within the lagoon off the Queensland coast to depths of about 12 m, and columns of reef limestone have grown up from the lagoon floor to form patch reef platforms a little above low tide level. These include the scattered platforms of the Bunker and Capricorn Groups, and the complex pattern of reefs that border the Steamer Channel N of Cairns. The shapes of these reef platforms are related to patterns of waves generated by the prevailing SE trade winds in Queensland coastal waters; several have a horseshoe form, with arms trailing northwestwards, away from these prevailing winds (Fig. 122). Cairns Reef has this form, and a more advanced stage is represented by Pickersgill Reef, the arms of which have curved in almost to enclose a shallow lagoon. In some respects, Pickersgill Reef resembles an incomplete atoll, but the lagoon is

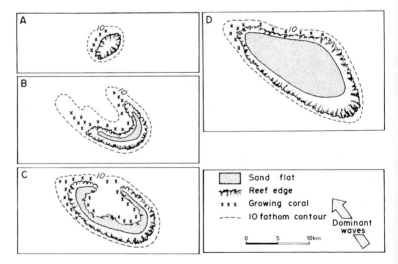

122   *Evolution of horseshoe reefs. Initial reef patches (A), common in coastal waters off Queensland (Fig. 127), tend to grow into forms with marginal deflection by the dominant waves. Stage B is exemplified by Cairns Reef, stage C by Pickersgill Reef, off NE Queensland. Eventually a larger reef platform may develop (D). After Fairbridge, 1950*

only a few feet deep, whereas the atolls commonly found in tropical seas enclose lagoons that are generally at least 35 m deep (Wiens, 1962).

Other major barrier reefs include those that run parallel to the coasts of New Caledonia for over 600 km, enclosing a lagoon up to 12 km wide and 100 m deep; the Great Sunda Reef south-east of Kalimantan; and the Great Sea Reef, 260 km long, to the north of Fiji.

Atolls are annular reefs built up to sea level, typically circular or ovoid in plan. Fairbridge (1967) recognised three kinds of true atolls: *oceanic atolls* which have localised, generally volcanic, foundations at depths exceeding 550 m, *shelf atolls* which rise from the continental shelf, with foundations at depths of less than 550 m, and *compound atolls* where the ring-shaped reef surrounds or encloses relics of earlier atoll formations. Oceanic atolls are common in the W Pacific, and are present in the Coral Sea and the N Tasman Sea, including Middleton and Elizabeth Atolls. Shelf atolls are found off the N coast of Australia, where barrier reefs have not developed. Seringapatam, 460 km north of Broome, is an excellent example rising abruptly from a depth of almost 550 m near the outer edge of a broad, sloping continental shelf. The enclosing reef is about 900 m wide, and the lagoon, 9.6 km long and 6.4 km broad, has an average depth of 35 m. Scott Reefs, not far away, consist of a similar enclosed atoll and a second atoll that is incomplete, with the superficial form of a horseshoe reef. Water more than 180 m deep surrounds and separates the two reefs, but the enclosed and partly enclosed lagoons have floors at a depth of 35–45 m. Shelf atolls are also well developed in the Indonesian region, especially in the Flores Sea. Compound atolls are represented by the Houtman Abrolhos Group, which consists of a complex of reef platforms, with remnants of emerged reefs of Pleistocene age. Typical features of an oceanic atoll are shown in Fig. 123. The reef flat on the windward side is often wider, with a *Lithothamnion* rampart in the breaker zone, and sometimes one or more low islands of coral debris. Outlets to the ocean are usually on the leeward side. The lagoon floor is generally a smooth depositional surface, from which pinnacles and ridges of live coral may protrude (Fig. 124). There are, however, many variations as indicated by the many detailed studies of atolls recorded in the *Atoll Research Bulletin*.

Small-scale atoll-like annular reefs up to a kilometre in diameter and enclosing lagoons less than 20 m deep are known as *faros* in equatorial regions (especially in the Maldive Islands), and possibly originated from living reefs that persisted through the Last Glacial low sea level phase in these low latitudes. Still smaller are the *microatolls*, intertidal ring-shaped organic reef

123   *Kapingamarangi Atoll, Caroline Islands. After Wiens, 1962*

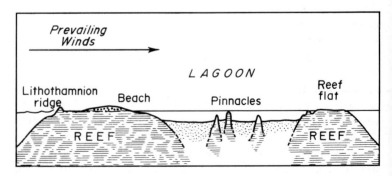

124   *Diagrammatic section across a typical atoll*

structures, typically 1 to 6 m in diameter, with slightly raised rims of living coral, built up to about low neap tide level, and standing above the general level of a reef flat.

Origins of reef forms
The central problem of reef development is the upward growth of reefs from below the depths at which reef-building corals now live. The foundations of barrier reefs and atolls, if not of fringing reefs, are well below the present limit of coral growth, and yet the formation of coral structures has been essential for their construction. In 1835 Charles Darwin, during his voyage in the *Beagle*, proposed the subsidence theory, which regarded barrier reefs and atolls as the outcome of upward growth from ancient fringing reefs bordering islands and continental margins that had since subsided gradually beneath the oceans. In these terms, the outer barrier reefs off the Queensland coast commemorate the alignment of a former land margin that has subsided tectonically. Atolls, some of which still have a central island ('almost-atolls'), are thus regarded as the built-up fringing reefs encircling islands lowered by crustal subsidence: an island with a fringing reef subsides to become an island surrounded by a barrier reef and enclosing a lagoon, and finally an atoll, with the central island lost from view (Fig. 121). The reefs we see are those that have been able to maintain upward growth as subsidence took place. Those that have been carried down too rapidly are now submerged beneath the depth at which reef-building organisms can live. Such submerged barrier reefs and atolls have been detected by soundings in the ocean particularly off the SE coast of New Guinea and in the Coral Sea. Many of the sea-mounts which rise from the deep floor of the Pacific Ocean have been planed off to form flat-topped *guyots* with surfaces at depths of 550–900 m. As some bear fossil corals of Cretaceous age, they have evidently subsided below the limit of reef growth during Tertiary and Quaternary times.

The subsidence theory provided a better explanation for atolls than earlier theories of cup-shaped coral growth (Chamisso) or upgrowth from rims of submarine volcanic craters (Lyell). Later theories included Murray's idea that atolls formed after corals had colonised submarine banks built up to a suitable depth by sea floor accretion or uplift, and Agassiz' suggestion that they developed as a veneer on shallow platforms produced by planation of volcanoes. Davis (1928), reviewing the various ideas, preferred Darwin's theory of upgrowing reefs on subsiding foundations, noting Dana's observation that coastlines bordered by barrier reefs, as in Queensland, show abundant evidence of submergence by the sea, in the form of inlets, embayments, and drowned valley mouths. The general absence of cliffing on such coasts is evidence that the barrier reefs grew up as the continental shelf subsided, so that the coast was consistently protected from the action of strong ocean waves. This would explain the contrast between the Queensland coast, with its numerous promontories and 'high islands' offshore, and the New South Wales coast, farther S and beyond the protection of the barrier reefs. On the Queensland coast, the limited cliffing is clearly related to waves generated by the prevailing SE trade winds in coastal waters behind the Great Barrier Reefs. On the New South Wales coast, where submergence is equally in evidence, there are fewer offshore islands and the headlands are more strongly cliffed. It is evident that the Queensland coast has never been exposed to the full force of ocean waves that have shaped the coastal landforms of New South Wales, and the building of a barrier reef during a phase of subsidence provides an explanation for this. Where coastlines bordered by barrier reefs have fringing reefs as well (as in NE Queensland) it is necessary to regard the latter as secondary forms, initiated along the coast after the submergence which led to the upgrowth of the barrier reef came to an end (Davis, 1928).

Many of the features that Darwin ascribed to subsidence can equally well be explained by a rising sea level, and, with this in mind, Daly (1934) proposed a glacial control theory to account for reef development. Major glacio-eustatic changes of sea level have taken place during Pleistocene and Holocene times (Chapter III), and when sea level fell, possibly as much as 140 m during the Last Glacial phase, any reefs previously formed must have been exposed to the atmosphere and eroded. As ocean temperatures also fell, the growth of coral could have continued only in the warmer parts of the oceans, probably in latitudes to 10°–15° N and S. The present patterns of reef landforms are thus regarded as the outcome of reef building during and since the Holocene marine transgression, and the barrier reefs and atolls we see are those that grew rapidly enough to keep pace with the rising sea, or at least to remain within the zone where ecological conditions permit coral and algal growth. The narrowness (400–800 m) of many reefs could be a function of relatively rapid upward growth, of the order of 120 m in the last 20,000 years (cf. Fig. 15). In support of his hypothesis, Daly claimed that depths of lagoons enclosed by reefs showed a considerable degree of accordance, few being more than 75 m deep. They originated, he suggested, as reef platforms planed off by the sea when it stood at a lower level. When the marine transgression began, live coral at the margins of the planed-off surface developed an encircling reef, which grew upwards as sea level rose. Fringing reefs, in these terms, have developed only since the Holocene marine transgression established the general outlines of the present coast, although some of them probably embody the relics of Pleistocene fringing reefs which developed at an earlier stage close to the present shore level, and escaped destruction during low sea level phases.

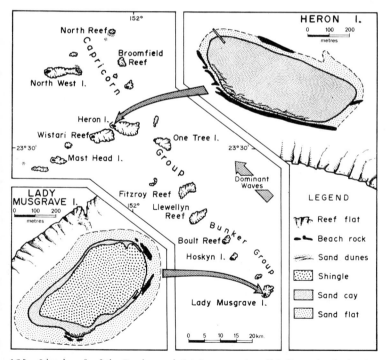

125 *Island reefs of the Bunker and Capricorn groups, off S Queensland, showing Heron Island (a sand cay) and Lady Musgrave Island (a shingle cay). After Steers, 1937*

Further evidence of the origin of atolls and barrier reefs has been obtained from deep borings in reef structures. In 1926 a boring at Michaelmas Cay (off Cairns) proved reef material to a depth of 123 m, resting upon unconsolidated sand, and a similar boring at Heron Island (Fig. 125) in 1937 penetrated 154 m of reef material before entering sand. In 1959 a much deeper boring on nearby Wreck Island enabled samples to be dated from their content of fossil foraminifera. The top 121 m consisted of Holocene reef debris, beneath which Pleistocene sand extended to 162 m, Tertiary deposits, including ancient fragments of coral, to 422 m, then Tertiary sandstone and siltstone to 547 m, where older volcanic basement rocks were encountered. Deep borings on Bikini and Eniwetok Atolls in the Marshall Islands in 1952 indicated a great thickness of shallow coralline materials resting on a volcanic basement about 1,400 m below present sea level. The sequence represented reef growth since Eocene times, interrupted by phases of subaerial exposure

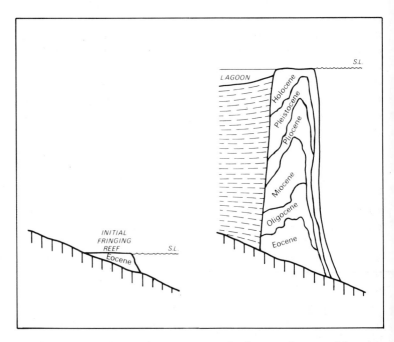

126   *A fringing reef initiated in Eocene times has become a barrier reef formed in several stages, built up in high sea level phases and subject to karstic dissection in low sea level phases, through a period of overall subsidence*

indicated by land snails and weathering features. As the foundations lie deeper than any possible glacio-eustatic lowering of sea
level, Darwin's theory of tectonic subsidence of the ocean floor
is necessary to explain these reefs; but the subaerial phases
represent accompanying oscillations of sea level, especially in
Quaternary times. Such reefs must have been exposed and
shaped into karstic ridges by rainwater solution and marginal
marine erosion during low sea level episodes, then submerged,
recolonised and recapped by coralline growth in succeeding
phases of sea level rise. Many more borings and stratigraphical
analyses of reef formations are needed to decipher this alternating sequence, but it is evident that the reefs we now see were
built up to their present level during and since the Holocene
marine transgression, when a modern coral veneer was plastered on to the stumps of earlier reef formations developed
during high interglacial stands of sea level during Pleistocene
times, and dissected during low sea level episodes (Fig. 126).

A satisfactory explanation of reef landforms evidently
requires a combination of Darwin's subsidence theory (to
account for the depth of reef foundations) and Daly's glacial
control theory (since sea levels have certainly risen and fallen
during the period of reef building). The allocation of the respective roles of sea level rise, sea floor subsidence, the provision of
foundations suitable for reef building, and the extent of ecological conditions favourable to reef growth, may be possible when
more detailed studies have been made of the distribution and
stratigraphy of reef structures.

The distribution of reefs raises a number of questions. On the
world scale the pattern reflects the distribution of coral larvae
by ocean currents, the paucity of reefs in the E Atlantic and
Pacific areas being related to the westward flow of equatorial
currents, and the richness of the reefs off Queensland being
related to abundant larval supply in currents arriving from the
W Pacific and the Coral Sea. It is more difficult to account for
the poor development of coral reefs off the W coast of Australia,
where the reefs parallel to the mainland coast are submerged
ridges of aeolian calcarenite with only a veneer and fringe of
living coral and calcareous algae, similar to the sandstone reefs
off NE Brazil. Fairbridge (1967) thought that here, too, the supply
of coral larvae had been poor, both the northward summer
current and the southward winter current arriving from reefless

or relatively reefless ocean areas. The prevailing offshore winds may have helped keep away the coral larvae, and a further limiting factor may be the relatively low nutrient status of the sea off the low-lying, semi-arid coast of Western Australia compared with the steep, high-runoff coast of Queensland. The patchy development of reefs off N Australia may be due to excessive subsidence in the Timor Sea. A submerged barrier reef exists off the Sahul Shelf, indicating that sea floor subsidence has been too rapid for reef growth to be maintained.

Reefs and platforms built largely by algae have been described from subtropical coasts close to, and beyond, the limits of coral growth, as in Florida and Brazil, around the Mediterranean, and in the hypersaline waters of Shark Bay, W Australia. In addition to promoting carbonate precipitation from sea water, some algae have sediment-trapping structures.

Emerged reefs

The fact that reef platforms are built up to a strict level in relation to low tide makes them good indicators of emergence where they are found at a higher level, but it is necessary to decide whether this emergence is the result of tectonic uplift or of eustatic lowering of sea level. The latter explanation is preferred by Fairbridge for the emerged reef that forms part of the Pelsart Group in Houtman Abrolhos, off the coast of Western Australia, which was evidently built to the level of a Late Pleistocene interglacial (or interstadial) stillstand of the sea about 7.5 m above present sea level. It is bordered by modern reef platforms, which are still developing just above low tide level. Similar emerged Pleistocene reefs have been found farther S, on Rottnest Island, beyond the present range of reef-building.

Emerged reefs extending up to 3 m above present low tide level have been reported at various places around the Australian coast, including the shores of Melville Island, the reefs in Torres Strait, and several islands off the Queensland coast, notably Raine Island. They have generally been regarded as reef platforms built up to a slightly higher sea level, then laid bare as a consequence of a succeeding drop in sea level. Steers (1937) reported emerged reef platforms between 1.5 and 3 m above low tide level from islands off the NE coast of Queensland: for example, on Enn Island (inset, Fig. 127), where a raised reef up to 2.75 m above the present reef platform is being undercut

127   *Reefs off NE Queensland. Inset: Enn Island, a Low wooded island. After Steers, 1937*

marginally by wave action. Benches have been observed at a similar level, cut in older non-coralline rocks on the shores of islands off this coast, and also on the flanks of headlands, notably Cape Flattery. In his analysis of the reef landforms of Australian coastal waters, Fairbridge (1967) found evidence of emerged reef platforms corresponding with the sequence of Holocene higher sea levels he had previously inferred from terraces cut in aeolian calcarenite at 3, 1.5 and 0.5 m above present low tide level on the coast of Western Australia. The validity of these Recent higher sea levels was discussed in Chapter III; if the Holocene marine transgression attained present sea level without ever exceeding it, it is necessary to find some other explanation for these emerged reef platforms. Two possibilities remain. The reef platforms may have been built up to higher sea levels during Pleistocene times, but if they are really of Holocene age they must have been raised out of the sea by tectonic movements during the past few thousand years.

The intricacies of the problem are well illustrated by the question of the emerged reef that borders Peel Island, in Moreton Bay (27°30'S), S of the present limit of coral growth in Queensland coastal waters. It is tempting to regard this as a reef platform that had been built up to the surface of a higher (and probably a warmer) sea when the Holocene marine transgression attained a maximum level. A radiocarbon date for a sample of dead coral placed it at 3,710 ± 250 years B.P., but critics have questioned the validity of datings of emerged coral. The Peel Island coral may owe its emergence to localised tectonic uplift. Alternatively, it may be a much older reef platform that was built up in Pleistocene times to the level of a higher (and warmer) interglacial or interstadial sea. Near Tokyo uplifted Holocene coral formations are found well to the north of living coastal reefs, implying a similar alternation in the limits of Holocene coral growth in the north Pacific.

Examples of emerged reefs that have certainly been elevated by tectonic movements are found on the mountain slopes of NE New Guinea where reefs extend more than 1,500 m above sea level, far above the levels attained by any previous eustatic movements of the sea. They rest unconformably on an uplifted sea floor, and are being rapidly consumed by subaerial processes of denudation, notably solution by rainwater. On the coast of the Huon peninsula a stairway of emerged reefs forms terraces which diverge laterally across an axis of upwarping, attaining a maximum elevation of about 750 m in the vicinity of the Tewai gorge. A similar sequence of uplifted fringing reefs is seen on the tilted coral cap of the island of Barbados. Christmas Island, 320 km S of Java, is an emerged atoll 390 m high, uplifted tectonically to such an extent that underlying Eocene marine limestones are exposed. The Loyalty Islands, NE of New

Caledonia, include uplifted atolls such as Maré, where the former lagoon floor is an interior plain surrounded by an even-crested rim of reef limestone 30 m high, the steep outer coast-line showing 15 terraces indicative of stages in its uplift, and Uvéa, which has been intermittently tilted during upheaval so that the terraced eastern rim has emerged while the western rim, submerged, has a newer loop of developing reefs. Emerged reef landforms such as these are being attacked marginally by marine erosion processes, with the result that low tide shore platforms are being developed similar to those that border Australian calcarenite coasts (Chapter IV). The Isle of Pines, S of New Caledonia, is fringed by emerged reefs with typical notch-and-visor coastal profiles, and a shore platform that is being extended seaward by the addition of a modern fringing reef.

Evidence of lower stillstands of sea level is less easily obtained from within reef landforms, but platforms developed during such episodes may be indicated in borings by unconformities, weathered layers, or horizons of reef sediment. That reef plat-forms are quickly responsive to sea level changes is shown by the renewed upward growth of coral on reefs in Houtman Abrolhos, W.A., as a result of a relative rise of sea level.

Islands on reef platforms
In addition to islands formed by the emergence of reefs, various kinds of 'low island' have been built up on reef platforms by accumulation of sand, shingle, and boulders formed from reef debris that has been eroded by wave action and cast up on the platform. Some of these low islands are built of sediment der-ived from the destruction of emerged reefs, but many are not, and it is clear that although emergence would facilitate their development, it is by no means essential, for they can be built without any change in the relative level of the sea. A variety of carbonate sediments make up the depositional features on these islands, including large lumps of broken reef material, sticks of staghorn coral, discoidal *Halimeda* shingle, the grits and sands into which coralline material disintegrates, and fine-grained carbonate muds.

The simplest kinds of low island are exemplified on the patch reef platforms of the Bunker and Capricorn groups off the Queensland coast (Fig. 125). The prevailing winds here are the SE trades, and the islands have generally been built near the NW

64   *Beach rock exposed on the shore of a sand cay at Low Isles, off the N Queensland coast*

65   *An aerial view of Heron Island, a sand cay on a reef platform off the coast of S Queensland (L. & D. Keen Pty Ltd)*

corner of the reef platform, because debris eroded from the reef is washed across the platform by waves from the SE at high tide. Refraction of waves around the reef platform produces a convergence on the lee side, building up waves in such a way that they prevent the reef debris from being swept over the lee edge of the platform. At first the island is nothing more than a sandbank or a heap of coral shingle awash at high tide, but gradually the sediment accumulates, and once it has been built above high tide level, it is colonised by grasses and shrubs, and then by trees, notably palms (*Pisonia* and *Pandanus* species), and *Casuarina*. An island of this type is termed a cay. It is often elongated at right angles to the prevailing winds, but its configuration is subject to change as erosion and deposition alternate on its shores.

Between high and low tide levels, sand and shingle are often cemented by secondary deposition of calcium carbonate in the zone of repeated wetting and drying. The sand forms the compact sandstone layer known as beach rock (Plate 64), described in Chapter V, whereas the shingle becomes a lithified conglomerate. The greater resistance of these formations stabilises a

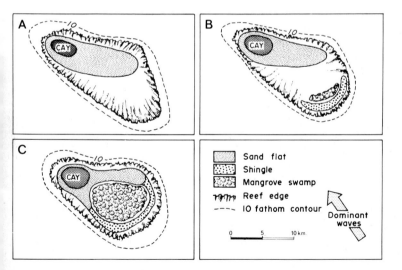

128 *Evolution of a low wooded island on a reef platform. A, platform with sand cay (e.g. Fife Island); B, addition of shingle ridges on seaward side; C, development of a mangrove swamp (e.g. Enn Island; Low Isles)*

cay to a certain extent, although waves generated during tropical cyclones may still sweep it away, or modify its outline, leaving only the patterns of eroded beach rock or shingle conglomerate to commemorate its former configuration.

The Bunker and Capricorn groups are not protected from ocean waves by any barrier reef. On the Bunker Group, exposure to ocean waves is evidently responsible for the predominance of coarse shingle over sand in such islands as Lady Musgrave Island (Fig. 125), while on the less exposed platforms of the Capricorn Group, sand cays such as Heron Island (Fig. 125 and Plate 65) are more common. Both these islands show evidence of slight changes of configuration, their former outlines being marked by lines of beach rock, and on Heron Island wind action has built some of the eroded coral sand into low dunes.

More complex low islands are found off NE Queensland, on reef platforms in the lagoon N of Cairns (Fig. 127). In addition to sand cays similar to Heron Island (Fife Island, N of Port Stewart, and Green Island, off Cairns, are examples of these), there are islands consisting of a sand cay on the leeward (NW) side, a shingle embankment on the windward side, and an

66   *Low Isles, a low wooded island off Port Douglas, Queensland, showing the shingle rampart on the SE shore in the foreground, the mangrove swamp, the lagoon, and the sand cay on which the lighthouse stands*

129   *Section across a low wooded island on a reef platform*

intervening depression, or shallow lagoon, in which mangrove swamps (chiefly the red mangrove *Rhizophora*, but some of the smaller white mangrove, *Avicennia*, marginally) have become established. These are known as 'low wooded islands' (Figs. 128, 129), and Enn Island (Fig. 127) and Low Isles (Plate 66) are good examples. Their development is evidently related to the greater shelter afforded by the outer barrier reef here, compared with the Capricorn and Bunker groups. Sand cays develop first, on the leeward side, and then shingle ridges are thrown up on the windward side, built from debris eroded from the edge of the reef platform. Mangroves then colonise the intervening depression and there is evidence that they 'dig themselves in' as organic acids exuded from the roots corrode the underlying reef limestone, replacing it with soft carbonaceous mud. In some cases there are several shingle ridges; the older ridges are dark in colour and largely cemented as conglomerate, but the younger are white or cream, and relatively loose. Addition of such freshly-formed coralline debris is often a consequence of tropical cyclones.

It is conceivable that much of the coral shingle on these low wooded islands was formed as wave action destroyed reefs that had previously been built up, or lifted tectonically, above present sea level, but Stoddart (1965) has shown that it is not necessary to invoke Holocene emergence, either tectonic or eustatic, to account for the distribution of cays and low wooded islands off the Queensland coast. They are related to wave energy conditions. On the outer reefs, in a high wave energy environment, these islands are not formed. The inner reefs, partly protected from ocean waves, have a limited fetch and a medium wave energy environment conducive to sand cay formation by refracted waves generated by local winds. The reef platforms in the Steamer Channel are in deep water with a relatively broad fetch over which the SE trade winds can generate waves strong enough to build shingle ramparts on the windward side and cays on the leeward side. Similar patterns of cays and low wooded islands occur in similar conditions of wave energy variation in the reefs off British Honduras.

These low islands are by no means stable features. During exceptional storms they are much reduced, displaced, or even swept completely off the reef platform. Their reconstruction in similar, if not identical, patterns is a relatively slow process; it can be studied by making repeated surveys of particular islands. On Low Isles, such surveys have shown that changes in configuration resulting from accretion during relatively calm conditions and erosion during a few severe storms. In Fiji the coralline cay of Makuluva off Suva has migrated NW across the reef flat; the windward (SE) coast has been cut back, so that lighthouse foundations and water tanks stand offshore, while the leeward coast has a broad prograding beach. Stoddart (1965) made a detailed study of the effects of Hurricane Hattie (October 1961) on the atolls and barrier reef islands off the British Honduras coast, comparing their subsequent configuration with surveys of their physiography and vegetation made in 1959–61. The hurricane swept westwards across the reefs towards the coast S of Belize, accompanied by gusts exceeding 320 km/hr. A 72 km wide storm surge attained up to 4.5 m above normal high water. Reef islands which had a dense littoral vegetation were modified less than those on which the natural vegetation had been cleared and replaced by coconut plantations: the former were eroded on the windward side with shingle and coral debris piled up against the vegetation, but the latter were more severely damaged, and seven cays were swept away completely. Stoddart estimated that the natural restoration of damaged areas would take between 25 and 30 years. However, studies of cays in the Great Barrier Reef region (Stoddart and Steers, 1977) have shown a prevalence of erosion on their coastlines in recent decades, confirmed by extensive outlying exposures of beach rock: in general, these sandy cays have been diminishing in size, perhaps as the result of a sea level rise.

In many respects these low islands are similar to the spits and barriers built by coastal deposition as described in Chapter V; their distinctive features are largely a response to the special environment of the reef platforms on which they have been built.

X

CLASSIFICATION OF COASTAL LANDFORMS

Various attempts have been made to classify coastal landforms (including shores and shoreline features), but none of them has been entirely successful. This is partly because of a widespread belief in the superiority of genetic classifications, in terms of the origin of the landforms, over purely descriptive classifications, in terms of landforms as observed: cliffed coasts, delta coasts, mangrove coasts, and so on. The difficulty is that a genetic classification can only be applied satisfactorily when the mode of origin of coastal landforms is known; the attempt to use particular types or associations of landforms as indicators of particular modes of origin has frequently led to errors that have been revealed by subsequent coastal research.

130   *The Kimberley coast, NW Australia, a ria coastline with intervening ridges and promontories related to the geological strike*

One of the early attempts at coastal classification was that put forward by Suess (1906). He distinguished 'Atlantic' coasts, which run transverse to the general trend of geological structures, from 'Pacific' coasts, which run parallel to structural trends. The former are characteristic of the Atlantic shores of Europe; the latter of the Pacific coast of North America. In Australia, the Atlantic type is exemplified by the coast between Broome and Darwin, particularly around Yampi Sound and the Buccaneer Archipelago (Fig. 130), and the Pacific type, appropriately, by the Pacific coast of New South Wales, which is parallel to the N–S strike of the rocks of the Eastern Highlands.

An updated version of the Suess scheme has been proposed by Inman and Nordstrom (1971), who devised a geophysical classification based on plate tectonics, whereby the earth's crust is seen as a pattern of plates separated by zones of spreading and zones of convergence. A distinction is made between collision coasts (plate-edge coasts) at zones of convergence and trailing-edge coasts (plate-embedded coasts) retreating from the zones where crustal spreading is in progress. The former are typically steep and tectonically active, with structures parallel to the coast (cf. Pacific coasts), the latter gentler and more stable, often with transverse structure (cf. Atlantic coasts). These are broad-scale classifications, however, dealing with first-order (continental) features (ca. 10^3 km long $\times$ 10^2 km wide $\times$ 10 km high) whereas coastal geomorphologists are usually concerned with second-order features (ca. 10^2 km long $\times$ 10 km wide $\times$ 1 km high) such as deltaic structures, and coastline features of higher order.

Another method of classification distinguishes coasts formed by submergence from coasts formed by emergence. This distinction was made by Gulliver (1899), and developed into a genetic classification of *shorelines* by Johnson (1919), who proposed four categories:

1. *Shorelines of submergence*
2. *Shorelines of emergence*
3. *Neutral shorelines*, with forms due neither to submergence nor emergence, but to deposition or tectonic movement: delta shorelines, alluvial plain shorelines, outwash plain shorelines, volcano shorelines, and fault shorelines.
4. *Compound shorelines*, which have an origin combining two or more of the preceding categories.

There are difficulties in applying this classification, particularly if it is restricted to shorelines as previously defined ('the water's edge, migrating to and fro with the tide'). Johnson apparently took a wider view than this, including offshore barriers as shoreline features, and his scheme may be more conveniently considered as a classification of coasts. Difficulties remain, however, for most coasts show evidence of both emergence, following high sea levels in interglacial phases of the Pleistocene period, and submergence, due to the Holocene marine transgression. Many show 'neutral' features as well, so that most fall into the 'compound' category. Johnson applied the classification in terms of the most strongly marked characteristics; the majority of coasts must fall into the category of submerged coasts, shaped by the Holocene marine transgression. The possibility of a slight emergence following this transgression (Chapter III) should be borne in mind, but strongly marked characteristics of emerged coasts can really be expected only in regions that are rising because of isostatic recovery following deglaciation, as in Scandinavia, or in regions subject to uplift associated with tectonic deformation, as in parts of Indonesia and New Guinea, or around the Caspian Sea, where emergence results from sea level lowering (Fig. 20).

Johnson suggested certain characteristics of 'shorelines of submergence', such as an initially indented outline formed by the drowning of valley mouths, which are readily recognised from maps, nautical charts, and air photographs. The proposed characteristics of 'shorelines of emergence', initially simple and smooth in outline, with barriers likely to form offshore where the depth has been reduced by emergence, evidently apply only to coasts of gentle offshore gradient. Emergence of steep coasts with irregularities in the sea floor offshore could produce a *more* indented outline, as on the Californian coast, but barriers are certainly not restricted to 'shorelines of emergence': they are most common on recently-submerged coasts. While Johnson did not insist that these characteristics were diagnostic of 'shorelines of emergence' the exceptions show that application of this genetic classification is hazardous until coasts have been investigated in sufficient detail to determine their geomorphological history.

In 1899 Gulliver proposed a distinction between initial and subsequent coast forms, the initial forms to be those that existed when the present relative levels of land and sea were established and marine processes began work, and the sequential forms to be those that have since developed as the result of marine action. Shepard devised a more precise classification on these lines, which made a basic distinction between coasts shaped primarily by non-marine agencies and coasts that have been modified to their present form by the activity of marine processes. It was essentially a genetic classification, with descriptive detail inserted to clarify the sub-divisions, and it recognised that, because of the world-wide Holocene marine transgression, the sea has not long been at its present level relative to the land, and many coasts have been little modified by marine processes. His aim was to devise a classification that would 'prove useful in diagnosing the history and origin of coasts and shorelines from a study of charts and airplane photographs', but it is dangerous to assume that the history and origin of a coast can be deduced from such evidence without a field investigation. A straight coast may be produced by deposition, faulting, emergence of a featureless sea floor, or submergence of a coastal plain; an indented coast may be formed by submergence of an undulating or dissected land margin, emergence of an irregular sea floor, differential marine erosion of hard and soft outcrops at the coast, or transverse tectonic deformation (folding and faulting) of the land margin. It is doubtful whether configuration can be accepted as a reliable indication of coastal evolution.

Previous editions of this book have summarised and criticised the successive versions of the classification put forward by Shepard in 1937, 1948, and 1963 in order to illustrate the difficulties encountered in the search for a comprehensive classification. The most recent version (Shepard, 1976) is given here, with illustrative examples:

I. *Primary coasts*, with configuration resulting from non-marine processes:
    A. *Land erosion coasts*, shaped by erosion of the land surface and subsequently drowned by sea-level rise or sinking of the land:
        1. *Drowned river-cut valleys*—relatively shallow estuaries, usually with V-shaped cross-sections, deepening seaward: Chesapeake Bay, Carrick Roads (Fig. 86), and the ria coast of NW Spain.
        2. *Drowned glacial erosion coasts*—including fiords and glacial troughs, deep with U-shaped cross-sections but shal-

lower towards the mouths: Norwegian fiord coast, Southland fiord coast (Fig. 87), Gulf of St Lawrence glacial trough.

3. *Drowned karst topography*—embayments with oval depressions representing sinkholes, common in limestone areas: Dalmatian coast, Yugoslavia.

B. *Land deposition coasts*, prograded by land-derived deposits:

1. *River deposition coasts:*

    a. *Deltaic coasts*—usually form a lobe into the sea with distributary stream channels: birdfoot Mississippi delta cuspate Tiber delta, lobate Rhône delta, arcuate Nile delta.

    b. *Compound alluvial fan*—coastal plain at base of mountains, usually straightened by wave erosion: east coast of South Island, New Zealand.

    c. *Outwash plain*—alluvial deposition along outer margin of large glaciers: seaward margin of Malaspina Glacier, Alaska.

    d. *Mud lumps:* small, short-lived islets resulting from upthrust of mud off distributary mouths of Mississippi delta.

C. *Ice coasts*, where glacier fronts extend into the sea: most of Antarctic coast and locally in Greenland.

II. *Secondary coasts*, with configuration resulting mainly from marine agencies or marine organisms:

A. *Wave erosion coasts:*

1. *Straightened by wave erosion*—contrast with fault coast in having gently sloping sea floors and shore platforms: Atlantic shores of Cape Cod, Chalk coasts bordering English Channel.

2. *Made irregular by wave erosion*—indentations differ from drowned river valleys in minor character of penetration (not necessarily at river mouths): cliffed coast of Port Campbell, Victoria.

B. *Wave deposition coasts:*

1. *Coastal plains built seaward by waves*—contrast with river deposition coast in lacking deltaic bulges: Disaster Bay, New South Wales.

2. *Barrier coast*—separated from mainland by lagoons or swamps: Gulf and Atlantic coasts, U.S.A.; East Gippsland, Victoria.

3. *Cuspate forelands*—large projecting sand (or shingle) points with or without lagoons on the inside: Cape Hatteras, Dungeness (Fig. 58).

4. *Mud flats or salt marshes*—where very gentle offshore slope stops waves from breaking near the coast: Bridgwater Bay, England.

C. *Coasts prograded by organisms:*

1. *Coral reef coast*—built out by corals and algae and later brought above sea level by storm waves: fringing reefs on tropical coasts, as at Yule Point, NE Queensland.

2. *Serpulid reef coast*—sectors of beach sand cemented by serpulid worms: found in Bermuda.

3. *Oyster reef coast*—built by oyster shells: bays on Gulf Coast, U.S.A., notably Atchafalaya Bay, Mississippi delta margin.

4. *Glacial deposition coasts:*
   a. *Partially submerged moraine*—hummocky topography, usually straightened by marine deposition and/or erosion: parts of Long Island, New York.
   b. *Partially submerged drumlins*—oval hills, elongate in direction of ice movement: Boston Harbour, Massachusetts.

5. *Wind deposition coasts:*
   a. *Dune prograded coast*—rare: part of south side of San Miguel Island, California, and the southern shores of Corner Inlet, Victoria.
   b. *Dune coast*—where dunes are bordered by a beach: mouths of many river valleys in central California and Oregon, most beaches in SE Australia.

6. *Landslide coasts*, where masses fallen from cliffed coasts form projections into the ocean: Humbug Mountain, Oregon; head of Lyme Bay in England.

D. *Coasts shaped by volcanic activity:*

1. *Lava-flow coast*—convex protrusions at volcano, usually slopes continue steeply seaward: south coast of Hawaii.

2. *Volcanic collapse or explosion coast*—concave bays on side of volcano: Hanauma Bay, E of Honolulu; Krakatau in Sunda Strait.

3. *Tephra coast*—where fragmental volcanic material has built out the coast: San Benedicto Island W of Mexico; Surtsey off Iceland (Fig. 131).

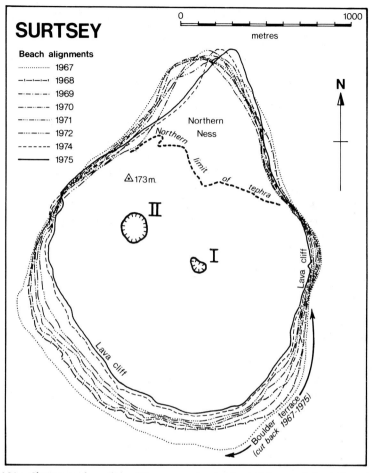

SURTSEY

Beach alignments
- 1967
- —·—·—· 1968
- —··—··—· 1969
- —···—···— 1970
- —····—···· 1971
- —·····—····· 1972
- – – – – 1974
- ———— 1975

0 ———————————— 1000
metres

N

Northern Ness

Northern limit of tephra

△173 m.

II

I

Lava cliff

Lava cliff

Boulder terrace (cut back 1967-1975)

131 *Changes in the outline of the young volcanic island of Surtsey, Iceland (formed by eruptions in 1966-67) where cliff recession on the more exposed southern coast has generated sand and gravel, deposited in the cuspate foreland to the north. After Norrman, 1980*

E. *Coasts shaped by diastrophic movements:*
  1. *Fault coast*—straight fault scarps continuing steeply below sea level: NW San Clemente Island, California.
  2. *Fold coast*—where coast has been recently folded: Wellington district, New Zealand.
  3. *Sedimentary intrusion coasts:*
     a. *Salt domes:* oval-shaped islands in southern Arabian Gulf.

67   *Beach of concrete tetrapods at Atami, near Tokyo, Japan, to protect the coastline against typhoon surges*

68   *Artificial coastline near Dymchurch, south-east England*

4. *Mangrove coast*—where the shore is occupied by mangroves, which may accrete sediments: SW Florida, Port Darwin (Fig. 91), Westernport Bay (Fig. 98).

5. *Marsh grass coast*—like mangroves, marsh grass may grow in shallow embayments and along gently sloping sea floors where wave energy is minimal: Suwannee Sound, Florida; bays in S Finland.

Shepard's classification has been much used in class work, and its applications in devising practical exercises are obvious, but, in terms of coastal research, a classification is useful if it provides a set of descriptive categories requiring investigation and explanation. There are dangers when descriptive categories based on interpretation of maps or aerial photographs are fitted into a prearranged genetic framework; in successive revisions Shepard has increased the descriptive categories and made his scheme as comprehensive as is possible while remaining within the limitations of a genetic approach. Snead (1982) has published a collection of 247 annotated photographs illustrating the various categories of Shepard's classification.

An omitted category which has recently been receiving closer attention is the category of ice coasts, well developed in Antarctica, where the Ross Ice Shelf terminates in cliffs up to 35 m high. In summer, icebergs calve from these cliffs and in winter the adjacent sea freezes, a fringe of sea ice persisting until winds and the spring thaw break it into floes. Melting in late spring is hastened by diatomaceous growths which darken the ice and increase its solar heat absorption. Protruding snouts of glaciers which reach the sea form floating ice tongues, somewhat richer in morainic debris, which is released and deposited on the adjacent sea floor. Wave action is weakened by the predominance of winds blowing offshore from the ice cap. Permanently frozen ground (permafrost) influences coastal evolution in northern Alaska and the arctic coasts of Canada and the U.S.S.R., where the summer thawing of interstitial ice contributes to rapid degeneration of 'tundra cliffs' of peaty and morainic material, which may retreat tens of metres in a few weeks.

Another omitted category of increasing importance is the category of artificial or man-made coasts (Plates 67 and 68). These are extensive in the Netherlands, where reclaimed lowlands are bordered by lengthy sea walls along the shoreline, and are becoming extensive in such areas as Hong Kong, Singapore, and the head of Tokyo Bay, where the coastline has been artificially prograded sequentially since the sixteenth century.

Of the several classifications that have been proposed by Cotton, the 1952 scheme is the most straightforward (Cotton, 1974). Aware of the importance of tectonic movements in shaping the coasts of his homeland, New Zealand, he made a distinction between coasts of 'stable' and 'mobile' regions, 'stable' regions being those thought to have escaped the Quaternary tectonic movements that had certainly affected the 'mobile' regions, where earth movements may still be continuing. The classification of coasts bordering these regions is as follows:

A.   Coasts of stable regions. These have all been affected by the Holocene marine submergence:
    1.   coasts dominated by features produced by Holocene submergence
    2.   coasts dominated by features inherited from earlier episodes of emergence
    3.   miscellaneous coasts (fiord, volcanic, etc.)

B.   Coasts of mobile regions. These have been affected by uplift or depression of the land as well as by Holocene submergence:
    1.   coasts on which the effects of marine submergence have not been counteracted by uplift of the land
    2.   coasts on which recent uplift of the land has led to emergence
    3.   fold and fault coasts
    4.   miscellaneous coasts (fiord, volcanic, etc.)

This system is most useful as a clarification of Johnson's scheme, the analysis of submergence and emergence enabling certain types of 'compound' coast to be separated.

De Martonne (1909) used the morphological distinction between 'steep' and 'flat' coasts as a basis for classification, suggesting a number of sub-types, some descriptive (estuary coasts, skerry coasts), others genetic (fault coasts, glacially-sculptured coasts). Ottmann (1965) followed a similar approach, recognising five classes with some subdivisions:

A—steep coasts which plunge to oceanic depths (Alpes-Maritimes)
    A_1—terraced or faulted steep coasts (California, Algeria)
    A_2—steep coasts of volcanic islands and (emerged) atolls

B—vertical cliffs with shore platforms at sea level (Normandy)
C—steep coasts which plunge to submerged platforms (Marseilles)
    C_1—with steep-sided inlets (calanques of Provence)
    C_2—with fiords (Patagonia)
D—partially submerged coasts without notable cliffing (parts of Brittany)
    D_1—ria coasts (SE Corsica)
    D_2—dissected coasts (Dalmatia)
    D_3—glacial drift coasts (S Scandinavia)
E—low, depositional coasts
    E_1—estuaries (Loire)
    E_2—deltas (Orinoco)
    E_3—marshlands and mangroves (Amazon)
    E_4—dunes (Landes)
    E_5—with barrier reefs (NE Brazil)

Classes A to D are rocky coasts, and class E coasts that have advanced as the result of deposition.

Classification of rocky coasts on the basis of lithology was advocated by Russell (1967). In the course of his very extensive coastal travels, he had noted a striking similarity in features developed on crystalline rocks, irrespective of their climatic and ecological environments: crystalline rocks that outcrop on parts of the coasts of Scandinavia, SW Australia, South Africa and Brazil all show similar domed surfaces related to large-scale spalling and conspicuous joint-control. Limestones (including chalk and coral), basalts, and sandstones each yield distinctive kinds of coastal landforms, with contrasts related to structure, wave energy, and weathering regimes, while unconsolidated formations show another range of landform types. Bedrock coasts are commoner in cold, arid, and temperate regions than in the humid tropics, where depositional fringes are extensive, and the limited sectors of coastal rock outcrop are usually profoundly weathered.

Advance or recession of coastlines was the theme developed by Valentin (1952), who noted that an advancing coast may be due to coastal emergence and/or progradation by deposition, while a retreating coast is due to coastal submergence and/or retrogradation by erosion. He first devised a system of coastal classification that could be used on a world map (scale 1 : 50,000,000) of coastal configuration types (Valentin, 1952, Plate 1):

A. Coasts that have advanced:
   1. due to emergence:
      a. *emerged sea floor coasts*
   2. due to organic deposition:
      b. phytogenic (formed by vegetation): *mangrove coasts*
      c. zoogenic (formed by fauna): *coral coasts*
   3. due to inorganic deposition:
      d. marine deposition where tides are weak: *lagoon-barrier and dune-ridge coasts*
      e. marine deposition where tides are strong: *tideflat and barrier-island coasts*
      f. fluvial deposition: *delta coasts*

B. Coasts that have retreated:
   1. due to submergence of glaciated landforms:
      g. confined glacial erosion: *fiord-skerry coasts*
      h. unconfined glacial erosion: *fiard-skerry coasts*
      i. glacial deposition *morainic coasts*
   2. due to submergence of fluvially-eroded landforms:
      k. on young fold structures: *embayed upland coasts*
      l. on old fold structures: *ria coasts*
      m. on horizontal structures: *embayed plateau coasts*
   3. due to marine erosion:
      n. *cliffed coasts*

The classification is partly genetic and partly descriptive, and examples of each type of coast shown on Valentin's world map are listed below:

a. *emerged sea-floor coasts* border the S shores of Hudson Bay, Canada, where the land is emerging as the result of isostatic recovery following deglaciation of the Canadian Shield.

b. *mangrove coasts* are found in sheltered embayments especially on tropical coasts.

c. *coral coasts* are exemplified by the Queensland coast, bordered by the Great Barrier Reefs.

d. *lagoon-barrier and dune ridge coasts* are well developed on the SE coast of Australia and the Gulf and Atlantic coasts of the United States.

e. *tideflat and barrier-island coasts* are found on the Dutch, German, and Danish North Sea coasts.

f. *delta coasts*, such as the Mississippi and the Nile, and the confluent deltas of N Java.

g. *fiord-skerry coasts* are best developed in Norway and British Columbia; the W coast of New Zealand's South Island has fiords, but skerries (fringing islands) are relatively rare. Port Davey, in Tasmania, shown as a fiord by Valentin, is actually a drowned river valley.

h. *fiard-skerry coasts* are found on the Baltic shores of Sweden and Finland and on the Arctic coasts of Canada.

i. *morainic coasts* are exemplified by the S Baltic coast.

j. *embayed upland coasts* are found on the W coast of the United States, in Chile, and in the Mediterranean, notably in Greece and Turkey.

k. *ria coasts* are represented by S Ireland, SW England, Brittany, and NW Spain, and by the coasts of Tasmania, New South Wales, and S Queensland.

l. *embayed plateau coasts* border the Red Sea and W India, Argentina, and parts of N Russia; the Hampshire coast in S England was placed in this category.

m. *cliffed coasts* are extensive on the Nullarbor Plain margin in S Australia, in parts of S and W Africa, and locally on the shores of the Mediterranean, the Black Sea, the English Channel, and the North Sea.

Valentin's classification has the merit of taking account of changes in the relative levels of land and sea, and being based on observed evidence of the gain or loss of land. He also considered the evidence of changes in progress, which can be expressed as an interaction of vertical movements (emergence and submergence) and horizontal movements (erosion and deposition), shown diagrammatically in Fig. 132. On this diagram the line ZOZ' indicates coasts that are neither advancing nor retreating, either because emergence is cancelled out by erosion (ZO) or because submergence is cancelled out by deposition (OZ'): the point O represents an absolutely static coast on which no changes of any kind are in progress. Changes are most marked towards A, where emergence accompanied by deposition leads to rapid advance of the coast, and towards R, where erosion accompanying submergence results in rapid retreat. Rapid erosion may lead to recession of an emerging coast (X), while rapid deposition may prograde a coast that is being submerged (Y).

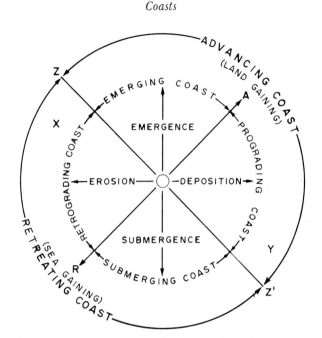

132   *Valentin's scheme for analysing coastline changes (for explanation, see text)*

Bloom (1965) suggested an elaboration of Valentin's scheme by the addition of a time-axis passing through O. On the three-dimensional diagram thus produced, it is possible to portray the course of evolution of a particular coast where relationships between emergence and submergence, erosion and deposition, have varied through time. An example is given from the Connecticut coast, where radiocarbon dates from buried peat horizons have yielded a chronology of relative changes of land and sea level in Holocene times. At some stages the sea gained on the land during submergence, even though deposition continued; at other stages deposition was sufficiently rapid to prograde the land during continuing submergence. Now there is widespread erosion on the seaward margins of salt marshes, possibly because of resumed submergence. Each condition gives different points on Valentin's diagram, and Bloom's three-dimensional scheme offers a means of portraying coastal evolution as a wavy line drawn from a selected origin on the time axis and linking successive positions on the intersected planes.

Valentin attempted to measure present-day emergence and submergence from tide gauge records, accepting the evidence for a world-wide eustatic rise of sea level in progress at a rate of about 1 mm per year. Where mean tide levels are rising more rapidly than this, submergence is being accelerated by tectonic subsidence; where they are rising less rapidly, and where they are falling, submergence is being partly offset by tectonic uplift and the coast is emerging. Tide gauge records are not available for many sections of coast, and this kind of analysis remains somewhat speculative. Valentin's map showing present-day coastal evolution distinguished between emerging, prograding, submerging, and retrograding coasts, and gave figures for changes of level where possible.

Valentin's scheme was a definite advance on earlier classifications made in terms of theoretical 'marine cycles', initiated by submergence or emergence as propounded by Johnson in terms of the Davisian 'cycle' concept (Davis, 1912), and reproduced in the older textbooks. This cyclic hypothesis has now outlived its usefulness, even as a teaching device, and can be seen in retrospect to have stultified coastal research. The essential idea was that a coast formed by submergence, initially indented, would pass through stages of 'youth' as promontories were cut back and sediment derived from them built laterally into spits and barriers enclosing embayments, 'sub-maturity' as the barriers retreated and coastal erosion drove back the headlands, and 'maturity' when all traces of the original indentations were destroyed, and the barriers came to rest as beaches along a smoothed, cliffed coast. It is quite possible that certain coasts have evolved in this way, but the hypothetical sequence cannot be accepted as 'normal' or 'typical'. The objections are that newly-submerged coasts are not necessarily indented; that crenulation by marine erosion can be a prolonged phase, not necessarily followed by this smoothing and simplification of coastal outlines; that where spits and barriers have formed the sediment is not necessarily derived from erosion of intervening cliffed headlands; that spits and barriers, formed on a submerged coast, are not necessarily driven landwards, and will prograde seawards if sediment supply is abundant; that the theoretical scheme is not a 'cycle', returning to the initial form, but a postulated 'sequence', the general validity of which has never been demonstrated; and that such idealised theoretical schemes of coastal evolution prompt facile interpretation of observed coastal features, which appear to fit the theoretical sequence, and are accepted as evidence of it without proper investigation of their geomorphological evolution. Similar objections apply to the hypothetical sequence of evolution of coasts following emergence, and neither scheme is satisfactory unless the coast becomes stable, following submergence or emergence. The advantage of 'non-cyclic' classifications, such as those proposed by Valentin and Bloom, is that they pose problems and stimulate further research instead of fitting observed features into presupposed evolutionary sequences. The liberation of coastal geomorphology from premature assumptions of 'cyclic' development was timely; it has been taken a stage farther by McGill (1958) in compiling a map of the coastal landforms of the world.

McGill's map (scale 1 : 25,000,000), published by the American Geographical Society in 1958, showed the major landforms of the coastal fringe, 5–10 miles (8–16 km) wide, with selected shore features and certain other information relevant to analysis of coastal evolution. It was a useful aid to research, prompting further inquiry and comparative study of coastal landforms as a means of isolating and measuring the factors at work.

Major coastal landforms were classified in terms of their hinterlands as follows:

I. Lowlands:
    A. Constructional (depositional) plains:
        1. dominantly flat-layered structure:
            a. existing ice
            b. plains of glacial deposition
            c. plains of fluvial deposition (including deltas)
            d. dune plains
            e. coral flats
            f. lava plains

    B. Destructional (erosional) plains:
        1. flat-layered structure:
            a. sedimentary plains formed by glaciation
            b. sedimentary plains formed by fluvial erosion
            c. volcanic plains formed by glaciation
            d. volcanic plains formed by fluvial erosion
        2. complex structure:
            a. formed by glaciation
            b. formed by fluvial erosion

II. Uplands:
  A. Plateaus:
    1. flat-layered structure:
      a. glaciated sedimentary plateau
      b. fluvially-eroded sedimentary plateau
      c. glaciated volcanic plateau
      d. fluvially-eroded volcanic plateau
    2. complex structure:
      a. formed by glaciation
      b. formed by fluvial erosion

  B. Hills:
    1. flat-layered structure, remnant hills:
      a. glaciated sedimentary plateau
      b. fluvially-eroded sedimentary plateau
      c. glaciated volcanic plateau
      d. fluvially-eroded volcanic plateau
    2. complex structure:
      a. formed by glaciation
      b. formed by fluvial erosion

  C. Mountains: subdivisions as for hills

  D. Constructional (depositional) uplands:
      a. ice plateau
      b. dune hills
      c. elevated coral flats
      d. lava plateau
      e. volcanoes (active and inactive).

This information is supplemented by indications of selected shore features, constructional or destructional, in the backshore, foreshore, and offshore zones, classified by the agent responsible: sea, wind, coral, or vegetation. This enables such features as backshore dunes, tidal flats, sedimentary and coral barriers, and 'tidal woodlands' (usually mangrove swamps) to be indicated. Finally, the map indicates such relevant features as:

  1. the limits of present-day glaciation and the maximum extent of ice during the Last Glacial phase;
  2. the approximate limit of permafrost;
  3. the average limit of polar sea ice, with spring maximum and autumn minimum of pack ice;

4. the approximate limit of reef coral (here taken as the 20°C isotherm of sea water in the coldest month);

5. tide ranges larger than 10, and larger than 20 feet, both general and where localised in embayments;

6. certain characteristics of coastal embayments, their form and orientation to the coastal margin;

7. the coastal areas affected by isostatic recovery following deglaciation; and

8. the location of karst topography on limestone coasts.

McGill's map has stimulated further investigation of coastal landforms, and the making of much more detailed morphological maps of coastal features. The American Geographical Society also published 1 : 50,000,000 maps of the world showing coastal climates (Bailey, 1958) and coastal vegetation (Axelrod, 1958), which give a valuable background to the analysis of coastal geomorphic systems, and these could also be developed on a local scale for research on particular coasts. Alexander (1966) devised symbols for detailed mapping of the shore zone, and illustrated his method with reference to the coast of Tanzania. Wiseman *et al.* (1973) divided the Alaskan Arctic coasts into 157 eight-kilometre segments for morphometric analysis, and by grouping segments with similar landform suites generated 22 provinces ranging from 15.6 to 159.6 km in shoreline length and separated by well-defined boundaries. This concept is analogous to the land systems approach in terrain studies, and can

133   *Changes on the Louisiana coastline between 1812 and 1954, based on a map by J. P. Morgan (Shepard and Wanless, 1972)*

similarly be applied hierarchically, with recurrent associations of minor compartments grouped into longer coastal sectors.

Another approach to detailed studies is the mapping of coastal changes over specified periods, illustrated here by Morgan's map of the Louisiana coast (Fig. 133). Other examples are given by Shepard and Wanless (1972), and Zunica's (1971) study of patterns of change along the Venetian coast in Italy and McLean's (1978) analysis of coastline changes in New Zealand show what can be achieved using historical information. The I.G.U. Commission on the Coastal Environment has been documenting world-wide coastline changes during the past century (Bird, 1976; Bird and Koike, 1981). An understanding of such changes will provide the background required for the future management of coastal environments and the conservation of coastal resources.

SELECTED BIBLIOGRAPHY

The scientific literature on coastal geomorphology is extensive, and is currently increasing at the rate of about four hundred publications a year. This selected bibliography of works mentioned in the text is intended as an introduction to the research literature. Advanced students will need to consult bibliographies issued every four years by the International Geographical Union Commission on the Coastal Environment, and bibliographies published by the Commission on Shorelines of I.N.Q.U.A. (International Association for Quaternary Research), as well as the relevant sections of *Geographical Abstracts (Geomorphology)*, published by K. M. Clayton (University of East Anglia, Norwich, England). Useful material will also be found in *Coastal Research Notes*, published thrice yearly by the Geology Department of Florida State University, Tallahassee, U.S.A. and in the *Encyclopedia of Beaches and Coastal Environments* (Schwartz 1982).

AHNERT, F. 1960. Estuarine meanders in the Chesapeake Bay area. *Geogrl Rev.* **50**: 390-401.

ALEXANDER, C. S. 1966. A method of descriptive shore classification and mapping as applied to the northeast coast of Tanganyika. *Annals Assn Amer. Geogrs.* **56**: 128-40.

ALLEN, J. R. L. 1965. Coastal geomorphology of eastern Nigeria: beach-ridge barrier islands and vegetated tidal flats. *Geologie Mijnb.* **44**: 1-21.

— and WELLS, J. W. 1962. Holocene coral banks and subsidence in the Niger delta. *J. Geol.* **70**: 381-97.

ARBER, M. A. 1940. The coastal landslips of south-east Devon. *Proc. Geol. Ass.* **51**: 257-71.

AXELROD, D. I. 1958. Coastal vegetation of the world. Map issued with *Second Coastal Geography Conference* (ed. R. J. Russell). Washington.

BAILEY, H. P. 1958. An analysis of coastal climates, with particular reference to humid mid-latitudes *Second Coastal Geography Conference* (ed. R. J. Russell). Washington: 23-56.

BAKER, G. 1956. Sand drift at Portland Harbour, Victoria. *Proc. R. Soc. Vict.* **68**: 151-98.

— 1958. Stripped zones at cliff edges along a high wave energy coast, Port Campbell, Victoria. *Proc. R. Soc. Vict.* **71**: 175-9.

BASCOM, W. N. 1951. Relationship between sand size and beach face slope. *Trans. Am. geophys. Un.* **32**: 866-74.

— 1954. The control of stream outlets by wave refraction. *J. Geol.* **62**: 600-5.

— 1959. Ocean waves. *Scient. Am.* **201**: 74-84.

BAUER, F. H. 1961. Chronic problems of terrace study in southern Australia. *Z. Geomorph.* Supp. 3: 57-72.

BAULIG, H. 1956. *Vocabulaire Franco-Anglo-Allemand de Géomorphologie.* Strasbourg.

BEACH EROSION BOARD. 1961. *Shore Protection Planning and Design.* Washington.

BENSON, W. N. and RAESIDE, J. D. 1963. Tidal colks in Australia and New Zealand. *N.Z.J. Geol. Geophys.* **6**: 634-40.

BIRD, E. C. F. 1967. Coastal lagoons of southeastern Australia. *Landform Studies from Australia and New Guinea* (eds. J. N. Jennings, J. A. Mabbutt): 366-85.

— 1970. The steep coast of Macalister Range, North Queensland, *J. trop. Geogr.* **31**: 33-9.

— 1971. The origin of beach sediments on the North Queensland coast. *Earth Sci. J.* **5**: 95-105.

— 1973. Australian coastal barriers, in *Barrier Islands* (ed. M. L. Schwartz): 410-26.

— 1976. *Shoreline Changes during the Past Century*. I.G.U. Working Group, University of Melbourne.

— 1978a. *The Geomorphology of the Gippsland Lakes Region*. Ministry for Conservation, Victoria, Environmental Studies Series, 186.

— 1978b. The nature and source of beach materials on the Australian coast. *Landform Evolution in Australasia* (eds. J. L. Davies and M. A. J. Williams): Canberra, 144-57.

— 1979. Coastal processes. *Man and Environmental Processes* (eds. K. J. Gregory and D. E. Walling): 82-101.

— 1981. Coastal landforms in the humid tropics. *Perspectives in Geomorphology* (ed. H. S. Sharma). **1**: 351-73.

— and BARSON, M. M. 1975. Shoreline changes in Westernport Bay. *Proc. Roy. Soc. Vict.* **87**: 15-28.

— and DENT, O. F. 1966. Shore platforms on the south coast of New South Wales. *Aust. Geogr.* **10**: 71-80.

— and HOPLEY, D. 1969. Geomorphological features on a humid tropical sector of the Australian coast. *Aust. geogr. Studies* **7**: 89-108.

— and KOIKE, K. (eds.) 1981. *Coastal Dynamics and Scientific Sites*. Komazawa University, Tokyo.

— and RANWELL, D. S. 1964. The physiography of Poole Harbour, Dorset. *J. Ecol.* **52**: 355-66.

— and ONGKOSONGO, O. S. R. 1980. *Environmental Changes on the Coasts of Indonesia*. United Nations University, Tokyo.

— and SCHWARTZ, M. L. (eds.) 1983. *The World's Coastlines*. Stroudsburg, Pennsylvania.

BLOOM, A. L. 1965. The explanatory description of coasts. *Z. Geomorph.* **9**: 422-36.

— 1967. Pleistocene shorelines: a new test of isostasy. *Bull. geol. Soc. Am.* **78**: 1477-94.

— 1979. *Atlas of Sea Level Curves*. Cornell University, New York.

BOURCART, J. 1952. *Les Frontières de l'Océan*. Paris.

BRUNSDEN, D. and JONES, D. K. C. 1980. Relative time scales in formative events in coastal landslide systems. *Z. Geomorph., Suppl.* **34**: 1-19.

BRUUN, P. 1962. Sea level rise as a cause of shore erosion. *Proc. Am. Soc. civ. Engrs* (Waterways and Harbours Divn) **88**: 117-30.

— 1967. *Tidal Inlets and Littoral Drift*. Oslo.

CAMBERS, G. 1976. Temporal scales in coastal erosion systems. *Trans. Inst. Brit. Geogr.* **1**: 246-56.

CARR, A. P. 1962. Cartographic record and historical accuracy. *Geography* **47**: 135-44.

— 1965. Shingle spit and river mouth: short-term dynamics. *Trans. Inst. Br. Geogr.* **36**: 117-30.

— and BLACKLEY, M. W. L. 1973. Investigations bearing on the age and development of Chesil Beach, Dorset, and the associated area. *Trans. Inst. Br. Geogr.* **58**: 99-112.

CHAPMAN, V. J. 1960. *Salt Marshes and Salt Deserts of the World*. London.

CHAPPELL, J. 1967. Recognizing fossil strand lines from grain size analysis. *J. sedim. Petrol.* 37: 157-65.

— 1974. Geology of coral terraces, Huon Peninsula, New Guinea: a study of Quaternary tectonic movements and sea-level changes. *Bull. geol. Soc. Am.* 85: 553-70.

— 1983. A revised sea level record for the last 300,000 years. *Search.* 14: 99-101.

— and VEEH, H. H. 1978. Late Quaternary tectonic movements and sea level changes at Timor and Atauro Island. *Bull. geol Soc. Am.* 89:356-68.

CHURCHILL, D. M. 1959. Late Quaternary eustatic changes in the Swan River district. *J. Proc. R. Soc. West Aust.* 42: 53-5.

COALDRAKE, J. E. 1962. The coastal sand dunes of southern Queensland. *Proc. R. Soc. Qld.* 72: 101-16.

COLEMAN, J. M. and SMITH, W. G. 1964. Late Recent rise of sea level. *Bull. geol. Soc. Am.* 75: 833-40.

— and WRIGHT, L. D. 1977. Research techniques in deltas. *Geoscience and Man.* 18: 35-51.

COOPER, W. S. 1958. Coastal sand dunes of Oregon and Washington. *Mem. geol. Soc. Am.* 72.

COTTON, C. A. 1952. Criteria for the classification of coasts. *Proc. 17th Conf. Internat. Geogrl. Union* (Washington): 315-19.

— 1956. Rias *sensu stricto* and *sensu lato. Geogrl. J.* 122: 360-4.

— 1963. Levels of planation of marine benches. *Z. Geomorph.* 7: 97-111.

— 1974. *Bold Coasts.* Wellington, New Zealand.

CRUZ, O. 1982. Spits and bar formation in Caraguatatuba Bay, Sao Paulo. *I.G.U.-C.C.E. Field Symposium on the Brazilian Coast* (eds. E. C. F. Bird and K. Suguio): 58-65.

CURRAY, J. R. 1960. Sediments and history of Holocene transgression, continental shelf, northwest Gulf of Mexico. *Recent Sediments, northwest Gulf of Mexico* (Tulsa, Okla.): 221-66.

DALY, R. A. 1934. *The Changing World of the Ice Age.* Yale.

DARBYSHIRE, J. 1961. Prediction of wave characteristics over the North Atlantic. *J. Inst. Navig.* 14: 339-47.

DAVIES, J. L. 1957. The importance of cut and fill in the development of sand beach ridges. *Aust. J. Sci.* 20: 105-11.

— 1959. Wave refraction and the evolution of shoreline curves. *Geogrl Stud.* 5: 1-14.

— 1964. A morphogenic approach to world shorelines. *Z. Geomorph.* 8 (Mortensen Sonderheft): 127-42.

— 1972. *Geographical Variation in Coastal Development.* Edinburgh.

— 1974. The coastal sediment compartment. *Aust. Geogr. Studies.* 12: 139-51.

— 1978. Beach sand and wave energy in Tasmania, *Landform Evolution in Australasia* (eds. J. L. Davies and M. A. J. Williams): Canberra, 158-67.

DAVIS, W. M. 1896. The outline of Cape Cod. *Proc. Am. Acad. Arts Sci.* 31: 303-32.

— 1928. *The Coral Reef Problem.* American Geographical Society Special Publication 9.

DE BOER, G. 1964. Spurn Head: its history and evolution. *Trans. Inst. Brit. Geogr.* 34: 71-89.

DE MARTONNE, E. 1909. *Traité de Géographie Physique.* Paris.

DIETZ, R. S. 1963. Wave-base, marine profile of equilibrium, and wave-built terraces: a critical appraisal. *Bull. geol. Soc. Am.* 74: 971-90.

DIONNE, J. C. 1972. Caractéristiques des schorres des régions froides. *Z. Geomorph.* 13: 131-62.

DONN, W. L. and SHAW, D. M. 1963. Sea level and climates of the past century. *Science* 142: 1166-7.

—, FARRAND, W. R. and EWING, M. 1962. Pleistocene ice volumes and sea level lowering. *J. Geol.* **70**: 206-14.

DONOVAN, D. T. and STRIDE, A. H. 1961. Erosion of a rock floor by tidal streams. *Geol. Mag.* **98**: 393-8.

DUNBAR, G. S. 1956. *Geographical History of the Carolina Banks.* Coastal Studies Institute, Louisiana State University, Technical Report 8.

EDWARDS, A. B. 1958. Wave-cut platforms at Yampi Sound in the Buccaneer Archipelago. *J. Proc. R. Soc. West Aust.* **41**: 17-21.

EMERY, K. O. 1960. *The Sea off Southern California.* New York.

— 1961. Submerged marine terraces and their sediments. *Z. Geomorph.* Supp. **3**: 17-29.

— and STEVENSON, R. E. 1957. Estuaries and lagoons. *Mem. geol. Surv. America* **67**: 673-750.

EMILIANI, C. 1966. Isotopic palaeotemperatures. *Science*, **154**: 851-7.

EVANS, O. F. 1942. The origin of spits, bars, and related structures. *J. Geol.* **50**: 846-63.

FAIRBRIDGE, R. W. 1950. The geology and geomorphology of Point Peron, W.A. *J. Proc. R. Soc. West Aust.* **34**: 35-72.

— 1961. Eustatic changes in sea level. *Physics and Chemistry of the Earth* **4**: 99-185.

— 1967. Coral reefs of the Australian region. *Landform Studies from Australia and New Guinea* (eds. J. N. Jennings, J. A. Mabbutt): 386-417.

FISHER, J. J. 1980. Shoreline erosion, Rhode Island and North Carolina coasts. *Proceedings of the Per Bruun Symposium* (eds. M. L. Schwartz and J. J. Fisher), Rhode Island: 32-54.

FISK, H. N. 1958. Padre Island and the Laguna Madre flats, coastal south Texas. *Second Coastal Geography Conference:* 103-51.

— and McFARLAN, E. 1955. *Late Quaternary Deltaic Deposits of the Mississippi River.* Geological Society of America Special Publication **24**: 279-302.

FLEMING, C. A. 1965. Two-storied cliffs at the Auckland Islands. *Trans. R. Soc. N.Z.(Geol.)* **3**: 171-4.

FLINT, R. F. 1966. Comparison of interglacial marine stratigraphy in Virginia, Alaska, and Mediterranean areas. *Am. J. Sci.* **26**: 673-84.

FOLK, R. L. and WARD, W. C. 1957. Brazos River bar; a study in the significance of grain size parameters. *J. sedim. Petrol.* **27**: 3-26.

FRIEDMAN, G. M. 1961. Distinction between dune, beach, and river sands from their textural characteristics. *J. sedim. Petrol.* **31**: 514-29.

FUENZALIDA, H. *et al.* 1965. *High Stands of Quaternary Sea Level along the Chilean Coast.* Geological Society of America Special Publication **84**: 473-96.

GALLOWAY, R. W. and BAHR, M. E. 1979. What is the length of the Australian coast? *Australian Geogr.* **14**: 244-47.

GELL, R. A. 1978. Shelly beaches on the Victorian coast. *Proc. Roy. Soc. Vict.* **90**: 257-69.

GIERLOFF-EMDEN, H. G. 1961. Nehrungen und Lagunen. *Petermanns geogr. Mitt.* **105**: 81-92; 161-76.

GILBERT, G. K. 1890. *Lake Bonneville.* U.S. Geological Survey Monograph 1.

GRESSWELL, R. K. 1953. *Sandy Shores in South Lancashire.* Liverpool.

GUILCHER, A. 1953. Essai sur la zonation et la distribution des formes littorales de dissolution du calcaire. *Annls Géogr.* **62**: 161-79.

— 1956. Les travaux de Berthois sur l'estuaire de la Loire. *Norois* **3**: 87-90 and **4**: 106-7.

— 1958. Coastal corrosion forms in limestone around the Bay of Biscay. *Scott. geogr. Mag.* **74**: 137-49.

— 1979. Marshes and estuaries in different latitudes. *Interdisciplinary Sci. Reviews.* **4**: 158-68.

— and BERTHOIS, L. 1957. Cinq années d'observations sédimentologiques dans quatre estuaires-témoins de l'ouest de la Bretagne. *Revue Géomorph. dyn.* **8**: 67-86.

— and NICOLAS, J. P. 1954. Observations sur la langue de Barbarie et les bras du Sénégal aux environs de St Louis. *Bull. Inf. Com. cent. Océanogr. Etude Côtes* **6**: 227-42.

GULLIVER, F. P. 1899. Shoreline topography. *Proc. Am. Acad. Arts Sci.* **34**: 151-258.

GUTENBERG, B. 1941. Changes in sea level, postglacial uplift and mobility of the earth's interior. *Bull. geol. Soc. Am.* **52**: 721-72.

GUZA, R. T. and INMAN, D. L. 1975. Edge waves and beach cusps. *J. Geophys. Research* **80**: 2997-3012.

HARRIS, R. L. 1955. *Restudy of Test Shore Nourishment by Offshore Deposition of Sand, Long Branch, New Jersey.* Beach Erosion Board Technical Memorandum 62.

HARRISON, W. 1970. Prediction of beach changes. *Progress in Geography.* **2**: 209-35.

HEALY, T. R. 1968. Bioerosion on shore platforms in the Waitemata formation, Auckland. *Earth Sci. J.* **2**: 26-37.

HELLE, J. R. 1958. *Surf Statistics for the Coasts of the United States.* Beach Erosion Board Technical Memorandum 108.

HEY, R. W. 1978. Horizontal Quaternary shorelines of the Mediterranean. *Quaternary Research.* **10**: 197-203.

HILLS, E. S. 1949. Shore platforms. *Geol. Mag.* **86**: 137-52.

— 1971. A study of cliffy coastal profiles based on examples in Victoria, Australia. *Z. Geomorph.* **15**: 137-80.

HJULSTRÖM, F. 1939. Transportation of detritus by moving water. *Recent Marine Sediments* (ed. P. D. Trask): 5-31.

HODGKIN, E. P. 1964. Rate of erosion of intertidal limestone. *Z. Geomorph.* **8**: 385-92.

HOPLEY, D. 1971. The origin and significance of North Queensland island-spits. *Z. Geomorph.* **15**: 371-89.

— 1974. Coastal changes produced by tropical cyclone Althea in Queensland, December 1971. *Aust. Geogr.* **12**: 445-56.

— 1979. Deltaic barrier spit. *Australian Geogr.* **14**: 248-51.

— 1982. *Geomorphology of the Great Barrier Reef.* Wiley Interscience, New York.

HOSSFELD, P. S. 1965. Radiocarbon dating and palaeoecology of the Aitape fossil human remains. *Proc. R. Soc. Vict.* **78**: 161-5.

HOYT, J. H. 1967. Barrier island formation. *Bull. geol. Soc. Am.* **78**: 1125-36.

HUBBARD, J. C. E. 1965. Spartina salt marshes in southern England, VI: Pattern of invasion in Poole Harbour. *J. Ecol.* **53**: 799-813.

HUTCHINSON, J. 1976. Coastal landslides in cliffs of Pleistocene deposits between Cromer and Overstrand, Norfolk. *Laurits Bjerrum Memorial Volume*, Oslo: 155-82.

INGLE, J. C. 1966. *The Movement of Beach Sand.* Elsevier.

INMAN, D. L. and NORDSTROM, C. E. 1971. On the tectonic and morphologic classification of coasts. *J. Geol.* **79**: 1-21.

JENNINGS, J. N. 1957. On the orientation of parabolic or U-dunes. *Geogrl J.* **123**: 474-80.

— 1959. The submarine topography of Bass Strait. *Proc. R. Soc. Vict.* **71**: 49-72.

— 1967. Cliff-top dunes. *Aust. Geog. Studies* **5**: 40-9.

— and BIRD, E. C. F. 1967. Regional geomorphological characteristics of some Australian estuaries. *Estuaries* (ed. G. H. Lauff): 121-8.

JOHNSON, D. W. 1919. *Shore Processes and Shoreline Development.* New York.

— 1925. *The New England-Acadian Shoreline.* New York.

JOHNSON, J. W. 1956. Dynamics of nearshore sediment movement. *Bull. Am. Ass. Petrol. Geol.* **40:** 2211-32.

— 1959. The littoral drift problem at shoreline harbours. *Proc. Am. Soc. civ. Engrs* (Waterways and Harbours Divn). **124:** 525-55.

JOLLIFFE, I. P. 1961. The use of tracers to study beach movements and the measurement of littoral drift by a fluorescent technique. *Revue Géomorph. dyn.* 12: 81-95.

JONES, O. A. and ENDEAN, R. (eds.) 1977. *Biology and Geology of Coral Reefs.* Academic Press, New York.

KAYE, C. A. 1959. Shoreline features and Quaternary shoreline changes, Puerto Rico. U.S. Geological Survey Professional Paper 317-B: 49-140.

KHAFAGY, A. and MANOHAR, M. 1979. Coastal problems of the Nile delta. *Nature and Resources.* 15: 7-13.

KIDSON, C. 1963. The growth of sand and shingle spits across estuaries. *Z. Geomorph.* 7: 1-22.

— and CARR, A. P. 1962. Marking beach materials for tracing experiments. *Proc. Am. Soc. civ. Engrs* (Waterways and Harbours Divn). **88:** 43-60.

KING, C. A. M. 1959. *Beaches and Coasts.* London. (2nd ed. 1972).

— and McCULLACH, M. J. 1971. A simulation model of a complex recurved spit. *J. Geol.* **79:** 22-36.

KING, L. C. 1962. *The Morphology of the Earth.* Edinburgh.

KIRK, R. M. 1973. An instrument system for shore process studies. *Brit. Geomorph. Res. Gp. Tech. Bull.* 10.

KOLB, C. R. and VAN LOPIK, J. R. 1966. Depositional environments of the Mississippi River deltaic plain. *Deltas in their Geological Framework* (ed. M. L. Shirley): 18-63.

KOMAR, P. 1976. *Beach Processes and Sedimentation.* New Jersey.

KRAFT, J. C., ASCHENBRENNER, S. E. and RAPP, G. 1977. Palaeo-geographic reconstructions of coastal Aegean archaeological sites. *Science.* 195: 941-7.

KRUMBEIN, W. C. 1963. *The Analysis of Observational Data from Natural Beaches.* Beach Erosion Board Technical Memorandum 130.

LANDON, R. E. 1930. An analysis of beach pebble abrasion and transportation. *J. Geol.* 38: 437-46.

LAUFF, G. H. (ed.) 1967. *Estuaries.* Publication of the American Association for the Advancement of Science 83.

LEATHERMAN, S. P. (ed.) 1981. *Overwash Processes.* Stroudsburg, Pennsylvania.

LE BOURDIEC, P. 1958. Aspects de la morphogénèse plio-quaternaire en basse Côte d'Ivoire. *Revue Geomorph. dyn.* 9: 33-42.

LEWIS, W. V. 1932. The formation of Dungeness foreland. *Geogrl J.* 80: 309-24.

LINDSAY, J. F. 1976. Sound-producing dune and beach sands. *Bull. Geol. Soc. America.* 87: 463-73.

LONGUET-HIGGINS, M. S. and PARKIN, D. W. 1962. Sea waves and beach cusps. *Geogrl J.* 128: 195-201.

LUCKE, J. B. 1934. A theory of evolution of lagoon deposits on shorelines of emergence. *J. Geol.* 42: 561-84.

LYMAREV, V. I. 1958. Reed beds on a coast of accumulation. *Izv. Akad. Nauk. SSSR., Ser. Geogr.* 4.

McGILL, J. T. 1958. Map of coastal landforms of the world. *Geogrl Rev.* 48: 402-5.

McINTIRE, W. G. and WALKER, H. J. 1964. Tropical cyclones and coastal morphology in Mauritius. *Annals Assn. Amer. Geogrs.* 54: 582-96.

McLEAN, R. F. 1978. Recent coastal progradation in New Zealand. *Landform Evolution in Australasia.* (eds. J. L. Davies and M. A. J. Williams): Canberra, 168-96.

MARSDEN, M. A. H. (ed.) 1979. Sedimentary processes and water circulation in Westernport, Australia. *Marine Geol. Special Issue.* **30.**

MASON, C. C. and FOLK, R. L. 1958. Differentiation of beach, dune and aeolian flat environments by size analysis, Mustang island, Texas. *J. sedim. Petrol.* **28:** 211-26.

MAY, V. J. 1977. Earth cliffs. *The Coastline* (ed. R. S. K. Barnes): 215-36.

MILLER, D. J. 1960. Giant waves in Lituya Bay, Alaska. U.S. Geological Survey Professional Paper 354-C: 51-86.

MILLER, R. L. and ZEIGLER, J. M. 1958. A model relating dynamics and sediment pattern in equilibrium in the region of shoaling waves, breaker zone, and foreshore. *J. Geol.* **66:** 417-41.

MØLLER, J. T. 1963. Accumulation and abrasion in a tidal area. *Geogr. Tidsskr.* **62:** 56-79.

MÖRNER, N. A. 1976. Eustacy and geoid changes. *J. Geol.* **84:** 123-51.

MOSS, A. J. 1962–63. The physical nature of common sandy and pebbly deposits. *Am. J. Sci.* **260:** 337-73 and **261:** 297-343.

MUNK, W. H. *et al.* 1963. Directional recording of waves from distant storms. *Phil. Trans. R. Soc.* Series A **255:** 505-84.

NICHOLAS, R. L. 1948. Flying bars. *Amer. J. Sci.* **246:** 96-100.

NIEDORODA, A. W. and TANNER, W. F. 1970. Preliminary study of transverse bars. *Marine Geol.* **9:** 41-62.

NORRMAN, J. O. 1980. Coastal erosion and slope development in Surtsey Island, Iceland. *Z. Geomorph. Suppl.* **34:** 20-38.

NOSSIN, J. J. 1965. The geomorphic history of the northern Padang delta. *J. trop. Geogr.* **20:** 54-64.

OAKS, R. A. and COCH, N. K. 1963. Pleistocene sea levels, southeastern Virginia. *Science* **140:** 979-84.

OLSON, J. S. 1958. Lake Michigan dune development. *J. Geol.* **66:** 254-63, 345-51, and 473-83.

ORLOVA, G. and ZENKOVICH, V. P. 1974. Erosion of the shores of the Nile delta. *Geoforum* **18/74:** 68-72.

OTTMANN, F. 1965. *Introduction à la géologie marine et littorale.* Paris.

PASKOFF, R. 1981. *L'érosion des côtes.* Paris.

PETHICK, J. S. 1981. Long-term accretion rates on tidal salt marshes. *J. Sed. Pet.* **51:** 571-8.

PHILLIPS, A. W. 1970. The use of the Woodhead sea bed drifter. *Brit. Geomorph. Res. Gp. Tech. Bull.* 4.

PIRAZZOLI, P. A. 1977. Sea level relative variations in the world during the past 2000 years. *Z. Geomorph.* **21:** 284-96.

PRÊCHEUR, C. 1960. *Le Littoral de la Manche: de Ste Andresse à Ault. Etude morphologique. Norois* special volume.

PRICE, W. A. 1947. Equilibrium of form and forces in tidal basins of the coast of Texas and Louisiana. *Bull. Am. Ass. Petrol. Geol.* **31:** 1619-63.

PRINGLE, A. 1981. Beach development and coastal erosion in Holderness, N. Humberside. *The Quaternary in Britain* (eds. J. Neale and J. Flenley): 194-205.

PSUTY, N. P. 1965. Beach-ridge development in Tabasco, Mexico. *Ann. Ass. Am. Geogr.* **55:** 112-24.

RANWELL, D. S. 1972. *Ecology of Salt Marshes and Sand Dunes.* London.

REDFIELD, A. C. 1972. Development of a New England salt marsh. *Ecol. Monogr.* **42:** 201-37.

REVELLE, R. and EMERY, K. O. 1957. Chemical erosion of beach rock and exposed reef rock. U.S. Geological Survey Professional Paper 260-T: 699-709.

ROBINSON, A. H. W. 1955. The harbour entrances of Poole, Christchurch and Pagham. *Geogrl J.* 121: 33-50.

— 1960. Ebb-flood channel systems in sandy bays and estuaries. *Geography* 45: 183-99.

— 1961. The hydrography of Start Bay and its relationship to beach changes at Hall-sands. *Geogrl J.* 121: 63-77.

— 1966. Residual currents in relation to shoreline evolution of the East Anglian coast. *Marine Geology* 4: 57-84.

RUSSELL, R. C. H. and MACMILLAN, D. H. 1954. *Waves and Tides.* London.

RUSSELL, R. J. 1958. Long straight beaches. *Eclog. geol. Helv.* 51: 591-8.

— 1962. Origin of beach rock. *Z. Geomorph.* 6: 1-16.

— 1963. Recent recession of tropical cliffy coasts. *Science* 139: 9-15.

— 1964. Techniques of eustasy studies. *Z. Geomorph.* 8 (Mortensen Sonderheft): 25-42.

— 1967. *River Plains and Sea Coasts.* California.

— and MCINTIRE, W. G. 1965a. Beach cusps. *Bull. geol. Soc. Am.* 76: 307-20.

— and — 1965b. Southern hemisphere beach rock. *Geogrl Rev.* 55: 17-45.

— and — 1966. *Australian Tidal Flats.* Louisiana State University Coastal Studies Series 13.

— and RUSSELL, R. D. 1939. Mississippi River delta sedimentation. *Recent Marine Sediments* (ed. B. D. Trask): 153-77.

SAVILLE, T. 1950. Model study of sand transport along an infinitely long straight beach. *Trans. Am. geophys. Un.* 31: 555-65.

SCHOFIELD, J. C. 1975. Sea level fluctuations cause periodic postglacial progradation, South Kaipara barrier, New Zealand. *N.Z. Jl Geol. Geophys.* 18: 295-316.

SCHOU, A. 1945. *Det Marine Forland.* Copenhagen.

— 1952. Direction determining influence of the wind on shoreline simplification and coastal dunes. *Proc. 17th Conference of the International Geographical Union.* Washington: 370-3.

SCHWARTZ, M. L. 1967. The Bruun theory of sea level rise as a cause of shore erosion. *J. Geol.* 75: 76-92.

— (ed.) 1972. *Spits and Bars.* Stroudsburg, Pennsylvania.

— (ed.) 1973. *Barrier Islands.* Stroudsburg, Pennsylvania.

— (ed.) 1982. *Beaches and Coastal Environments.* Stroudsburg, Pennsylvania.

SHACKLETON, N. J. and OPDYKE, N. D. 1973. Oxygen isotope and palaeomagnetic stratigraphy of Equatorial Pacific core V-28-238. *Quaternary Research* 3: 39-55.

SHEPARD, F. P. 1963. *Submarine Geology.* New York (2nd ed.).

— 1976. Coastal classification and changing coastlines. *Geoscience and Man* 14: 53-64.

—, EMERY, K. O., and LA FOND, E. C. 1941. Rip currents: a process of geological importance. *J. Geol.* 49: 337-69.

— and WANLESS, H. R. 1972. *Our Changing Coastlines.* New York.

— and YOUNG, R. 1961. Distinguishing between beach and dune sands. *J. sedim Petrol.* 31: 196-214.

SILVESTER, R. 1956. The use of cyclonicity charts in the study of littoral drift. *Trans. Am. geophys. Un.* 37: 694-6.

SMITH, T. H. and IREDALE, T. 1924. Evidence of a negative movement of the strand line of 400 feet in New South Wales. *J. Proc. R. Soc. N.S.W.* 58: 157-68.

SNEAD, R. E. 1982. *Coastal Landforms and Surface Features.* Stroudsburg, Pennsylvania.

SPRIGG, R. C. 1959. Stranded sea beaches and associated sand accumulations of the upper south-east of South Australia. *Trans. R. Soc. S. Aust.* **82**: 183-93.

STEARNS, H. T. 1961. Eustatic shorelines on Pacific islands. *Z. Geomorph.* Supp. **3**: 3-16.

— 1974. Submerged shorelines and shelves in the Hawaiian islands. *Bull. geol. Soc. Am.* **85**: 795-804.

STEERS, J. A. 1937. The coral islands and associated features of the Great Barrier Reefs. *Geogrl J.* **89**: 1-28 and 118-46.

— 1953. *The Sea coast.* London.

— (ed.) 1960. *Scolt Head Island.* Cambridge.

— 1964. *The Coastline of England and Wales.* Cambridge.

—, STODDART, D. R., BAYLISS-SMITH, T. P., SPENCER, T. and DURBRIDGE, P. M. 1979. The storm surge of 11 January 1978 on the east coast of England. *Geogr. J.* **145**: 192-205.

STEVENSON, R. E. and EMERY, K. O. 1958. *Marshlands at Newport Bay, California.* Allan Hancock Foundation Publication 20.

STIPP, J. J., CHAPPELL, J. M A., and McDOUGALL, I. 1967. K/Ar age estimate of the Plio-cene-Pleistocene boundary in New Zealand. *Am. J. Sci.* **265**: 462-74.

STODDART, D. R. 1965. Re-survey of hurricane effects on the British Honduras reefs and cays. *Nature, Lond.* **207**: 589-92.

— 1969. Ecology and morphology of Recent coral reefs. *Biol. Rev.* **44**: 433-98.

— and CANN, J. R. 1965. Nature and origin of beach rock. *J. sedim. Petrol.* **35**: 243-7.

— and STEERS, J. A. 1977. Nature and origin of reef islands. *Biology and Geology of Coral Reefs* (eds. O. A. Jones and R. Endean) **4**: 59-105.

SUESS, E. 1906. *The Face of the Earth* (trans. W. J. Sollas). Oxford.

SUNAMURA, T. 1977. A relationship between wave-induced cliff erosion and erosional force of waves. *J. Geol.* **85**: 613-18.

SWAN, B. 1979. Sand dunes in the humid tropics: Sri Lanka. *Z. Geomorph.* **23**: 152-71.

TANNER, W. F. 1963. Origin and maintenance of ripple marks. *Sedimentology* **2**: 307-11.

—, EVANS, R. G., and HOLMES, C. W. 1963. Low-energy coast near Cape Romano, Florida, *J. sedim. Petrol.* **33**: 713-22.

THOM, B. G. 1973. The dilemma of high sea levels during the last glaciation. *Progress in Geography* **5**: 170-246.

— 1974. Coastal erosion in Eastern Australia. *Search* **5**: 198-209.

—, BOWMAN, G. M., GILLESPIE, R., POLACH, H. and BARBETTI, M. 1981. Progradation histories of sand barriers in New South Wales. *Search* **12**: 323-5.

TIETZE, W. 1962. Ein beitrag zum geomorphologischen problem der strandflate. *Peter-manns geogr. Mitt.* **106**: 1-20.

TRICART, J. 1956. Aspects morphologiques du delta du Sénégal. *Revue Géomorph. dyn.* **7**: 65-85.

— 1959. Problèmes géomorphologiques du littoral oriental du Bresil. *Cah. océanogr.* **11**: 276-308.

— 1962. Observations de géomorphologie littorale à Mamba Point, Liberia. *Erdkunde* **16**: 49-57.

TRICKER, R. A. R. 1964. *Bores, Breakers, Waves and Wakes.* London.

VALENTIN, H. 1952. Die Küsten der Erde. *Petermanns geogr. Mitt (Erg.)* 246.

— 1961. The central west coast of Cape York Peninsula. *Aust. Geogr.* **8**: 65-72.

VANNEY, J. R., MENANTEAU, L. and ZAZO, C. 1979. Physiographie et évolution des dunes de Basse-Andalousie. *Les côtes Atlantiques de l'Europe* (ed. A. Guilcher) Brest: 277-85.

VAN STRAATEN, L. M. J. U. 1953. Megaripples in the Dutch Wadden Sea and in the Basin of Arcachon. *Geologie Mijnb.* **15**: 1-11.

— 1959. Littoral and submarine morphology of the Rhône delta. *Second Coastal Geography Conference Proceedings:* 233-64.

— 1965. Coastal barrier deposits in south and north Holland. *Meded. geol. Sticht.* **17**: 41-75.

VERSTAPPEN, H. 1953. *Djakarta Bay: A Geomorphological Study in Shoreline Development.* La Haye, Ohio.

VLADIMIROV, A. T. 1961. The morphology and evolution of the lagoon coast of Sakhalin. *Trudy Inst. Okeanol.* (Moscow) **48**: 145-71.

WARNKE, D. A., GOLDSMITH, V., GROSE, P. and HOLT, J. J. 1966. Drastic beach changes in a low energy environment caused by Hurricane Betsy. *J. Geophys. Res.* **71**: 2013-16.

WEBB, J. E. 1958. The ecology of Lagos lagoon. *Phil. Trans. R. Soc.* **241**: 307-18.

WENTWORTH, J. K. 1939. Marine bench-forming processes: solution benching. *J. Geomorph.* **2**: 3-25.

WEXLER, H. 1961. Ice budgets for Antarctica and changes of sea level. *J. Glaciol.* **3**: 867-72.

WIENS, H. J. 1962. *Atoll Environment and Ecology.* Yale.

WILLIAMS, W. W. 1956. An east coast survey: some recent changes in the coast of East Anglia. *Geogrl J.* **122**: 317-34.

WILSON, G. 1952. The influence of rock structures on coastline and cliff development around Tintagel, North Cornwall. *Proc. Geol. Assoc.* **63**: 20-48.

WISEMAN, W. J. *et al.* 1973. Alaskan arctic coastal processes and morphology. *Coastal Studies Institute, Louisiana State University, Tech. Rep.* **149**.

WRIGHT, L. D. and COLEMAN, J. M. 1972. River delta morphology: wave climate and the role of the subaqueous profile. *Science* **176**: 282-89.

—, GUZA, R. T. and SHORT, A. D. 1982. Dynamics of a high-energy dissipative surf zone. *Marine Geol.* **45**: 41-62.

—, and THOM, B. G. 1977. Coastal depositional landforms: a morphodynamic approach. *Progress in Physical Geography* **1**: 412-59.

—, CHAPPELL, J., THOM, B. G., BRADSHAW, M. P. and COWELL, P. 1979. Morphodynamics of reflective and dissipative beach and inshore systems, south-eastern Australia. *Marine Geol.* **32**: 105-40.

YASSO, W. E. 1965a. Plan geometry of headland-bay beaches. *J. Geol.* **73**: 702-14.

— 1965b. Fluorescent tracer particle determination of the size-velocity relation for foreshore sediment transport, Sandy Hook, New Jersey. *J. sedim. Petrol.* **35**: 989-93.

ZENKOVICH, V. P. 1959. On the genesis of cuspate spits along lagoon shores. *J. Geol.* **67**: 269-77.

— 1967. *Processes of Coastal Development* (trans. O. G. Fry; ed. J. A. Steers), Edinburgh.

— 1973. Geomorphological problems of protecting the Caucasian Black Sea coast. *Geogrl. J.* **139**: 460-6.

ZEUNER, F. E. 1959. *The Pleistocene Period.* London.

ZUNICA, M. 1971. *Le spiagge del Veneto.* Padua.

AUTHOR INDEX

307

SUBJECT INDEX